toward professionalism in advertising

The Story of
Alpha Delta Sigma's
Aid to Professionalize Advertising
Through Advertising Education

1913-1969

Donald G. Hileman
Southern Illinois University

Billy I. Ross
Texas Tech

Published by
Alpha Delta Sigma
1969

Cover Design by
Jerry D. Kelly, Texas Tech

Copyright 1969

Printed in the U.S.A. by
Taylor Publishing Company
Dallas, Texas
Library of Congress Catalog Card Number: 71-78435

Foreword

Usually when the word "history" is mentioned, most of us think in terms of thousands or at least hundreds of years and accept the fact that the majority of individuals and organizations combining to comprise the history have long disappeared. Not so in the case of a history of advertising as we know it and the people and the fraternity of Alpha Delta Sigma. We are speaking in terms of barely more than a half century.

True, advertising in one form or another has been with mankind for thousands of years. However, until scarcely over a hundred years ago, most advertising was hit and miss and depended upon the inspiration of each individual who had goods or services to sell. Records indicate that it was not until the beginning of the twentieth century that institutions of higher learning began to include courses of study in advertising in the curriculum. 1913 is the earliest date we find organization among the teachers and students of advertising to form a fraternity with the aim of increasing common knowledge among its members and improving the quality of both education and production in the field. Alpha Delta Sigma was the first such fraternity and was for male members while Gamma Alpha Chi (founded in 1920) was the counterpart for female members.

In the short span of fifty-five years, Alpha Delta Sigma has seen thousands of young men and their professor-advisors enter its ranks. In later years chapters for practitioners or professional members from the field of advertising business have been formed.

Not long before ADS was started, clubs or local organizations with membership made up of men and women in advertising began appearing across the nation and soon joined to form regional and national associations for the same purpose as ADS had been formed on campuses. With several changes in names, the associations evolved as the Advertising Federation of America with clubs east of Denver and the Advertising Association of the West with clubs west of Denver. The Advertising Club of Denver was the only club to hold membership in both. This dual membership enabled Denver advertising practitioners to be active in both AFA and AAW.

After serving as President of the Advertising Club of Denver and Governor of the Ninth District of AFA, it was my privilege to continue active work in AAW and become elected President (later changed to Chairman) of that association. At the same time I was in office as Vice President of AFA. In the late 1950's AFA and AAW took an active interest in a new organization formed by advertising educators and called the American Academy of Advertising. At the same time (1960) I was invited to become a "professional" member of the Lowell Thomas Chapter of ADS at the University of Colorado. All of these organizations and my interest in them brought me to know officers of the ADS fraternity who were also active in the AAA.

In 1962 the AFA and AAW held the first (and only) joint national convention in Denver, Colorado. ADS and AAA officers and members were a part of the two organizations by now, and educators and practitioners were becoming better acquainted and working more closely than ever before toward a common goal of making courses in advertising more meaningful and employment of advertising graduates more likely in the business field.

1963 saw the ADS national convention in New York celebrating the golden anniversary of the founding of the fraternity and increased recognition of both educators and practitioners through awarding of "Golden Fifty" medallions to numerous individuals for their contribution to advertising during that half-century. This brought the business world of advertising and the advertising education world closer and set the stage for cooperative effort toward "professionalization of advertising" on and off campus.

In 1965-66 it was my honor to serve as Chairman of the Advertising Federation of America and a few months later to Chair a Joint Commission which successfully merged AFA and AAW to form the American Advertising Federation. The formal merger took place in Washington, D.C., in February, 1967. On the boards of the predecessor organizations for a number of years,

ADS moved into the merger as an important part of the new board.

The 1967 national convention of ADS, held in Houston, Texas, honored me by electing me to the office of National President. (I had served four years in an advisory capacity). The outgoing National President, Dr. Billy I. Ross, who had been working on gathering material for a history of Alpha Delta Sigma since the decision to publish such a volume was made in New York at the 1963 national convention, now became Chairman of the National Council of ADS and, relieved of some of the routine duties of the President, devoted even more time to preparation of the history. Dr. Donald G. Hileman, presently Executive Director of ADS, has also spent many hours digging through the columns of *Linage* to help make the history current and complete. Assistance was given by a number of men, including Milt Gross, long-time National Secretary.

As will be shown in the History, ADS initiations of professional members have now become a regular part of the proceedings at regional and national conventions of the American Advertising Federation, and AAF members are becoming active as professional members of ADS. Thus, as this first history of Alpha Delta Sigma comes off the press, we have proof that educators and practitioners are working hand in hand as never before toward true professionalization of advertising through education. I, for one, consider it a real honor to have been even a small part of the group making this come to be.

—Lee Fondren

Dedication

This book is dedicated to the professional advertising educator who has, is and will serve in the future as an advisor to the Alpha Delta Sigma chapter on the university campus. If Alpha Delta Sigma is to continue its service to advertising, to the academic community, and to the students for which it exists, it will do so primarily through the efforts of interested and concerned advisors dedicated to the higher purposes of the organization.

TABLE OF CONTENTS

FOREWORD

DEDICATION

INTRODUCTION

SECTION I — History of National Organization

1	Countdown	1
2	Founding Chapter	7
3	Founders	14
4	Going National	22
5	Rejuvenation	31
6	Post War	40
7	The Present	123
8	The Future	144

SECTION II — Appendixes

A	Founding Dates of Undergraduate Chapters	155
B	National Officers	163
C	Golden Fifty Award Recipients	165
D	Sidney R. Bernstein Advisor Award	169
E	The Sixth Degree Key Awards	171
F	The G. D. Crain Jr. Awards	173
G	Outstanding Chapter Awards— The Donald Davis Awards	184

SECTION III — Chapter Histories

Histories of Undergraduate Chapters 189

Histories of Professional Chapters 248

This book is a historical document and can be read from that point of view. It attempts to record the events of Alpha Delta Sigma for more than a half century. One can trace these events chronologically, relating each event to a person or persons responsible for its happening.

Certainly each individual who has taken his initiation into ADS with the seriousness it was intended will find satisfaction in the events and in the people themselves. It is intended to give recognition to the many who have served advertising, advertising education and ADS well. Yet, we feel that such an approach can and should be secondary.

The book can provide a philosophical understanding of advertising education in this country. It reflects the struggle of those in advertising education wishing to gain acceptance of the advertising program in the university both by the academic community itself and by practitioners of advertising.

It can be argued that education alone does not made a profession and that the requirements of a profession require more than education; but it is quite obvious that education is one of the primary and basic foundations for a profession.

We agree with the many who feel that advertising has not yet gained the acceptance of the traditional professions—law, medicine, teaching and the ministry; yet we also point out that great strides "towards professionalization in advertising" have been taken in the last half century.

Many individuals and organizations are responsible for these steps forward. Among them is Alpha Delta Sigma, its leaders and members. These persons and organizations are discussed in the ensuing chapters. We have come a long way, but we still have a long way to go.

While each of us—student, practitioner or educator—must continue individually to develop our skills, to pursue excellence in the performance of our careers and to seek our self-interests, required will be a deeper concern for our fellowman, be it practitioner, teacher, student or consumer.

One of the higher purposes of professions has and always will be "what can I give to my chosen field?" It is no less true for advertising; it is no less true for ADS. In fact, this is the spirit of Alpha Delta Sigma.

Read the following pages for the significance of the events and the people involved, but read also to acquire the feeling of the philosophy which motivated these men and events. We think it reflects a most important movement "towards the professionalization of advertising."

We cannot predict the next fifty years of Alpha Delta Sigma or any other advertising-oriented organization. We cannot even guarantee that Alpha Delta Sigma will continue to exist. We do believe strongly, however, that the philosophical considerations discussed in the historical development of the organization to date and the sense of direction expressed by its National Council in recent years to be essential if we are to continually progress "toward professionalization in advertising."

Donald G. Hileman

Billy I. Ross

"...and, now a word from our sponsor."

Regardless where one looks in the history of the world he can find evidence that advertising was manifest. Documents dating back to circa 3000 B.C. indicate a form of advertising on early Babylonian bricks. Later, advertising was practiced orally in villages by town criers or barkers. And later still, signs over shops proved to be an effective medium for the time.

Probably one of the most important breakthroughs in advertising, as in most other fields, was the advent of printing. This discovery led to the mass printing of newspapers and magazines, all needing the financial support of advertising. These early printed forms of news media made it easy for radio and television to make dramatic appearances in the 1900's with their "word from the sponsor."

The middlemen of advertising, the agencies, began to appear in the middle 1800's to help the advertiser reach the public more effectively. At the end of the Civil War advertisers in the United States were spending only about fifty million dollars in this new form of business communication. Total expenses for advertising mounted rapidly with more than one-half billion dollars being spent at the turn of this century. Most of the advertising dollars were being spent to advertise such items as soap, railroad travel, patent medicine and books.

There is little wonder why the public and those working in

advertising began to worry about the ethics of a business that was growing so rapidly. Many persons started to band together into local advertising clubs and to ask among themselves what could and should be done with this little giant. In 1903 the Pacific Advertising Association was founded, which later became the Advertising Association of the West. This organization united the local advertising clubs in the West. A similar move was started in the East with the founding of the American Federation of Advertising Clubs in 1905. Both organizations had name changes during their early years with the organization in the West finally becoming the Advertising Association of the West and the other becoming the Advertising Federation of America.

In 1966 these two organizations merged into the American Advertising Federation, serving more than 175 advertising clubs with approximately 30,000 members.

Recognizing the need for more public confidence in advertising at the turn of this century the advertising clubs of these two organizations launched a program built around the theme, "Truth in Advertising." This, in part, stimulated the publishers of *Printers' Ink*, the leading trade journal of that day to publish a set of Model Statutes, which in years to come were adopted into original or modified forms of law in more than forty states. Through the efforts of the advertising clubs the Better Business Bureau was established in 1913. The Bureau is still today the watchdog over local advertising practices.

These are only a few of the historical landmarks along the path of advertising, a major industry today. It is anticipated that in a few years, advertisers will spend more than twenty billion dollars to reach the American public with their business messages.

COUNTDOWN

While advertising was growing, as were many other newly-founded industries and professions in this country, professional education was beginning to find its place on the college campus. Law, engineering, theology, and science were already established in the curriculum, but courses in such fields as advertising, journalism, and marketing were just beginning.

Although there is no direct tie between an advertising organization such as Alpha Delta Sigma and advertising education, the history of one has had a direct bearing on the history of the other. As advertising education found its way into the curriculum, Alpha Delta Sigma found its way to the college campus.

Historically, advertising education has been directly connected with the academic areas of journalism and business, with its subdivision marketing. Today, these two academic areas control nearly all advertising education. In *Advertising Education* by Billy I. Ross, a brief history of journalism and business education was presented.

Journalism Education

A course in news writing and editing given in 1869 at Washington College (now Washington and Lee University) was the meager beginning of journalism education. Kansas State College followed in 1873 with a course in newspaper printing. In 1878 the Department of English at the University of Missouri offered a journalism course taught by its chairman, Professor David Russell McAnally.

In 1893 the first journalism curriculum in the U.S. was developed by Joseph French Johnson at the Wharton School of Business, University of Pennsylvania. The program of study included five courses:

Journalism — Art and History of Newspaper Making. One Hour. Professor Johnson.

Journalism — Law of Libel, Business Management, Typographical Union, Cost and Revenue, Advertising, Method of Criticism, etc. One hour. Professor Johnson.

Journalism — Newspaper Practice, Exercises in Reporting, Editing of Copy, Conversations, etc. Three hours. Professor Johnson.

Journalism — Current Topics, Lectures on Live Issues in the United States and Foreign Countries. Three hours. Professors Johnson, Cheyney, Falkner, and Robinson, Dr. Adams, and Mr. Munro.

Journalism — Public Lectures by Men Engaged in the Active Work of the Profession.

The mention of advertising in the second course is among the first notations of its inclusion in a college course. Similarly, the first journalism course at the University of Illinois, offered in 1902 by the Department of Rhetoric and Oratory, is described as

Rhetoric 10. Business Writing-Business Correspondence, the making of summaries and abstracts, advertising, proofreading, and the preparation of manuscripts for the press. I, III, Tu. Th. 4; (2) Professor Clark. (Open only to students in the business courses.) Required: Rhetoric and Oratory 1 or 2.

One of the pioneers of professional education in journalism was Dr. Charles W. Eliot, president of Harvard University, who prepared a course of study for journalism education which included:

Editorial work, including news and editorial writing
Operation of the business office
Operation of the advertising office
Close connection with the mechanical department

Although Eliot's plan was not tried at Harvard, it was put into operation at the University of Missouri in 1908 when Walter Williams became dean of the first school of journalism in the world. Courses in journalism had been taught at Missouri for more than thirty years at that time. The catalogue of 1898, 1899, and 1900 mentioned advertising content in one course:

Newspaper Making: Business management, cost and revenue, advertising, editorials, reporting, clipping from exchanges, methods of criticism.

Dean Williams, who included advertising as a part of journalism education, wrote in his *Journalists' Creed*:

I believe that advertising, news, and editorial columns should alike serve the best interests of the readers; that a single standard of helpful truth and cleanness should prevail for all; that the supreme test of good journalism is the measure of its public service.

That advertising courses have continued to flourish under journalism education is noted in Dr. James L. C. Ford's unpublished thesis on the subject, which states that in 1926-27 90 per cent of twenty journalism schools were offering advertising courses; by 1936-37 the figure had risen to 93 per cent of thirty-two schools.

Business and Marketing Education

As with journalism education, business education was rarely found in the college curricula before the turn of the century. James E. Hagerty, one of the pioneer teachers of marketing, wrote in 1936 that only three colleges of business administration existed before 1900. The first, the Wharton School of Business at the University of Pennsylvania, was started in 1881; the universities of California and Chicago started schools in 1898.

There is disagreement about which institution offered the first marketing course. H. H. Maynard contends that the first course was offered by the Economics Department of the University of Michigan in 1902. The course, entitled "The Distributive and Regulative Industries of the United States," was taught by Assistant Professor E. D. Jones.

Simon Litman, also an early marketing teacher, claims that the course called "The Techniques of Trade and Commerce," which he taught during the 1902-03 school year at the University of California, was overlooked by Professor Maynard. He also claims that Professor G. M. Fisk offered a similar course at the University of Illinois the same year.

Apparently a number of courses in marketing were offered during the first ten years of the new century; however, few of them carried the title of marketing. Probably the first course with the title of marketing was offered at the Wharton School, University of Pennsylvania, in 1904. This course, "The Marketing of Products," included advertising in its content. The course description reads:

The method now practiced in the organization and conduct of the selling branch of industrial and mercantile business. The principal subjects in the field are publicity, agency, advertising, forms and correspondence, credit and collections, and terms of sale.

The 1904-05 school year was also the starting date for courses at Dartmouth and Ohio State universities. A special bulletin on Business Administration and Social Service, issued in 1906 by Ohio State University, listed a course that mentioned advertising content.

> 40. Mercantile Institutions. 3 credit hours, 1st and 2nd terms. Mr. Hagerty.
>
> . . . advertising, its psychological laws, its economic importance and the changes it has introduced in selling goods.

In the spring of 1909, Professor Paul T. Cherington taught a course at Harvard College on "Commercial Organization and Methods" that included lectures on advertising. The University of Pittsburgh offered its first marketing course, "The Marketing of Products," in 1909.

By the beginning of the second decade of the twentieth century, marketing courses were being taught in several institutions.

Advertising Education

Advertising education made its appearance on the college campus only five years after the turn of the new century. New York University was the first institution to offer a course listed as "advertising." In fact, the course was titled just that and was taught by W. R. Hotchkin, advertising manager of the John Wanamaker Company during the 1905-06 school year.

In 1908, Northwestern University offered a course in advertising taught by Walter Dill Scott, an outstanding teacher of advertising for many years and later the president of Northwestern. During the same year the University of Missouri's School of Journalism offered its first advertising course. Charles G. Ross, later President Harry S. Truman's press secretary, taught the course.

Indiana University and the University of Kansas followed quickly the pattern and offered courses in advertising the next year. Iowa State University and the University of Wisconsin followed with courses in 1910. By 1930 more than thirty colleges and universities had an advertising course in their curriculum. Today it is estimated that more than 800 have at least one advertising course.

As found in most other professional fields of education, advertising courses preceded the formation of formalized programs in advertising. It is generally conceded that the School of Journalism at the University of Missouri had the first organized major program in advertising. The specific date is hard to establish since students were preparing for advertising careers as early as the time of the first course. Many believe it was established as a major program around 1913.

New York University developed an advertising major in 1915, followed by Marquette University (1916), University of Wisconsin (1917), Northwestern University (1919), and the University of Oklahoma (1919). By 1930 ten schools were listing major programs in advertising. Today more than 75 schools have major programs.

With the field of advertising expanding so rapidly in those early years and with the courses in advertising finding their way into the curriculum, it was little wonder that a need was found for an advertising fraternity on the college campus.

Chapter 2

Founding Chapter

The new century was only thirteen years old when interested students of advertising at the University of Missouri founded Alpha Delta Sigma. In fact one founder, Rex Magee, remembered that at that time of the founding only one airplane had ever landed in Columbia, Missouri.

This was a time when radio commercials were still a few years away, and no one dreamed of an advertising medium as powerful as television. Still, this period felt a need for rapid development of a powerful persuasive selling tool—advertising.

Since the first school of journalism had been founded on the campus of the University of Missouri and since the first advertising program was started on that campus, it is not difficult to understand why Alpha Delta Sigma was founded there. Not only was the Fraternity started on the Missouri campus, but for the majority of the first fifty years the national office was also there. Its faculty members have given guidance for the direction of the Fraternity over much of the years of its growth. The deans of the School have been most understanding in providing facilities as well as time for faculty to work with the organization.

The first news story about the founding of Alpha Delta Sigma ran in the *Columbia Missourian* on March 3, 1914. It read.

"Alpha Delta Sigma is a new honorary fraternity in the School of Journalism. It has the distinction of being the first advertising fraternity in the world. The fraternity will be extended to other universities in the country. It will study special problems in advertising. All the members intend to make advertising their life-work. The fraternity probably will be made a member of the Associated Advertising Clubs of America.

"The charter members are: J. B. Powell, H. J. MacKay, T. E. Parker, Oliver Gingrich. J. Harrison Brown, J. W. Jewell, Rex Magee, Guy Trail, and A. C. Bayless."

When a fraternity such as Alpha Delta Sigma begins, there is seldom a single reason for such action, and one is never really sure what is the prime motivating source. No one can be completely sure what ran through the minds of John B. Powell and the other founders in the early meetings. At the founding meeting on November 14, 1913 the charter group set down on paper three major objectives:

1. to combine in one fraternal body students and actual workers in a field including many diversified interests, and regarded by the lay public as the "advertising business,"

2. to have college training for advertising given greater recognition, both by college administrations and people actively engaged in the business of advertising, and

3. to raise by every legitimate means the prestige of advertising as a business and the prestige of those who earned their living from it.

It must be remembered that the founding fathers were pioneers in the real sense. Advertising, as a field of endeavor was very young, and certainly as a subject matter for the university, it was higly questionable.

Some of the founding members recorded random thoughts and feelings about ADS during those beginning days. Guy Trail, former newspaper writer and now retired in New Haven, Missouri, said that his first knowledge about an advertising organization came in the fall of 1914 when John B. Powell, an instructor in advertising, discussed the need for such an organization for the advertising students at the University.

He said that after class one day a few of the students discussed the idea while sunning on the steps of Switzler Hall. They agreed that such an organization was a good idea and told Mr. Powell that they were willing to pursue plans for the Fraternity.

Rex B. Magee, a founding father who died in the summer of 1965, first heard about the founding of the Fraternity from a fellow advertising student, Oliver Gingrich. Called "Ginrickey" by fellow students because of his dry hometown, Columbia, Oliver never seemed dry for ideas in handling his advertising accounts for the college daily.

Gingrich stopped Magee one day on the campus and said, "Say, you know the Missouri School of Journalism is the first in the world, why shouldn't we organize the first advertising Greek-

ALPHA DELTA SIGMA

Founded at the University of Missouri, November 15, 1913
Honorary Advertising Fraternity

THOMAS BALMER CHAPTER

JEWELL		SCHOFIELD		TRAIL
	BAYLESS		GINGRICH	
BROWN	PARKER		McKAY	MAGEE

Chapter Roll

J. B. POWELL
HUGH J. MACKAY
OLIVER GINGRICH
J. HARRISON BROWN
REX B. MAGEE

THOMAS E. PARKER
J. E. SCHOFIELD
JOHN W. JEWELL
GUY TRAIL
ALEX C. BAYLESS

Honorary

FRANK L. MARTIN
CHARLES G. ROSS

*Fraternities
Journalistic*

From a page in the 1914 SAVITAR, University of Missouri yearbook

FISHER
WARFIELD
HALL
FIELDER
WELLS
STRONG
COCKRELL
SMITH
PROUTY

Alpha Delta Sigma

HONORARY JOURNALISTIC FRATERNITY

Devoted to Practical Advertising

ILLINOIS CHAPTER

Founded at the University of Missouri, 1913

Established March 24, 1914

MEMBERS IN THE FACULTY

HARRISON MC JOHNSON

MEMBERS IN THE UNIVERSITY

Seniors

FRANCIS MARION COCKRELL
RUSSELL PRITCHETT HALL
VERNON HUFF WARFIELD
ARTHUR C. STRONG

BENJAMIN SIDNEY FISHER
WILLIAM FULLER FIELDER
EDWIN CHESTER PROUTY
WILSON MARSHALL SMITH

Junior
FRED SHEAFF WELLS

521

A page from the 1915 ILLIO, University of Illinois yearbook

10

letter fraternity?'' Magee agreed it was a good idea and said to count him in when the group decided to meet.

On the night of November 15, 1913 (other records indicate November 14), the group met with the faculty approval in Dean Walter Williams' office, according to Magee. Magee was handed a creed that had been written by one of the other members to be read at that time. This was followed, he says, by "some vows" which initiated the first chapter of ADS. The Greek letters of ADS were used to form the initials of the English word ads, meaning advertisements.

Another charter member, J. Harrison Brown, who is retired and living in Long Beach today, commented: "I do remember one very definite feeling of satisfaction as far as I was concerned. It was that recognition of the 'business' side of journalism was available . . .''

". . . J. B. Powell was the advertising instructor. Some of us were soon interested in advertising and managing. His energy and personality attracted those of us who might show feeble signs of selling. He was a great teacher and to this day I thank Heaven for his training.''

Guy Trail commented on early meetings of the Fraternity in this way: "Fraternity meetings were rather studious in contrast to social affairs. We pondered advertising ethics and such dubious practices as offering a suit of long underwear for $2.59 when only yesterday it was priced at $3.08.''

A page from the 1914 *Savitar*, official University of Missouri yearbook, shows the chapter name of the fraternity as the Thomas Balmer Chapter. A few years later the chapter name was changed to the John W. Jewell Chapter, which was the name it carried until 1947 when changed to the John B. Powell Chapter in honor of the founder.

Little is known about Thomas Balmer, yet a story in the *Columbia Missourian* on January 6, 1920, tells about John W. Jewell, who was killed on the night of January 11, 1918, at Camp Funston, Kansas. The story announced a gift from the Jewells to the School of Journalism to establish a scholarship fund in John W. Jewell's name. The story read:

"Mr. Jewell attended the University in 1913-14-15. In 1915 he served as business manager of the *Evening Missourian*. After he left school he held the same position on his father's paper in Springfield. In 1917 he accepted an offer to become editor of the Y.M.C.A. Army paper at Camp Funston.

"On the night of January 11, 1918, he went to the Army Bank at Camp Funston to see his classmate and fraternity brother in the University, Kearney Wornell of Kansas City, and officer of the bank. There he found Mr. Wornell at work. It was a bitter cold night and he volunteered to wait and take Mr. Wornell home in his car. At 11:00 an unmasked army officer entered the building. After robbing the bank with a hand ax, and wounded Mr. Wornell so dangerously that his life was despaired of for the time. Besides Mr. Jewell the other victims were: C. F. Wineres of Kansas City, cashier, O. M. Hill and Carl Ohleson, clerks.

"Mr. Wornell was at the point of death for several days but later recovered.

"The robber, Captain Lewis Whistler of Salina, Kansas, committed suicide after the robbery had been traced to him. It was said that he had gone insane.

"Mr. Jewell was married in June 1916, to Miss Jean McGregor of Springfield. While in the University he was a member of Sigma Alpha Epsilon, Chi Chi Chi, Alpha Delta Sigma and Kappa Tau Alpha fraternities. The last two are honorary journalism societies. He was also a member of Matrix society and of the board of directors of the *Evening Missourian.*

"Few students in the University took a greater interest in school activities or were more popular among students, members of the faculty and the citizens of Columbia than Mr. Jewell."

Advertising apparently shared common problems with the editorial side of journalism. There is no doubt that awareness of problems as well as the idea for a professional fraternity for advertising came from the sister organization in journalism education, Sigma Delta Chi.

Many of the charter members at the University of Missouri were also members of Sigma Delta Chi chapter. While the aims and goals for professionalism were the same, members of Sigma Delta Chi expressed no interest in the business side of journalism. One can conjecture that if SDX had not demonstrated such interest ADS may never have been.

A mimeograph account distributed on the Missouri campus at the time of founding commented:

"The Sigma Delta Chi Fraternity was already active on the campus of the School of Journalism and although some of the charter members of Alpha Delta Sigma were already members of Sigma Delta Chi, there was a feeling on the part of Mr. Powell that some special recognition should be given to those students who had selected advertising as their major.

It was reported that Powell had said that his object was to provide a fraternity for men who would make advertising their life work. He considered Sigma Delta Chi the journalism fraternity, and said that ADS in no way conflicted and was really in harmony with Sigma Delta Chi.

The requirement for invitation to membership to ADS was simply an interest in advertising and the business side of publishing, but no one was asked to pledge himself to follow this as his life work. Early membership was drawn from the following three sources on the Missouri campus:

1. undergraduate and graduate students,

2. teachers of advertising and business, and
3. those actually in the practice of advertising and the business side of publishing.

Little is known about the activities of the first chapter during the first few years. The chapter did not completely die during WWI, but activities were few while the war was in progress. Many of the chapter's charter members served in the Armed Forces.

Chapter 3

Nine men met in Switzler Hall on the campus of the University of Missouri, November 14, 1913 to perfect the organization of Alpha Delta Sigma. Included also on the original charter were the names of three faculty members of the School of Journalism.

John B. Powell promoted the organization and was elected the first president of the mother chapter. At that time, Mr. Powell was an instructor in advertising at the school.

Walter Williams, founder and dean of the School of Journalism and later president of the University of Missouri, and Frank L. Martin, who later became dean of the School, replacing Williams, were charter honorary members. The remaining faculty member was Charles G. Ross, who in 1908 had taught the first advertising course at the University. Ross later became an editor of the *St. Louis Post Dispatch* and during the administration of Harry Truman served as press secretary to the President. All of these faculty members are now deceased.

Probably one of the most fitting tributes to the founder of ADS, John Benjamin Powell, was given by John A. Conde at a Founders Day dinner in Detroit on November 14, 1949. Conde used *Time, The Detroit News, The New York Times, Newsweek,* and *The Columbia Missourian,* as his sources.

John B. Powell: A Biography

A slight, long-suffering man, his body emaciated from starvation and cold, stood before a gathering of University of Missouri alumni in Washington, D.C. at noon in February two years ago. He weighed less than a hundred pounds. He stood on crutches; nearly all of both feet had been amputated.

The subject of his talk was the need for greater friendship between American and Chinese peoples. He concluded with this cogent warning:

"Today in the Pacific the situation has not changed—only the actors have changed . . . But there is no occasion for a war with Russia unless we do as we did after World War I—scrap our fighting forces and withdraw again within ourselves."

It was the last warning issued by a man who had spent the better part of his life crusading for a free world. A few seconds after he sat down, amid great applause, he slumped over, dead of a heart attack.

It is the spirit of this courageous American, John Benjamin Powell, that lives in Alpha Delta Sigma. His life reads almost like a detective story.

He was born April 18, 1886, on a farm near Palmyra, in Marion County, Missouri. He attended schools in Hannibal, Missouri, and Quincy, Illinois, and was graduated from the University of Missouri's School of Journalism in 1910—just one year after the famed school was founded by Walter Williams.

After graduation he was named advertising manager of the *Hannibal Courier-Post*, a position he held for two years. He then returned to the University's Journalism School where for five years he was an instructor in the technique of advertising. During this period, on November 13, he founded Alpha Delta Sigma, the national professional advertising fraternity.

In 1917, at the age of 31, he went to China to become editor of a weekly Chinese newspaper known as *Millard's Review*. In 1922 he changed its name to the *China Weekly Review*. In the following year he also became editor of the *China Press*.

The world first heard of Mr. Powell in 1923. He and 20 other Westerners were kidnaped and held 40 days in the mountains of Shantung Province by Chinese bandits who had made a daring raid on the famous Peking-Shanghai Blue Express. While he was in prison in an old ruined temple on the side of Mt. Pao Zu Ku, he wrote Dean Walter Williams: "As soon as we were captured, I began sending out letters by handing them to farmers we passed, and I learned that most of them got out. This is due to the old Chinese veneration for anything which is written, which even the bandits still observe."

Mr. Powell never let this incident affect his steadfastness of friendship for the Chinese. As a special representative of American commercial interests in China, he was largely responsible for enactment in Washington of the China Trade Act. He achieved this even though from 1917 until after World War II began, he did not return to this country.

During the Chinese Nationalist Revolution in Central and South China, which began in 1926, he defended the main purposes of the Chinese cause, despite the fact that in earlier phases of the war many anti-foreign incidents occurred.

Mr. Powell, reporting for his Chinese newspapers, also covered the Sino-Japanese conflict in 1932. In 1934 he traveled in the Soviet Union and in Japan. At no time during his journalistic career in China did he take anything but an absolutely forthright stand on matters affecting the country he adopted, and he was frequently criticized—even by the American Chamber of Commerce—for his comments regarding the siege of Shanghai in 1927.

From the time the Kwantung Army started its era of international violence by invading Manchuria, he denounced the military minions of the Mikado. Mr. Powell covered the campaign that transformed Manchuria into the puppet state of Manchukuo; he was in Shanghai when the Japanese made their first attack on the city. After the Sino-Japanese war opened in 1937, his clashes with the invaders were many.

Many were their attempts to eliminate him. On one trip to Shanghai, the first car in which he was riding, although plainly marked with an American flag, was bombed and machine-gunned from the air. In 1939 his name led all the rest in the black list of foreigners issued by the puppet Chinese government. In 1941 a hand grenade was tossed at him while he was walking near the American Club in the heart of Shanghai's International Settlement. This was shortly after Mr. Powell had written an article on corruption in the puppet regime for the *China Weekly Review*. After that episode, Mr. Powell wore a bullet-proof vest and walked with a bodyguard.

Shortly after Pearl Harbor, on December 20, 1941, the Japs marched into his hotel room and seized him. He was thrown into filthy Bridge House Prison. He then weighed 160 pounds. Between then and May, 1942, beriberi and gangrene maimed him pitifully.

When he was released by an exchange of prisoners, he weighed only 70 pounds. A starvation diet, beatings and the bitter cold of the prison produced painful infections of his feet. When he came back to America on the Swedish mercy ship, the Gripsholm, a series of operations over a three-year period finally resulted in the partial amputation of both feet.

American and Chinese journalists expressed their faith in the cause fought by Mr. Powell by raising a fund to help pay for his hospital and medical expenses. Chiang Kai-Shek gave $10,000. The

Chinese National Press Association gave $11,000. But Mr. Powell spent most of the money in promoting better American-Chinese relations. From a wheel chair he took part in many war bond rallies in the United States. Able at last to hobble on crutches, he returned to Tokyo in 1946 to testify at the war crimes of Hideki Tojo and 26 top-ranking Japanese war criminals.

After his dramatic death February 28, 1947, Chinese Ambassador Wellkington Koo expressed the grief of the freedom-loving world when he paid the following tribute:

"John B. Powell was not only a great friend of the Chinese people but a staunch supporter of China's cause throughout the long years of her struggle against aggression. His courage has been unexcelled. He died at the very moment of expressing the importance of Chinese-American friendship and understanding between our two peoples. The whole Chinese nation will join in mourning the loss of this great friend of China."

Undergraduate Charter Members

Alex C. (Tex) Bayless, (deceased 1952), student in the School of Journalism, 1913-17; Alpha Delta Sigma; married, Dec. 15, 1920, to Grace Leavell; children, Alex C. Jr., and James Leavell; business manager, *Columbia Evening Missourian*, 1915-16; advertising salesman, *Dallas News-Journal*, 1916; naval aviation, 1917-18; General agent, Southland Life Insurance Co., Houston, 1918-38; State Manager, American Bankers Insurance Co., Waco, Texas, 1938-52.

J. Harrison Brown, (currently living in Long Beach California), B.J. 1914; Sigma Delta Chi, Alpha Delta Sigma, Kappa Tau Alpha; married 1920, to Bernice C. Fairly; children, Marjorie C. and J. Harrison, Jr.; Service department, *Dry Goods Journal*, Des Moines, Iowa, 1914-16; Advertising manager, *The Farm News*, Colorado Springs, Colorado, 1917; Manager, Service Department, *Dry Goods Journal*, New York, 1917-18; Advertising Manager, Sales Manager, Vice President and General Manager, A. P. Green Fire Brick Company, Mexico, Missouri, 1918-47; Retired, 1947.

Oliver N. Gingrich, B.J, 1914; Alpha Delta Sigma; married, August 29, 1923, to Dorothy Houston; children, Thomas Newton, Susan Jane, and Mary Elizabeth; Advertising Manager, Maryville (Mo.) *Democrat;* Advertising Manager, *Tribune*, Fort Scott, Kansas; Sales Promotion Department, Ralston Purina Co., St. Louis; Merchandising Manager, *St. Louis Post Dispatch;* Sales Promotion Manager, Martin Senour Co., Chicago; Advertising Manager, Albert Dickinson Co., Chicago; General Manager; Phillip-Bernard Company, Sioux City, Iowa; Publications: various articles in trade magazines; also political and economic articles.

John W. Jewell, (killed at Camp Funston, January 11, 1918, and whose name the chapter carried for many years, replacing the original name of Thomas Balmer Chapter) ; former student in the School of Journalism, Manager of the *Columbia Missourian,* 1914-15.

Rex B. Magee, (deceased 1965, Washington, D. C.), student in the School of Journalism, 1910-14; Alpha Delta Sigma, Sigma Delta Chi; reporter, Joplin (Mo.) *News Herald.* 1914; Reporter *Merchants Trade Journal,* Des Moines, Iowa, 1915; City editor, *Jackson Daily News,* Jackson. Mississippi, 1916; U. S. Army Lieutenant and Captain, 1917-18; State editor, Night editor, Associated Press, New Orleans, 1919; Federal Prohibition Inspector for Mississippi, 1920; Managing Editor, *Jackson* (Miss.) *Daily News,* 1921-24; State Service Commissioner and Editor, *Mississippi Veteran,* 1925-27; Political Editor, 1928; Lamar Life Insurance Company, Jackson, Miss., 1928-unknown; retired, Washington, D.C.

Hugh MacKay, (deceased), B.J., 1913; A.B., University of Oklahoma, 1917; A.M., University of Oklahoma, 1918; Kappa Tau Alpha, Sigma Delta Chi, Alpha Delta Sigma; married, December 25, 1914, to Jennie Myrtle MacDougall; children, Myrthle and Archie Robert; University Publisher. University of Missouri, 1912-15; Alumni Recorder, 1915-16; Student at the University of Oklahoma, 1916-18; Petroleum Geologist and Operator, 1918-unknown.

Thomas E. Parker, B.J., 1914; Sigma Delta Chi, Alpha Delta Sigma; Fresno (Calif.) *Republican.* 1915; Fresno *Herald,* 1919-22; Joplin (Mo.) *News Herald,* 1922; Joplin *Globe,* 1922; *Kansas City Star,* 1925; Empire District Electric Co.. Joplin, Mo. 1926-30; State Editor, *Los Angeles Times,* 1933-unknown.

Guy Trail, (currently living at New Haven, Missouri), B.J., 1914; advertising jobs in Monett, Maryville, and Sedalia, Missouri, 1914-15; News desk at the Sedalia *Capital,* 1915-16; Reporter and Assistant to the News Editor, Springfield (Mo.) *Republican,* 1916-17; Miami (Okla.) *Record-Herald,* 1917-20; Edited camp paper, the *Dijon Hub,* Dijon, France, 1918; Tucson (Ariz.) *Star,* 1920-22; *Tucson Citizen.* 1922-27; student. agriculture journalism, University of Arizona, 1927-28; special writer for farm papers and retired to Ozark fruit farm. Reviewed books for *St. Louis Post-Dispatch,* 1944-48.

Other First Year Members

Howard W. Hailey, (currently living in Sebastopol, California) ; student in the School of Journalism, 1911-12; 1913-16; Sigma Delta Chi, Alpha Delta Sigma, Kappa Tau Alpha, Dana Press Club; married April 12, 1936, to Eunice Hulbert; Overseas with American Ambulance and Field Service and Air Service 1917-18; American Red Cross, Balkans, 1919; Fieldman, Western Farm Life, Denver, 1920-22; Account Executive and Salesman. Fawcett Advertising Agency, Colorado Springs and Denver,

1923-25; Principal owner, H. W. Hailey, Inc. Advertising Agency, El Paso, Texas and Phoenix, 1926-31; Asst. to Business Manager, El Paso *Herald Post*, 1931-32; Sales Promotion Manager, *San Francisco News*, 1932-36; Director Business Promotion and Research, Scripps-Howard Newspapers 1936-40; Business Manager, The Denver Publishing Co., 1941 to retirement.

Albert G. Hinman, (deceased 1955); B.J. 1917; A.M., University of Wisconsin, 1924; Ph.D., Northwestern University, 1931; Alpha Delta Sigma; married, July 17, 1930, to Edith Tupper; son, Kendall Alan; Assistant Chief of Copy Service, *The Chicago Tribune*, 1918-19; Copy Department, The Otto J. Koch Advertising Agency, Milwaukee, Wisconsin, 1920; Instructor in Business Administration, University of Wisconsin, 1921-24; Assistant Professor of Advertising and Sales Management, University of Nebraska, 1924-25; Research Associate, Institute for Research in Land Economics and Public Utilities, Northwestern University, 1925-31; Associate Professor of Advertising and Sales Management, University of North Carolina, 1931-32; Business Manager, *Real Estate*, Chicago, Illinois, 1932-34; Professor of Economics and Head, Economics Department, The Principia College, Elsah, Illinois; 1934—retirement. Pulications: *Real Estate Merchandising, Urban Land Economics. Merchandising of Office Space* (monographs) *Population Growth and Its Demands Upon Land for Housing in Evanston, Illinois* (monograph).

Joseph Blaike Hosmer, B.J., 1922; Kappa Tau Alpha, Alpha Delta Sigma; married July 18, 1922, to Nadeline Flint, daughters, Madeline Ross and Katherine Jo; professor in advertising, Georgia School of Technology, 1922-25; Account Executive, James A. Greene and Company, 1925-26; Research and promotion manager, *Atlanta Georgian*, 1925-28; Advertising Economist, Hearst Newspapers, 1929-31; Advertising Consultant, 1933-   ).

Alfonso Johnson, (deceased 1950). B.J., 1922; Kappa Tau Alpha, Alpha Delta Sigma, Sigma Delta Chi; married, July 14, 1915, to Dot Walker; Manager, University Co-operative Store, Columbia, Missouri, 1915-18; Business Manager, *The Japan Advertiser*, Tokyo, Japan, 1918-20; U. S. Trade Commissioner to Japan, ex-officio Assistant Commercial Attache to Japan, 1920; Manager, *The Columbia Missourian*, 1920-24; Business Editor of *The Dallas News*, 1924-28; Manager, Refrigeration, General Electric Company, Tulsa, Oklahoma, 1928-30; Organizer and first director of the Trade Extension Division, Dallas Chamber of Commerce, 1930; Manager, Dallas Insurance Agents Association, 1931-50. Executive Secretary-Treasurer, Southwestern Association of Advertising Agencies, 1931-50; Executive Secretary-Treasurer, Southwest (10th) District, Advertising Federation of America. President, Board of Trustees, Dallas Public Library; Secretary of the Dallas Fire Prevention Council; Secretary of the Freeman Memorial Clinic; Executive Secretary of Southwest School of Printing; Executive Secretary, Federal Tax Equality League of Texas;

President, Rotary Club of Dallas. Correspondent for *New York Journal of Commerce, Chicago Journal of Commerce* and some 15 insurance publications, 1931-50. Author of newspaper feature, "The Bible Says."

D. D. Rosenfelder, Field Manager, United National Clothiers, Chicago; Opa Locka, Florida. (no other records available).

James E. Schofield, B.J., 1914; Alpha Delta Sigma; married, February 5, 1919, to Julia K Taylor; daughter, Ena Helen; Editor, Edina (Mo.) *Sentinel*, 1914-20; Wells (Minn.) *Mirror*, 1920-30; Hobart (Ind.) *Gazette*, 1930-33; Jeffersonville (Ind.) *Post*, 1933-35; Helena (Ark.) *Daily World*, 1935-36; Owned and operated: Edina Coal & Ice Co.; partner, S. & S. Co., lumber manufacturers; 1500 acres farm land; and vice president Edina *Sentinel*, 1936- unknown.

R. K. Tindall, *Evening Sentinel*, Shenandoah, Iowa. (currently living at this address.

Chauncey Wynne, no records available.

Faculty Honorary Members

Frank Lee Martin, (deceased 1941), dean of the School of Journalism at the University of Missouri from 1930 to   ; Sigma Delta Chi, Alpha Delta Sigma, Kappa Tau Alpha, Chi Phi; married, Sept. 25, 1907 to Martha Maria Hall; children, Martha Anne and Frank Lee, Jr.; reporter *Kansas City Star*, 1902-06; Asst. telegraph editor, 1907; Asst. city editor 1908-09; member of the faculty at the University of Missouri, 1909-16; professor 1921-30; associate dean, 1930-35; dean, 1935; exchange professor in Journalism, Yenching University, Peiping, China, 1931-32; news editor, *Japan Advertiser*, Tokyo, 1915-16; editor of the *Quill* of Sigma Delta Chi, 1917-22; council for Research in Journalism; Director of Missouri-Yenching Foundation; council for Education in Journalism; president of Walter Williams Memorial Journalism Foundation; member of the Missouri Press Association; fellow to the Institute of British Journalists; member of the Foreign Press Association Correspondents; the National Press Club, Washington, D.C.; board of governors, the American Press Society; associate editor of the *Journalism Quarterly*; author, *The Practice of Journalism* (with Walter Williams.)

Charles G. Ross, (deceased 1950), A.B. University of Missouri, 1905; LL.D. George Washington University, 1935; Kappa Tau Alpha, Sigma Delta Chi, and Alpha Delta Sigma; married, August 20, 1913, to Florence Griffin; children, John Bruce and Walter Williams; *Columbia Herald* of Missouri, 1904-05; Victor (Colo.) *Record*, 1906-07; St. Louis *Post-Dispatch*, 1906-07; St. Louis *Republican*, 1907-08, member of the faculty of the University of Missouri, 1908-18; sub-editor of the Melborne (Australia) *Herald*, 1917-18; Washington correspondent of the *St. Louis Post Dispatch*, 1918-45; press secretary to President Harry S. Truman,

1945-50; *The Writing of the News;* winner of Pulitzer Prize, 1932.

Walter Wiliams, (deceased 1935) ; dean of the School of Journalism at the University of Missouri, 1908-35; president of the University, 1930-35; Kappa Tau Alpha, Sigma Delta Chi, and Alpha Delta Sigma; married, 1892, to Hulda Harned, who died in 1918; children, Walter Jr., and Helen Harned; remarried, 1927, to Sara Lawrence Lockwood; children, Edwin Moss; editor of *Boonville Advertiser;* editor *Columbia* (Mo.) *Herald;* established the *Country Editor,* 1895; joined the faculty of the University of Missouri in 1908 when he founded the School of Journalism; Missouri Press Association, 1887, as president; National Editorial Association, 1905; representative of North America at International Press Congress, Switzerland, 1902; organizer of World Press Parliament, St. Louis, 1904; Board of Curators of the University of Missouri, 1898-1908; traveled in Africa, Asia, and Europe, fellow to the Khan Foundation for Foreign Travel of American Teachers, 1913-14; director of the International Press Conference in San Francisco, 1915; First president of the World Press Congress, 1915-25; First president of the Pan-American Congress of Journalists, Washington, 1925; member of National Press, Washington; fellow British Institute of Journalists and National Union of Journalists of Great Britain; on special government mission to China and Siberia, 1918-19.

Chapter 4

Going National

News of the first campus advertising fraternity traveled quickly. Advertising students at the Universities of Kentucky and Illinois became interested in forming chapters of the new fraternity.

Late in 1914 a chapter was established on the campus of the University of Illinois, to be followed a few weeks later by the establishment of the third chapter at the University of Kentucky.

America's involvement in World War I stopped any additional growth of chapters during the rest of the 'teens. In fact, activities of the three chapters already started slowed down considerably and in some cases came to a complete halt. In *Twenty Years of Education for Journalism*, Mrs. Walter Williams, wife of Dean Williams of the Missouri School of Journalism, pointed out that another reason why the number of chapters did not increase in number during that period was due to the failure of advertising as a profession to attract enough attention to itself to be taught in universities and colleges. In 1928 she wrote that once the advertising curriculum at Missouri had been accepted, other schools were rapidly beginning to offer courses of instruction.

A brief note in the *Columbia Evening Missourian* on January 6, 1920, reported that officers of the John W. Jewell Chapter were beginning to make plans for the first national convention of Alpha Delta Sigma. The meeting was to be held in conjunction with the annual Journalism Week activities that are held each May on the Missouri campus.

By the time of this announcement in 1920 a chapter had been established at Georgetown (Ky.) College. Members of the chapter at Missouri had already taken it upon themselves to provide the facilities of a national organization for the other three chapters.

The prospective first convention did not materialize and the forming of a national organization, along with the election of national officers, was conducted by mail among the four chapters.

Oliver N. Gingrich, one of the charter members of the fraternity, was elected national president. Other officers elected included: Alfonso Johnson, Missouri, vice president; Herbert Graham, Kentucky, secretary; and Myron McCurry, Georgetown, treasurer.

Gingrich served as national president until 1926 when the chapters met together for the first time at a national convention.

Professional Endorsement

In 1921, officers of Alpha Delta Sigma and Gamma Alpha Chi were endorsed by the Associated Advertising Clubs of the World at their annual convention in Atlanta, Georgia. Gamma Alpha Chi, the women's professional advertising fraternity, had been founded as a counterpart of ADS on the campus of the University of Missouri in 1920.

Together, the two organizations made a report to the educational committee of the National Advertising Commission at which time they announced the first meeting of the Conference on Student Advertising Organization that was being held in connection with the Atlanta convention.

Joe B. Hosmer, chairman of the Student group, prepared a pamphlet that was distributed to the delegates of the convention. In a preface to the handout Charles H. Mackintosh, chairman of the educational committee, wrote: "Your committee desires to set forth the best way in which to make use of the honorary advertising fraternity as a means to promote the life of the advertising clubs in colleges. The mortality among college advertising clubs in the past has been high because of the constant change in personnel. It is too much to demand of faculty members that they shall take charge of a movement of this sort, and so the most successful plan has been found to follow the outline contained in the attached pamphlet prepared by Mr. Hosmer in collaboration with members of the Educational Committee of National Advertising Commission and also with members of the Conference of Student Advertising Organizations" (*Columbia Evening Missourian*, June 24, 1921).

Four universities were represented at the meeting: University of Texas, Amos Tuck School of Finance, Dartmouth College, Georgia School of Technology and the University of Missouri.

Hosmer, who was also president of the University of Missouri chapter of ADS, was re-elected chairman of the Conference for that next year. Louise Wilson, president of the Gamma Alpha Chi chapter of the University of Missouri, was elected secretary, and Miss Louise Gladney, of the University of Texas GAX chapter, was chosen treasurer. John B. Powell, at that time vice president for the Orient in Associated Advertising Clubs of the World was present at the meeting.

The next year, 1922, saw a fast growth of chapters. Dartmouth started their chapter that year with the universities of Michigan and Washington founding chapters in 1923.

Four chapters were added to the fast-growing fraternity in 1924: Georgia Tech, Columbia University, University of Oregon and the University of Oklahoma.

In 1925, four more chapters joined the national organization: Boston University, University of Kansas, University of Minnesota and Syracuse University.

The 1926 Convention

It was felt that the need for a national convention was a must in 1926 due to the lack of a centralized type of national structure for the fraternity. Arthur E. Horst, who had enrolled in the School of Journalism at Missouri as a special student was elected president of the Jewell chapter, began a movement to get the fraternity to hold its first national convention at Columbia, Mo., during the annual Journalism Week in May of 1926.

The *Columbia Missourian* reported that the national convention of ADS convened on the morning of May 12, 1926 in Jay H. Neff Hall, University of Missouri. Delegates came from University of Kansas, Boston University, Georgia Tech University, Washington University (St. Louis), University of Oklahoma, Georgetown University, University of Kentucky and the University of Missouri. Delegates by proxy came from Columbia University, New York; Syracuse University; and Dartmouth University.

Due to absence of national officers Professor Arthur Hallam, University of Oklahoma, was elected temporary chairman of the convention. Charles A. Freck, a student member of the Missouri chapter, was chosen as temporary secretary. The main topic of discussion for the first session was the present national status of the fraternity.

At the next session of the national body E. K. Johnston, assistant professor of advertising, University of Missouri, was elected grand national president. Other officers elected included: first vice president, William P. Langreich, instructor in advertising in Columbia University, New York City; second vice president, R. W. Jones, associate professor of advertising at the University of Washington; third vice president, D. C. Anderson, on the advertising staff of the *Dallas News,* Dallas, Texas; grand secretary, Arthur Hallam, professor of advertising at the University of Oklahoma; and grand treasurer, W. B. Cole, of the University of Minnesota.

The convention ended with a banquet at the Daniel Boone Tavern where thirty members heard speeches by the new officers. A national convention for the next year was planned to be held again in conjunction with the Missouri Journalism Week.

Only two new chapters were started during 1926: Washington University, St. Louis, Missouri, and Oregon State University. The universities of Alabama and California began chapters in 1927.

The 1927 Convention

The second annual convention of ADS was held May 9-10, 1927 on the campus of the University of Missouri. At the business session in the council room of Jay H. Neff Hall, delegates of the various chapters made reports on the progress of their chapter. Those present included: Joseph McBride, University of Oklahoma; John Sparks, Jr., of Kansas; Calvin P. Horn, Jr., Oregon; J. R. Dorig, California; R. A. Stipes, Illinois; and J. C. Duckworth, Alabama. Six of the nine national officers were in attendance.

Champaign, Illinois, was chosen as the site for the third annual convention of the fraternity. The meeting was arranged for immediately after Christmas while the members were on vacation.

E. K. Johnston was re-elected grand president of the fraternity. D. C. Anderson of the *Dallas Journal;* Robert W. Jones, professor of advertising at the University of Washington; and Roger Washburn, instructor of advertising at Boston University, were elected grand vice presidents. Other officers included: Arthur Hallam, grand secretary and grand editor; Oliver Gingrich, employment director and publicity director; Alfonso Johnson of the *Dallas News,* alumni director; and Roy Marshall, Seattle, Wash., extension director.

Dean Walter Williams, Missouri School of Journalism, spoke briefly at the closing banquet held at the Daniel Boone Tavern. He said, "Seek ye first the high standards of advertising and the needful things of life will be added to you." He outlined briefly the essential factors in a true advertising man's creed stating that the honest, truthful message is advocated above the other things in the advertising world.

Grand President E. K. Johnston and Treasurer Walter Cole were presented with Jeweled Alpha Delta Sigma pins in recognition of their efficient work.

The 1928 Convention

Dean C. M. Thompson of the College of Commerce, University

of Illinois, officially opened the 1928 convention at Champaign Urbana, Illinois. Some fifty members of the fraternity attended the third anual convention.

At the business session plans for the division of the United States into six ADS districts was deferred until each local chapter could discuss the question and repcrt back within one month. The national body decided to organize an employment bureau to aid their members upon graduation.

Bruce Barton, New York advertising agency executive, was clected as the first honorary professional member of the fraternity by the national body. Plans were laid to choose one honorary member a year in the future.

H. C. Peterson, president of the Illinois ADS chapter, arranged for the delegates to see a model initiation ceremony. Those initiated at that ceremony were: Horace Baker, George Goldstein, and E. G. Fruin.

At the business luncheon on the concluding day the delegates heard Irl H. Marshall of the Affiliated Newspapers, Chicago discuss the advantages and disadvantages of the advertising business.

Plaques were awarded to the University of Missouri and the University of Washington as the two chapters doing the most work as a chapter during that year.

Professor C. H. Fernald of the department of business organization, University of Illinois and advisor to that school's chapter, was elected grand president for the coming year.

Other officers elected included: Grand vice president, E. K. Johnston, Columbia, Mo.; W. F. Thacher, Eugene, Oregon; J. C. Anderson, Dallas, Texas; and R. D. Washburn, Boston University; grand secretary, Arthur Hallam, Madison, Wisconsin; grand treasurer, W. B. Cole, South Bend, Ind.; alumni recorder, Alfonso Johnson, Dallas, Texas; employment director, Oliver N. Gingrich, Sioux City, Iowa; extension director, R. S. Marshall, Seatle, Washington; and attorney, G. E. Sloan, Hammond, Indiana.

During 1928 five new chapters were added to the roles of the fraternity: Washington State University, University of Southern California, University of Nebraska, Ohio University, and the University of Texas.

The 1929 Convention

The Desha Breckinridge chapter, University of Kentucky, was the host to the 1929 convention held in Lexington, Ky. on October 4-5. President Frank L. McVey, University of Kentucky, welcomed the delegates at the opening session in the Phoenix Hotel.

Official representatives in attendance for the 1929 convention included: George Baker, University of Missouri; Walter Ackerman, University of Illinois; Wilford Valade, University of

Kentucky; Harold Stone, University of Washington; George Weber, University of Oregon; Stanley Roll, Washington State College; Millard Koogle, Oregon State College; Claire Fischell, University of California; John Dalzell, University of Southern California; Waymon Bishop, University of Alabama; Irving Teetsell, Syracuse University; and Dale Miller, University of Texas. Unofficial delegates and national officers brought the total attendance to about 50.

University of Kentucky professors R. D. McIntyre and J. B. Miner presided over parts of the program.

Robert W. Jones, professor of advertising at the University of Washington, was elected grand president of the fraternity for the next year. Other elected and appointed officers included: grand secretary, Arthur Hallam, Madison, Wisconsin; grand treasurer, James S. Shropshire, Lexington, Ky.; grand vice presidents, J. B. Miner, Southern division — H. H. Palmer, Eastern division — F. A. Russell, Big Ten division — E. K. Johnston, Missouri Valley division — W. F. G. Thacher, Western division.

It was at the Kentucky meeting that the national chapter decided to convene in national convention only every two years. The next planned convention was scheduled for the University of Washington in 1931.

While at Lexington the delegates were treated to a Blue Grass tour, a dance in their honor with about 250 turning out, and a football game between the University of Kentucky and Maryville College.

The University College of Los Angeles and the University of Wisconsin were the only chapters coming into the national organization in 1929. De Pauw's application for a chapter was approved at the national convention in 1929, but the chapter was not installed until 1930.

The 1931 Convention

National President Robert W. Jones called to order the fifth annual national convention of Alpha Delta Sigma on October 1, 1931 at the University of Washington campus in Seattle. Thirty-five delegates from 16 chapters were in attendance.

Dr. Henry A. Burd, professor of business administration at the University of Washington, was the principal speaker for the first noon luncheon. After business sessions in the afternoon the delegates were the guests of the Oregon and Oregon State ADS chapters at a banquet in the Wilsonian Hotel, followed by an initiation and theatre party.

Aside from the business activities of the convention the delegates attended a Gamma Alpha Chi dance at the Yacht club and the Washington-Montana football game, according to co-chairmen Glenn Goddard and Dick Williams.

Some of the speakers heard at the convention included: Lila Arnold, Seattle Gamma Alpha Chi alumna; Roy A. Hunter, Vancouver, B.C., president of the Pacific Advertising Club association; and Raymond P. Kelley, Spokane advertising and business counselor. Harold Stone, former president of the University Ad club, was toastmaster. Dick Williams, president of the Washington ADS chapter, presided at some of the events.

Mr. Hunter was initiated as an honorary member of the fraternity at the model initiation ceremonies.

The national convention body elected Professor Herbert Hall Palmer, Syracuse University, as the new national president. The newly elected vice presidents were: Arthur J. Brewster, Syracuse University; W. F. G. Thatcher, University of Oregon; E. K. Johnston, University of Missouri; Fred A. Russell, University of Illinois; and James Minor, University of Kentucky. Arthur Hallam continued as secretary and treasurer of the national organization.

Syracuse University was selected as the site for the next national convention.

The only new chapter to come into ADS in 1931 was sponsored by Butler University. In 1932 a new chapter was installed at Indiana University, to be followed by three more new chapters in 1933 at New York University, Temple University, and Pennsylvania State University.

The Conventionless Years (1932-1937)

After the national convention in 1931 the fraternity did not hold another convention until 1938. Arthur Hallam, national secretary and treasurer, indicated that during the depression years most of the business, including the elections of national officers, was carried on by mail.

Herbert Hall Palmer was the last advertising educator to serve as national president of the fraternity for the next decade. The top executive position of the fraternity went to outstanding advertising practitioners, who in many cases served only in honorary capacities.

Bruce Barton, one of the founding partners of Batten, Barton, Durstine, and Osborn, was elected national president for 1934. Mr. Barton had distinguished himself through the agency and through the many other national advertising organizations. He was the first honorary professional member taken into ADS.

In 1935 Paoli A. Smith, Sparrow Advertising Agency, Birmingham, Alabama, succeeded Barton as national president. Coming into office with Smith were vice presidents: George B. Hotchkiss, New York University; Everett A. Tapscott, advertising manager of the *Indianapolis Times;* Ralph Dorsett, advertising manager of S. Ferris Department Stores. Austin, Texas; and Carl A. Bundy, Bundy, Quill and Press, Los Angeles.

A former president of Advertising Federation of America, Charles C. Younggreen, became the 1936 national president for Alpha Delta Sigma. Mr. Younggreen had served as one of the principals for three different advertising agencies, but was president of Reincke-Ellis-Younggreen & Finn in Chicago while serving as ADS head. The October 13, 1932 issue of *Printers' Ink* carried a story about Younggreen's being selected to organize the advertising for the re-election of Herbert Hoover.

Mr. Younggreen's vice presidents included: A. G. Norment. *Fort Worth Press*, Marshall Adams, *Good Housekeeping*, New York; John Cuddy, Californias, Inc., San Francisco; and James W. Petty, Jr., Davison-Paxon Co., Atlanta.

Another former Advertising Federation of America president, E. H. McReynolds, served as national president of Alpha Delta Sigma in 1937. Mr. McReynolds served Missouri Pacific Lines, St. Louis, from 1924 to 1937. At the time of his departure to the James Mulligan Printing and Publishing Company in 1937 he was head of Missouri Pacific's advertising and publicity staff.

Mr. McReynolds' death in late 1937 brought about the second election for the national presidency in the same year. Completing the 1937 year as national president was Chester H. Lang, a vice president of the General Electric Company, Schenectady, N.Y. A native of Pennsylvania, Mr. Lang served as president of Advertising Federation of America from 1934 to 1936.

Serving as vice presidents under McReynolds, and later Lang, were: John J. Tigert, University of Florida, G. D. Crain, Jr., *Advertising Age*, and Don E. Gilman, National Broadcasting Company. Lang had served as a vice president prior to becoming president.

Franklin and Marshall College was the only new chapter installed in 1937. City College of New York was granted a charter in 1938.

Don E. Gilman took over the national reigns of ADS early in 1938. Gilman, who is now retired and living in Los Angeles, was with NBC until it divided into two networks. At that time he became a vice president with the American Broadcasting Company. Later he served as executive vice president of the Western Oil and Gas Association.

While serving as president of the Pacific Coast Advertising Association (later known as the Advertising Association of the West) Gilman was initiated as an honorary member of ADS by the University of Washington chapter.

It was during the early months of 1938 that plans were being made for a national convention of the fraternity.

Little has been said about the man who served as the unifying force for the fraternity from 1926 until 1938—secretary Arthur Hallam. Hallam had become interested in ADS while serving on the faculty of the University of Oklahoma from 1922 to 1925. Prior to joining the Oklahoma faculty he had served eight years in advertising and other business fields in Madison, Minneapolis, St. Paul, and Chicago.

Born in Sioux City, Iowa, Hallam received his early education there and in Wisconsin. He received a Bachelor of Arts degree from the University of Wisconsin in 1914. At Wisconsin he was extended membership to Phi Beta Kappa.

While secretary of ADS Hallam returned to Wisconsin to become an assistant professor of business administration in the University of Wisconsin Extension Division from 1927 to 1931. During the remainder of his term of office with ADS he worked with the Rex Theatre in Evansville, Wisconsin.

It was during Hallam's first term of office in 1928 that he became editor of the *Town Crier*, the official publication of ADS at that time.

Hallam moved to Pomona, California, in 1940 where he established his own sales promotion counseling business. He died in 1965 at a time when many of the records of the early years of ADS were destroyed. In a letter written before his death, Hallam makes the following comments pertinent to a history of ADS: "If you ever write a history, I can give you a lot of information. The fraternity had existed on paper for ten years prior to my election, but had not done much except charter a handful of chapters. All I had to go on was a small fibre box of mixed up papers."

Neither the small fibre box nor any other records were found after his death.

Chapter 5

Rejuvenation

The thirties with the depression and slow economic recovery in the United States saw little growth in Alpha Delta Sigma. It was a period as W. F. G. Thacher, a former national president pointed out, in which the affairs of the fraternity were nearly entirely in the hands of the national secretary, Arthur Hallam. Most of the fraternity's business was conducted by mail.

Only eight new chapters were added during the entire decade. DePauw University came in 1930, and was followed by: Butler University (1931), Indiana University (1932), New York University (1933), Temple University (1933), Pennsylvania State University (1933), Franklin and Marshall College (1937), and City College of New York (1938).

Realizing the poor financial status of the fraternity and the need for a stronger national organization, Don Francisco and Howard Willoughby lead the Los Angeles Alumni Association of ADS in instigating a national convention of the fraternity in Los Angeles in 1938.

A story in the April 18, 1938 issue of *Advertising Age* reads: "ADS will stage its first national convention in seven years in Los Angeles, June 24-30. Meetings during the last four days of this period will be held in conjunction with the Pacific Advertising Clubs Association."

1938 *Convention*

Don E. Gilman, then vice president of NBC Hollywood and a professional member from the University of Washington presided at the Silver Jubilee Convention. The main business at the convention was a discussion of the financial straits of the fraternity. It was in debt almost $2,000, and there was talk of re-organizing the organization in hopes of regaining a sound financial footing.

The first order of business was accepting the retirement of Arthur Hallam. Mr. Hallam had been the only paid member of the fraternity for many years.

In a news release President Willoughby disclosed that "Arthur Hallam of Harvard, Illinois, has been retired and is no longer secretary-treasurer of the fraternity. It is asked that all fraternity correspondence go to Professor Billig..."

Through the combined efforts of Mr. Gilman and the national officers elected at this convention a complete and more satisfactory plan of fraternity management was set up and put into operation. Gilman was awarded the Sixth Degree Key for being instrumental in the re-organization at this convention. Prior to Gilman's award, only Robert W. Jones and Bruce Barton had received the highest award of the fraternity.

Howard Willoughby, then with Foster & Kleiser Company and later with *Sunset* magazine, was elected national president. Willoughby later served as president of the Advertising Association of the West. He has since retired and is living on the West Coast.

Elected along with Willoughby were: secretary, William C. Billig, USC; treasurer, James S. Shropshire, Kentucky; vice presidents, Darrell B. Lucas, NYU; W. F. G. Thacher, Oregon; and Lee Groves, Missouri.

During the Willoughby administration the fraternity began to eliminate its debts and build up the national organization. An announcement was made during the year of a new quarterly publication that was to be called *Lineage* (now spelled *Linage*). The first issue appeared February 1, 1938. This was to be a sister publication to *The Town Crier* which had been edited by Hallam for more than ten years. *Lineage* was to be the voice of the fraternity and would enable subscribers to keep up with the advertising world. *The Town Crier* would continue to be a more internal publication.

By convention time in 1939 the total membership of the fraternity was nearly 3,500, including both alumni and undergraduate members. A publication for the Brewster Chapter, Syracuse University, written by David Dayette, Jr., in 1939 reported: "Since its re-organization last year, ADS has taken on new life with a stronger national organization that is earnestly seeking to bind its chapters together in a concentrated effort to give the fraternity an importance never before dreamed of."

Increased activities were seen in the rejuvenated national organization during 1938. An article in the November 21, 1938 issue of *Advertising Age* carried this story about a proposed research program.

"ADS will collaborate in the consumer research program now being carried on by the American Association of Advertising Agencies . . ." A resolution followed accepting the fraternity's assistance.

"This cooperation," Mr. Willoughby said, "will bear special reference to the Consumer Advertising Council Studies and to those being made by the Advertising Research Foundation at the School of Business of Harvard University.

"The fraternity's efforts are expected to be of dual value; first in providing an effective student channel for consumer research and second, in opening ports of contact between the advertising profession and faculty staffs of universities and colleges."

"The research program will be carried on by officers of the fraternity and the national office of the Four A's under the direction of President John Benson."

A follow-up story in the May 15, 1939 issue of *Advertising Age* told about the progress of the study:

New York, May 9—"In an effort to determine how much credence consumers place in advertising they read and to appraise general attitudes toward the field as a whole, Alpha Delta Sigma, advertising fraternity, has launched a nationwide survey on the subjects."

"The study, which is being made in cooperation with the Advertising Research Foundation, is directed by the Graduate School of Business Administration at Harvard University. Investigators are student members of the fraternity's 18 college chapters."

"The field men are equipped with two questionnaires, devised by Neil Borden, professor of advertising at Harvard, and approved by the American Association of Advertising Agencies. It is planned to interview 25,000 consumers before the study is completed next month . . ."

"Results of the survey will be presented at the fraternity's annual convention to take place in conjunction with the Advertising Federation of America's annual meeting June 18-22."

1939 *Convention*

ADS was a thriving organization when Willoughby brought the chapters to New York for the 1939 convention. Much of the debt had been repaid and an emphasis was now being made to bring new chapters into the organization as well as bringing new life to those chapters that had been inactive.

The 1939 convention program concerned the problems confronting advertising students and the general advertising industry. Speakers at the convention included Paul Hollister, executive vice president, R. H. Macy & Co.; Otto Kleppner, president, The Kleppner Co.; William H. Johns, Chairman of the Board, Batten Barton, Durstine and Osborn; William Robinson, advertising director, *New York Herald Tribune;* Ken R. Dyke, director of national sales promotion, NBC; and A. O. Buckinham, vice president, Cluett, Peabody & Co.

A progress report on the consumer opinion of advertising was made by Dr. Neil Borden.

In addition to Don Gilman the national body presented The Sixth Degree Key to George Burton Hotchkiss, New York University; Howard Willoughby, San Francisco; and Frank A. Nagley, University of Southern California.

Executive Vice President C. C. Younggreen, Reincke-Ellis-Younggreen and Finn, Inc., Chicago, was elected to lead the fraternity for the 1939-40 year. Younggreen had been initiated into ADS by the University of Wisconsin chapter.

Also elected as national officers for the next year were: secretary, Eric Smith, Burrows, Inc., Los Angeles; treasurer, James Shropshire, Kentucky; vice presidents: Frank A. Nagley, USC; J. T. Tigert, Kentucky; E. K. Johnston, Missouri; and Herbert H. Palmer, Syracuse.

A new position, chairman of publications board, was established at the convention with Robert Funk, USC, being appointed to the position.

Eric Smith, who today is a partner of Smith and Hemmings, Los Angeles, said that because of Willoughby and Gilman and their officers, the debt that plagued the fraternity at the 1938 convention was completely wiped out in the three years that followed. This was done through the unselfish service of many persons in advertising and in colleges who served during those years without compensation.

1940 *Convention*

National officers Eric Smith and C. C. Younggreen brought the 1940 national convention to Columbia, Missouri—the birthplace of the fraternity. May 7-10 was the first time the national body had met on the campus of its birth since 1927.

The enthusiastic efforts of the fraternity began to pay off with three new chapters brought in that year: Stanford University, San Jose State College, and Northwestern University.

The 1940 convention was to be the last meeting before World War II. Only one Sixth Degree Key was presented by the national body at the Columbia meeting. It was fitting that it went to E. K. Johnston, one of the real stalwarts of the fraternity. After his initiation in 1921 he served as national president, vice president, and secretary. No one man probably served the fraternity more faithfully.

Ken R. Dyke, vice president of National Broadcasting Company, was elected national president. Along with Dyke, E. K. Johnston was elected national secretary and Eric J. Smith was elected national treasurer. Joseph Starr, Wisconsin; Clyde Robinson, Washington; James Shropshire, Kentucky; and Donald W. Davis, Penn State; were elected vice presidents.

Younggreen was elevated from president to chairman of the Grand Council. G. B. Hotchkiss, Jr. was named editor of *Lineage* by the national body.

Dyke, who is now senior vice president of Hardy Jones, Smith Dingwall Associates in New York said that during his term of office a primary effort was directed toward stimulation of activity in chapters by the initiation of competition for an annual cup award.

In 1941 Dyke became Chief, Bureau of Campaigns, Office of War Information, Washington and then served as a Brig. General on General MacArthur's staff in the Southwest Pacific. He returned to NBC after the war, and before coming to his present position, was vice president for Young and Rubicam.

1941 *Convention*

The war forced the cancellation of the 1941 convention which had been planned for the University of Oregon. The national officers decided to conduct the business of the fraternity by mail since they could not hold a meeting.

Only Babson Institute was added to the chapter roles during 1941. This was to be the last chapter installed until after the war.

The national body bestowed the Sixth Degree Key upon W. F. G. Thacher, pioneer advertising educator of the University of Oregon. The school's chapter bears his name.

Lou R. Townsend, Bank of America, San Francisco, was elected national president through the mail ballot.

Johnston and Smith were re-elected as secretary and treasurer. Davis was re-elected as a vice president along with Thacher and Lloyd D. Harold, Northwestern.

1942 *Convention*

Another convention-by-mail was held in the spring of 1942. By this time policy had been established for the national president to move automatically to the position of chairman of the Grand Council.

W. F. G. Thacher was elected national president of the organization, a position that he retained until after the war. Also re-elected until after the war, was E. K. Johnston as national secretary. With exception of Thacher, all other vice presidents were re-elected. Replacing Thacher was Clifford Weigle, San Jose, as western vice president.

In January of 1943 Eric Smith resigned as national treasurer and was replaced by John Eggers. Eggers resigned a few months later and was replaced by Edward E. Keeler, Compton Advertising Agency, Los Angeles. Keeler retained the position until after the war and was honored by the fraternity in 1947 with the Sixth Degree Key.

The War Years

President Thacher's accounts of his activity while national president are best recounted in an article he prepared in 1963 to be published with other material during the 50th anniversary of the University of Oregon's School of Journalism. Mr. Thacher, now in his nineties, lives in Eugene, Oregon.

Mr. Thacher recalls:

"My election to the national presidency of Alpha Delta Sigma in the year 1942 came as a complete surprise. Up to that time I had taken only incidental interest in the affairs of the parent body, but had devoted whatever I had in the way of time and energy to the welfare of the local chapter, and to the stimulation of interest and support for the cause of education in advertising on the part of professional advertising on the Pacific Coast. Actually, I had never attended a national convention, and had but a cursory knowledge of the situation in the East and the Middle West. Nor is any possible credit due me for holding that office for a period of six years. When World War II struck, all such interests were, inevitably and properly, simply put into cold storage 'for the duration.' Plans for the national convention, which had been assigned to Eugene, were filed away for future reference.

"World War II did bring to me, however, an opportunity to serve my country *and* the cause of education in advertising at one and the same time. And that is a chapter in my life that I take great pride in recalling. Here, in brief, is the story:

"One afternoon in the early summer of 1945 I was called to the telephone to take a long-distance call from Washington, D.C. The voice I heard was that of a certain captain to ask me if I would be interested in an appointment to teach advertising in one of the two universities being set up in Europe in order to meet the needs of the great numbers of G. I.'s held there awaiting their turn to be brought home.

"Would I? If there was anything in the world I wanted at that time, that was it. I already knew something about the program. Dean Theodore Kratt, of the School of Music had already accepted such an appointment, and was on that account the envy of his colleagues.

"'But I'm forced to remind you that I'm sixty-seven years

36

old.' I said.

"We know that, Professor. In fact, we know a lot about you and your record. It was Mr. Otto Kleppner who recommended you. We're prepared to waive the age limit of sixty-five — 'if you can pass the physical examination, that is.

"That physical examination scared the daylights out of me. Still vivid in my memory was my experience when, in World War I, at the conclusion of two months training at the Presidio of San Francisco, I was pronounced ineligible for a commission because of various physical disabiilties, and plunged into the depts of disappointment—only to get rescued by a special dispensation from the Surgeon General's office.

"This time, however, I passed with no great difficulty, and after a brief period of feverish preparation, I found myself on a plane—my first, by the way—for New York City and what promised to be an exciting and challenging adventure.

"Anything like a detailed account of Shrivenham Army University would be far too long for this record—and, moreover, not germane to the paper's primary purpose. This one statement will suffice: Shrivenham is the one case in the history of educational institutions in which a full-panoplied university was created, matured, lived its full functional life, and died—within the space of one year.

"And one added note: When it became known that the national president of Alpha Delta Sigma was a member of the faculty, it came to light that there were a few members of the fraternity among the G.I. students, and at least one faculty adviser. With this small nucleus, it was proposed that a chapter be formed at Shrivenham. To that end I communicated with the national secretary—E. K. Johnston, at the University of Missouri, as I remember—and, with such a wealth of material to draw on from the highly qualified students in my classes, there is every reason to believe that the plan would have been carried into execution had it not been for the announcement of the termination of the University's life tenure. What had happened was that the process of demobilization had been so speeded up that there were no longer a sufficient number of qualified students among the G.I.'s remaining in the European theatre to justify a third 8-week term.

"The last class in advertising I ever taught was at Shrivenham. And it came as near to being a failure as any I could remember. It was one of those last-minute classes, set up in order to take care of students who had failed to find enrollment in regular classes. Moreover, the hour—three o'clock in the afternoon—was clearly unpopular. There was not a member of that small class who had any measurable interest in the subject, or any aptitude for it. Of course I did the best I could—working, as I had in my other classes, without text books, and with only a most meagre supply of the references, samples and other materials upon which any teacher comes to depend. But when I stepped out of that dismal classroom into the chill drizzle of a late December after-noon, it was with that sense of failure and frustration which every sensitive teacher is bound at times to experience. As a compensation, however, I had only to think of another class, regularly scheduled in the morning and covering the same field, which I have always considered the most brilliant class I ever attempted to teach. How could it have been anything else? On the roll of its membership of twenty-odd, every man, with one exception, had been in civilian life a practitioner of advertising in some form or other—writer, artist, salesman, and so on. And maybe they didn't keep me on my pedagogical toes!

"Although my contract with the Army was for one year, and my leave from the University for that period, I took advantage of the privilege to resign—but only after a three weeks assignment to a so-called lectureship in Europe. Most of that time I spent in Hochst, a suburb of Frankfurt, living in comparative luxury at an Officers' Club, and with nothing to do but serve in a nominal capacity on the staff of some regimental publication. But at least my trip afforded me an opportunity to visit Paris, and to witness the awful destruction wrought by war on Le Harve, Paris, Frankfurt, and other places."

1947 *Convention*

Largely through correspondence, Thacher and Johnston made arrangement for the first post-war convention to be held in Chicago in the spring of 1947. Twenty-one undergraduate chapters and one alumni-professional chapter were represented at the national meeting.

The constitution was revised; conventions were to be bi-annual instead of every year with regional meetings in the off years and a policy was adopted of choosing national presidents from the ranks of practicing teachers of advertising, rather than professional luminaries.

At the convention Johnston informed the national body that he no longer wished to succeed himself as national secretary. As Thacher recounted, Johnston suggested a young man recently added to the faculty of the School of Journalism at the University of Missouri who, in his opinion, would meet the requirements of the job. The man, Milton E. Gross, was contacted by phone and agreed to serve the fraternity. He maintained the office for 14 years during an expanding and meaningful era.

Not the least important was the election of Pennsylvania State University's Donald W. Davis as national president. Thacher became chairman of the Grand Council and was later made an honorary life member of that body, a position that he alone has received.

In addition to the election of Davis and Gross, B. R. Canfield of Babson Institute was elected treasurer.

At the time of the convention ADS consisted of 39 chapters, including the installation of a chapter at the State University of Iowa in 1946. Roosevelt University made the 40th chapter in 1947.

As Thacher stated, ''I think it is fair to say that the Alpha Delta Sigma we know and love was re-born at the Chicago convention.''

Don Davis' impact on Alpha Delta Sigma was tremendous. His memory is highly honored within the fraternity, and the fraternity's top chapter award carries his name. ADS was instrumental also in his election to the Advertising Hall of Fame, the first educator to be so honored.

For many, the national organization of Alpha Delta Sigma became a reality for the first time when Davis took a sabbatical leave from his position at Pennsylvania State University to travel, visiting each of the more than thirty active chapters during the last six months of 1949. Davis commented on his trip in his President's Corner which appeared in the December, 1948 issue of *Linage*.

As explained in the news story the purpose of the trip, as conceived by national officers, is two fold: (1) To meet with the membership of existing chapters; (2) To make calls at colleges and universities where interest has been shown in the formation of a new chapter or where new chapters might seem to be in order. To establish these objectives will be my major activity during an expected semester's sabbatical leave from my work here at Penn State.''

Davis' trip pointed up new opportunities for a revitalized Alpha Delta Sigma. The primary purposes for the fraternity as stated by the founding fathers were just as meaningful in 1949 as they were in 1913. Due to organizational and financial problems in the thirties and the interruption of the war years, however, the fraternity had not established a sound national program. Davis raised a number of questions to be considered at the 1949 convention in Eugene, Oregon, which were to provide momentum in this direction. Some of these considerations were outlined in the May, 1949 issue of *Linage*.

1. What about a more specific policy on new undergraduate admissions? Should there be definite advertising course requirements? Should we define more specifically the phrase of collegiate rank in Section 2, Article I of the constitution?

2. Shall we undertake an aggressive plan for the expansion of alumni chapters in larger cities? Should we define more specifically the relationships of the alumni chapter, the national chapter, and the undergraduate chapter? We have only four alumni groups now but many officers and advisors feel that more alumni chapters can become one of our strongest agencies in 'bridging the gap'.

3. Obviously we should re-activate the vice presidency of the Southern district. New chapters in Georgia, Florida, and Central Texas, point up the need for a Southern vice president. What should be the boundaries of a re-activated Southern district and to what extent if any should the boundaries of other districts be revised?

4. Shall we undertake additional activities in the office of the National Secretary? Various chapter officers have suggested the desirability of a special Idea Exchange and of a National Job Placement Bureau. Can we afford these services and if so to what extent? Are there other services that the national office should undertake?

During the 1947-49 biennium nine schools were granted new ADS charters. In order of acceptance they were: Baylor, De Paul, Wayne, Emory, Michigan State, Miami (Fla.), Colorado, Rhode Island State and Florida. Of the 49 charters granted, 35 chapters had active programs at this time. The chapter at Emory became the first charter granted to a university in the Southeast.

The President's Cup Competition, started in 1940 and discontinued due to the war after 1941, was revised and was presented in 1948 to Northwestern University and in 1949 to the new chapter at Emory University. *Linage* resumed publication with the February, 1948 issue with Earl Porter, editor for this issue. George K. Morgan and James D. Wilson, along with Porter, edited other issues during the biennium.

Officers during the biennium other than Davis, Gross and Canfield included W. F. G. Thacher, Chairman; Robert W. Kenyon, *The Boston Post*, Boston, Mass., Eastern Vice President; Arne Rae, School of Journalism, University of Illinois, Urbana, Ill, Midwestern Vice President; and Martin R. Klitten, Klitten & Thomas Advertising, Los Angeles, Calif., Western Vice President.

1949 *Convention*

The National Council, for the first time, agreed to pay round trip rail coach fare for each delegate to the June, 1949 convention in Eugene, Oregon. Thus, it assured the convention of good attendance, and the result was a giant step forward in the national ADS program.

The delegates voted to accept higher standards for membership, to grant a new scholarship, work toward the formation of more alumni chapters, begin regional meetings on the off-year, establish a professional advisory board, accepted an official charter from the Advertising Federation of America and the Advertising Association of the West, and make W. F. G. Thacher a lifetime member of the National Council.

B. R. Canfield, former treasurer, was elected as president for the 1949-51 biennium. Milton Gross and Arne Rae were re-elected as National Executive Secretary and Midwestern Vice President, respectively. New members of the National Council included: Carl C. Webb, secretary-manager of the Oregon Newspaper Publisher's Association, Eugene, Oregon, Treasurer; Frederic H. Glade, School of Commerce, Accounts and Finance, New York University, Eastern Vice President; Ernest A. Sharpe, School of Journalism, University of Texas, Southern Vice President; and Rod MacDonald, The Biow Co., San Francisco, Calif., Western Vice President.

Robert Haverfield replaced George K. Morgan and Fred Damon as editor of *Linage*. He held the position for 14 years.

In strengthening the admission requirements for new undergraduate chapters, making it easier for the National Council to maintain the high standards of the fraternity, the following change was made in the constitution as cited in the October, 1949 issue of *Linage*:

"Collegiate chapters may be established in colleges and universities which for a suitable length of time have been empowered to grant bachelor's degrees, and which in the opinion of the National Council offer adequate group of courses in advertising and related subjects."

The new ruling implied that most new chapters would be established in schools which offered full four-year courses with programs in advertising or marketing.

The fraternity established its first major scholarship, a $750 grant to be awarded annually to an outstanding undergraduate member of ADS who would use the award for graduate study in a school of his choice. Barkev Kibarian of Rhode Island State College was the first recipient of the scholarship. He did his graduate work at New York University. NYU member Fred Schreier received the 1951 award, and he continued his graduate work at his alma mater.

A committee headed by Rod MacDonald, newly-elected Western Vice President of ADS, submitted to the convention a complete report outlining suggestions for expansion of ADS alumni activities and establishment of more alumni chapters in cities where advertising activities are concentrated.

The report outlined benefits of alumni activity to undergraduates (expansion of educational potentialities, job placement, fellowship), and to alumni (attraction to area of qualified and responsible men, fellowship, and orientation of alumnus when moving to new location).

The committee recommended that ADS vice presidents and faculty advisors, as well as individual alumni, take the lead in formation of new alumni chapters.

That the fraternity accepted the challenge is seen in the following comment of President Canfield in March, 1951:

"One of the most significant current developments in Alpha Delta Sigma is the expansion of our alumni activities. From a nucleus of three professional chapters in San Francisco, Los Angeles and Boston, we have chartered seven new alumni chapters in Chicago, Dallas, Houston, Kansas City, Memphis, New York City and Seattle during the past year."

In establishing regional biennial meetings on the off-year from the national convention, the fraternity hoped to promote regional interests and contacts. Such gatherings were to emphasize local chapter activities in order to help chapters do a better all-around job by learning more about what other groups were doing.

The regional conferences proved to be a successful addition to the ADS program and remains an integral part of the program today. President Canfield's reaction to the first such regional meeting at Robert Allerton Park, Monticello, Illinois, is a descriptive statement that might well apply today. Its reproduction from the May, 1950 issue of *Linage*:

I have just returned from the first of four annual regional conferences of Alpha Delta Sigma to be held this Spring in the East, South, West and Midwest. Our first conference held at Robert Allerton Park, Monticello, Illinois, with the Charles H. Dennis Chapter, University of Illinois as host on April 14, 15, and 16, was attended by more than forty delegates from ten chapters in the Midwest in addition to fifty members of the host chapter.

This first annual regional conference in the history of Alpha Delta Sigma will long serve as an example of a successful meeting and establish a precedent for an ideal meeting place, practical information, high inspiration and good fellowship which will be hard to equal.

Few more attractive settings for a meeting could be found than the beautiful English Georgian manor house belonging to the University of Illinois and situated on a six thousand acre estate in the rolling woodlands of the Sangamon Valley of central Illinois. Surrounding the residence is a series of formal gardens embellished with Old World statuary standing at the end of long avenues of evergreens down which the delegates strolled between sessions in the warm, spring sunshine.

Our midwest meeting made many impressions. First, it was an inspiring example of the closer relationship developing between ADS and the advertising profession. Leading advertising executives from the midwest, active in the national councils of advertising, not only addressed the delegates but took active part in the business sessions, freely contributing from their wide experience to counsel our members on vocational opportunities in advertising. This opportunity afforded our midwest members to become acquainted with advertising leaders was one of the most valuable products of the conference. Equally significant was the interest and enthusiasm shown by these professional advertising men in the work of our fraternity. It is good to know that we have many loyal and helpful friends in high places in advertising.

The conference served to bring together members from all over the Midwest with a common interest in advertising for an interesting and mutually helpful exchange of ideas about advertising practice and vocational opportunities. Members from Iowa exchanged ideas about advertising with men from Ohio; while Kansans traded views with Hoosiers from Indiana. All came away with a broader, more intelligent interest in advertising. The unifying influence of our organization was obvious in the new friendships made and the good fellowship prevailing at all sessions.

At the business sessions where pledging, entertainment, financing, publicity and many other topics were discussed, fine ideas for chapter operation were exchanged which are sure to result in more efficient conduct of chapter affairs. I was particularly impressed with the ingenious and successful fund raising activities of many of our midwest chapters. The chairmen of our conference business sessions showed unusual skill in leading discussion and bringing out the best experience of our most active chapters. This discussion of improving chapter business management was one of the most valuable features of the meeting.

The conference also afforded chapter advisors an opportunity to exchange experiences and gain practical understanding of the operating problems of other chapters. The valuable contribution made by our chapter advisors in the work of the fraternity, their keen interest, competence, and the part they are playing in carrying on and expanding the activities and values of our fraternity was apparent to all who attended the conference.

The dignity and significance of our initiation ritual made a lasting impression on both old and new members in a model initiation ceremony in which a large pledge class and professional members were initiated by our national officers and advisors.

Furthermore, the Midwest conference demonstarted conclusively that good regional as well as individual chapter meetings do not just happen, but are the result of careful planning, good organization, genuine cooperation, hard work, and willingness to take responsibilities. Our Midwest conference was a tribute to these qualities of our Midwest Vice President, Arne Rae; Frank B. Sanger, Advisor of the Charles H. Dennis Chapter; Stuart Helffrich, President of the host chapter and all of the host chapter members who contributed to make the conference a success.

Never have I attended a conference of any organization which so well combined the values of good fellowship, sound, practical information and real inspiration. I know from the plans now being made in our Eastern, Southern and Western regions that equally successful conferences will be held this Spring in those areas. I urge every Alpha Delta Sigma member and advisor to make plans now to attend his regional conference. These meetings afford an opportunity too valuable to be missed. The benefits which you will receive, including contacts with professional advertising people, vocational guidance, good fellowship, real personal enjoyment and greater knowledge of advertising cannot be compared with the small expense involved. Make your regional conference a "must." You will never regret it. I'll see you there.

Three leaders in advertising—Don Belding, Wesley I. Nunn, and Robert B. Brown—became the first members of the Professional Advisory Board for Alpha Delta Sigma. President Canfield appointed the board, with the advice of the National Council, because of the desire of ADS to work in closer cooperation with men who are outstanding members of the advertising profession. A December, 1949 issue of *Linage* stated:

"Work of the board will make it possible for the fraternity to gain from advice and recommendations on joint chapter projects, as well as other regional and national operations."

Development of the idea of such a board grew out of a luncheon at the AFA convention in Cincinnati, in June, 1948, following the judging of that year's President's Cup Project. At that time, Nunn; Karl T. Finn of the *Cincinnati Times-Star;* Otto Kleppner, teacher, author, and agency head; and Fred F. Bowden of the *St. Louis Post Dispatch* conferred with members of the ADS National Council about plans for the 1949 Cup Project.

Nunn, Midwestern member of the Advisory Board, was advertising manager of the Standard Oil Company, Indiana. A graduate of the University of Oklahoma, he is a professional member of the Northwestern University chapter. Brown, a professional member of the New York University chapter, was Eastern member of the Board. He was vice president and general manager of the Bristol-Myers Company and a director of the Association of National Advertisers. Belding, then Chairman of the Executive Committee of Foote, Cone and Belding, a professional member of the UCLA chapter, represented the Western area on the board. Belding later took an active part in the 50th Anniversary celebration in 1963.

Russell Z. Eller, advertising manager of the California Fruit Growers Exchange, Los Angeles, and Elon G. Borton, President and General Manager of the Advertising Federation of America. New York, presented AAW and AFA charters to ADS at the 1949 convention in Eugene.

The official presentations formalized a working relationship of ADS, AAW and AFA prior to 1949 and remains today symbolic of the concern for advertising education expressed continually by each of these organizations. In discussing the new affiliation with AFA, the October, 1948 issue of *Linage* stated:

"It is expected that this arrangement will prove of considerable mutual benefit to both organizations. ADS will contribute the viewpoint of the advertising student to AFA activities, while the AFA will undoubtedly contribute both prestige and tangible assistance to ADS. The National president of ADS becomes a member of the Advertising Federation Board of Directors, which should be a benefit in working out mutual plans.

"It is the plan of the Advertising Federation to follow through with a closer tie-up between ADS chapters and advertising clubs. To this end affiliated membership cards will be issued to each undergraduate member of ADS so that they can identify themselves for admission at any meeting or convention of AFA groups or clubs.

"The Advertising Federation will also release the AFA News to chapter advisors in such quantities as they may wish for distribution to their undergraduate members.

"The general advantage of the tie-up of ADS with the AFA, which has been the parent organization of most of our national advertising clubs, is quite obvious. It is felt by the officers of both groups that this affiliation is distinctly a step forward in bridging the gap between advertising training and advertising practice."

In convention speeches, Borton discussed the relation of ADS to organized advertising and outlined means by which greater cooperation might be attained between working practitioners in advertising and schools which are training young men to enter the advertising field. Eller's talk emphasized the great responsibility of advertising executives to encourage the training of young men now in the colleges and universities, on whom the future character of advertising so largely depends.

Both men are professional members of ADS—Borton at Penn State and Eller at Stanford. Borton later received the fraternity's Nichols Cup Award in 1957 for his outstanding contribution to advertising education. The chapter at Florida State University is named in his honor. Both men later served on the ADS Advisory Board.

The Convention voted W. F. G. Thacher a lifetime membership on the National Council of ADS. The resolution appeared in the October, 1949 issue of *Linage*:

"Because of his quarter century of leadership in Alpha Delta Sigma, his six years as national president of this organization, and because Alpha Delta Sigma needs his leadership and influence —it is resolved that Mr. W. F. G. Thacher be made a lifetime member of the Alpha Delta Sigma National Council.''

Five new charters were granted during the 1949-51 biennium at Ohio State University, University of Arizona, Denver University, Southern Methodist University, and the University of Houston. Forty of the 54 universities with charters maintained active programs during the biennium.

In 1950 *Linage* was mailed for the first time to every member, some 8,000 at that date. The AAW opened its 3 minute speaking contest to ADS members and the President's Cup went to New York University in 1950 and the University of Florida in 1951.

The fraternity sent a representative, Ed Preston of the University of Miami to the International Advertising Conference in London July 7-13, 1951. "ADS'er" Jerry Simmon also attended as an unofficial delegate. The British Advertising Association invited ADS as one of 30 organizations in the U.S. associated with advertising to send a representative to the meetings. The conference itself was a part of the Festival of Britain. World advertising leaders discussed common problems besetting the industry, comparing notes on advertising campaigns, techniques and aims. Preston was selected by the National Council after each chapter was invited to nominate one of its members to be considered.

1951 *Convention*

The National Council took a major step in the development of the welfare of the fraternity when it announced that for the June, 1951 convention at Cape Cod, Massachusetts it would include a special advisors' discussion session and pay most of the expenses of advisors to the convention. All of the lodging and meal expense at the convention, plus one-half the cost of round-trip rail coach fare was paid for advisors of chapters paying the $100 official delegate assessment. Thirty-four chapters were represented with 66 student members, 15 chapter advisors, 9 alumni representatives and 8 national officers.

Ernest A. Sharpe who had served as Southern Vice President during the previous biennium was elected President for the 1951-53 biennium. Other members of the National Council returning were Gross, MacDonald, Haverfield, and Canfield as Chairman. Noel P. Laird, Department of Economics, Franklin and Marshall College, Lancaster, Pa., became treasurer, a position he holds today. With the division of the Southern region into the Southeast and Southwest regions, four new Regional Vice Presidents were elected. These included: Philip W. Burton, School of Journalism, Syracuse University, Syracuse, New York; Frank W. Senger, Illinois Publishing Co., Champaign, Illinois; William Ridley,

47

School of Journalism, University of Oklahoma, Norman, Okla.; and Elmer J. Emig, Department of Journalism, University of Florida, Gainesville, Fla. During the second year of the biennium MacDonald resigned and Vernon R. Frost served as Western Region Vice President. Frost was Director of the School of Communications, University of Washington, Seattle, Washington. Robert B. Brown and Wesley I. Nunn were reappointed to the Professional Advisory Board and Russell Eller of Sunkist replaced Don Belding.

The fraternity established one of its finest awards at the 1951 convention. It presented for the first time an award to the person whom the fraternity felt had made the most outstanding contribution to advertising education. The award was named the Nichols Cup after its sponsor, Charles C. Nichols, first president of the Bruce Barton chapter of ADS at Boston U. First recipient of the award was Otto Kleppner, agency head and author.

Three new national awards were established during this biennium—the Affiliated Advertising Agencies Network Scholarship; The Otto Kleppner ADS Award; and the *Linage* Award.

Thomas L. Yates, president, Thomas L. Yates Advertising, Fort Worth, for whom the Texas Christian chapter is named, served as the first chairman of the AAAN Scholarship Committee. Students were nominated for the $250 award by ADS chapters, although students other than ADS were eligible. Irwin Towers, City College of New York, received the first scholarship in 1952.

Otto Kleppner established a new incentive award for ADS to go to the most outstanding advertising student of the year. It was given two years. James E. Donovan of Wayne State University was the unaminous selection in 1952; William Novak, University of Illinois received the award in 1953.

Boston University captured the *Linage* award for consecutive years in 1952 and 1953. This award encouraged chapters to develop effective newsletters. Similar awards were given to the Chicago and Northern California alumni chapters. The President's Cup went to Roosevelt University in 1952 and to the University of Oklahoma in 1953. Charles K. Nogle of UCLA received the $750 ADS scholarship to do graduate work at the Los Angeles school. Original winner, George D. Duff of Penn State, was unable to accept the scholarship due to entrance into military service.

President Sharpe appointed Gene Duckwall, Foote, Cone & Belding, Los Angeles, California, National Alumni Coordinator. This new post was established when the alumni committee felt that one man should be responsible for maintaining the excellent relationship that exists between alumni and undergradate chapters. The duties of the office were outlined in the October, 1951 issue of *Linage*:

"Maintain liaison with alumni chapters and the regional vice presidents. Be in charge of and direct alumni publicity. Report directly to the National Council.''

Eight new chapters were added during the 1951-53 biennium. Undergraduate chapters were installed at the University of Mississippi, Arizona State College, Marquette University and Florida State University. Alumni chapters began operation in Milwaukee, Pittsburgh, Atlanta and New Jersey. The 1,281 members initiated in the biennium brought the total membership to 11,088. The number initiated was nearly 1,000 less than the record biennium of 1949-51 when 2,205 became associated with the fraternity.

Here are the member agencies of the Affiliated Advertising Agencies Network who in cooperation with ADS made possible the AAAN Scholarship Award:

Freitage Agency, Atlanta, Ga.
Emery Advertising, Baltimore, Md.
Cline Advertising Service, Boise, Idaho
Adam F. Eby Advertising, Buffalo, N.Y.
Alex T. Franz Advertising, Chicago, Ill.
Joseph Agency, Cincinnati, Ohio
Ralph Sharp Advertising, Inc., Detroit, Mich.
Howell Agency, Elmira, N.Y.
Mithoff Advertising, El Paso, Texas
Thomas L. Yates Advertising, Fort Worth, Texas
Jaqua Advertising Co., Grand Rapids, Mich.
Edward W. Robotham Co., Hartford, Conn.
Charles Crosson & Co., Houston, Texas
Marks & Neese, Inc., Jackson, Miss.
Selders-Jones-Covington, Inc., Kansas City, Mo.
Foltz-Wessigner, Inc., Lancaster, Pa.
Arthur Towell, Inc., Madison, Wisc.
Rosengarten & Steinke, Inc., Memphis, Tenn.
Al Herr Agency, Milwaukee, Wisc.
Addison Lewis Co., Minneapolis, Minn.
Howard Barney & Co., Mobile, Ala.
John Mather Lupton Co., New York
Philip Klein Advertising, Inc., Philadelphia, Pa.
Jennings & Thompson Advertising, Phoenix, Ariz.
W. Craig Chambers, Inc., Pittsburgh, Pa.
Adolph L. Block Advertising, Portland, Ore.
Thomas C. Wilson Advertising, Reno, Nevada
Padco Advertising Co., St. Louis, Mo.
R. T. Harris Agency, Salt Lake City, Utah
Armstrong Schram Co., San Diego, Calif.
Robert B. Young Agency, San Francisco, Calif.
The Burle Co., Seattle, Wash.
Virgil A. Warren Advertising, Spokane, Wash.
Henry Quednau, Inc., Tampa, Fla.
James Lovick & Co., Toronto, Ontario

Gibbons Advertising, Tulsa, Okla.
James Lovick & Co., Vancouver, B.C.
McCormick-Armstrong Co., Wichita, Kan.
Lowell & Hall Advertising, Greenville, S.C.
Hixson-Jorgensen, Inc., Los Angeles, Calif.
Savage-Lewis, Minneapolis, Minn.
Cargill & Wilson Advertising, Richmond, Va.
Hofer, Dieterich & Brown, San Francisco, Calif.
Hoag & Provandie, Boston, Mass.
Lessing Advertising Co., Inc., Des Moines, Iowa
Leonard M. Sive, Cincinnati, Ohio

The only chapter ever to be disbanded was the Richard Joe Chapter at Emory University in 1952. It was dissolved because of the dissolution by the Emory Board of Trustees of the school's Division of Journalism. *Linage*, Oct. 1952, reported the incident in this manner:

"The action came after the head of the division, Dr. Raymond Nixon, resigned to join the staff of the School of Journalism at the University of Minnesota.

"The ADS National Council protested to the Emory trustees in July, pointing up the accomplishments of the Emory ADS chapter throughout its four-year life. The protest also stated:

" 'Under the direction of Professor Nixon and Professor Richard Joel the development of advertising instruction at Emory has been extremely well handled. We also feel that the advertising work on your campus showed great promise in its possibilities of future contributions to the journalistic and economic life of the state of Georgia and the South.

" 'For these reasons Alpha Delta Sigma wishes to go on record as regretting deeply the proposed discontinuance of advertising instruction on the Emory campus and in expressing the hope that Emory University may see fit to reverse its decision and provide for continuance of the entire journalism program at Emory.'

"The protest was acknowledged by a long, mimeographed explanation of the trustees' reasons for their actions."

Advertising students, teachers and practitioners over the years have come to respect the philosophy of Ernest Sharpe of the University of Texas. Some expressions of this philosophy appear in the following excerpts of the President's Corner in *Linage* during his tenure as head of ADS:

The ADS chapters over the nation that stand out are the ones that plan big. The Robert W. Jones chapter of the University of Washington is making advertising history with its "Give a Pint of Blood" campaign. At the last tally, and it's probably more now, 881 pints had been donated to the student blood bank. About 80 percent of the blood goes overseas to the Armed Forces. What finer job can advertising do than saving lives! The project of the Washington chapter is an outstanding success because they planned big. Their goal is 3000 pints of blood. The campaign of "Capt. Corpuscle" and "Pvt. Plasma" continues into 1951-52.

A "Conestoga Wagon" may not mean much to many of you, but it's the rousing symbol of college spirit at Franklin and Marshall at Lancaster, Penn. Thanks to the big plans of the H. W. Prentis Jr. Chapter several years ago. Well known in that section of the country, the Conestoga wagon was "the ship of inland commerce" during the Revolution and post-Revolution period. It comes as near being elegant as a covered wagon can. The Franklin and Marshall chapter wanted to present a Conestoga wagon to the college to be used at pep rallies, parades, home-coming games, etc. They planned a colossal campus "Stunt Night", raised the necesary funds, bought a 140-year-old Conestoga wagon, painted it blue and orange, and deeded it to the college in appropriate ceremony. Because of some big plans by the ADS chapter, Franklin and Marshall now has its "Conestoga Wagon."

By planning big, the Emory chapter presents in one package more big-name speakers than most chapters bring to the campus in a decade.

I wish there were space to tell the stories of other chapters well known for their big plans . . . of the William Wrigley Jr., Chapter at the University of Oklahoma with its annual store-wide promotion at Rothchilds, a large department store in Oklahoma City . . . of the Philip Ward Burton Chapter at the State University of Iowa with its advertising agency . . . of the W. D. Moriarity Chapter at the University of Southern California, whose pledges perennially produce the best sandwich boards in the country . . . of the George Burton Hotchkiss Chapter at New York University and the Golden Jubilee Advertising Convention it put over. Of course there are other topflight chapters not mentioned here, but space limitation doesn't permit a complete account.

On the lifetime relationships of ADS he comments:

"And that, briefly, is ADS, except for one more thing, if you're still interested."

A student had inquired about ADS. Should he join?

"Still interested," he said.

"In addition, you get a bonus when you join ADS, a sort of lifetime bonus. Understand, ADS has no monopoly on this bonus. It's a package anybody can buy. But when you're an ADS man, you have a coupon that entitles you to a better package. What is it? It's a package of friendships that will last a lifetime, and serve you in many ways.

"Usually a fellow in college doesn't realize how extremely valauable an article a friendship is. Back in the home-town, you grew up with plenty of friends. In college, new friends come easy. But, when you leave the campus, the friends go off in all directions. For a time after college you'll be too preoccupied to notice that something important is missing. Chances are you'll serve a hitch with Uncle Sam. In a couple of years, however, you'll be back, out of the service, and looking for a job. That's one of the times, mister, when you can use that ADS bonus to good advantage. Cash in that coupon, and you can get the help of some friends you never knew existed, and the support of friendships it ordinarily takes years to build.

"Take the case of Ralph Davis. He left the campus here about two years ago . . . put some time in sweeping mines off the Korean coast . . . got his discharge last summer . . . and headed for the States. The big operation ahead of him was to get a job. For good reasons, he wanted a job in California, but he didn't have a single personal acquaintance on the West Coast to lend a hand in the search for a job. However, he had something better—that ADS coupon—and when he hit San Francisco, he cashed it in. From reading *Linage*, he knew Rod MacDonald was ADS Western Vice-President and lived in the Golden Gate City. He called on Rod, and here are the job interviews that resulted:

With Stu Harding of BBD&O, with Wilmont Rogers and Fred Hasemann of CAL-PAC, with Hugh Thomas of McCann-Erickson, with Linn Gross of Biow, Phil Arnot of O'Mara & Ormsbee, Russ Collier of Foote-Cone & Belding, George Briggs of the San Francisco News.

Every firm is a big name in advertising, and every man but one an ADS man. Result of the interviews: A hard-working job with one of the firms, and a job wtih a great future in advertising.

"So, Ralph Davis cashes in his ADS coupon, and, in a way, he gets two bonus packages. He finds the right job, and he has some real friends among the ADS alumni in the San Francisco area. They get together for luncheon on the fourth Tuesday of each month at Upton's Restaurant, 565 California Street, in downtown SF. They're officially organized as the San Francisco Alumni Chapter."

The inquiring student asked if the ADS coupon was good in any city in the United States. The answer had to be, "No, at least not for full value." At present, it's redeemable at full value in only fourteen cities. They are the cities where the ADS alumni are organized. But it could easily be twenty-five or fifty cities, because there are enough ADS alumni in the fifty largest cities in the country to have an alumni chapter in each of them. There should be alumni chapters in Philadelphia, Detroit, Minneapolis, Atlanta, Cincinnati, Indianapolis, Denver, New Orleans, and Oklahoma City, to name a few possibilities. It's in some good cities like these where ADS is missing out on the full value of that lifetime bonus. Some good friendships are drifting away, and some good ADS graduates looking for their first jobs are not getting that friendly boost that helps so very much and comes at a time when it's appreciated the most.

It only takes ten ADS alumni and a total of $10 for the

charter to start an alumni chapter. What city will be No. 15 to cash in those ADS coupons? Who's next in line for the lifetime bonus? Drop a card to the National Secretary, and he'll help you get the organization going.

1953 *Convention*

The 1953 delegates to the national chapter meeting held in Daytona Beach, Florida, made no major changes in organizational structure of the program of ADS. Through the administrations of Davis, Canfield and Sharpe, the National Council had established a strong program format for both undergraduate and alumni chapters. During the next two years ADS was to play an important part in making both the academic and advertising world aware of the importance of professional advertising educational programs in the nation's colleges and universities.

Phil Burton of Syracuse University, was elected to the first of his two terms at the Daytona Beach meetings. Gross, Laird, and Haverfield were to serve again as Executive Secretary, Treasurer and Editor of *Linage* respectively. Senger and Frost were re-elected as Vice Presidents of their regions, and the following three men were elected as Regional Vice Presidents for the first time: Roger Washburn, Boston University; Lester Rice, University of Oklahoma; and Richard Joel, Florida State University. When Frost died in March, 1954, Charles W. "Chick" Collier, Executive Secretary of the AAW, was appointed to fill out his term.

The first action to occur came shortly after the Daytona Beach meeting when forty active alumni and professional members of ADS met in a breakfast session of the Advertising Association of the West meetings in San Francisco. Western Vice President Vernon Frost reported on the highlights of the national convention in Florida, and then the following resolution from *Linage,* Oct., 1953, was proposed by Don Belding and unanimously approved by the members present, and later presented and adopted by the AAW:

WHEREAS, advertising is essentially a profession; and

WHEREAS, its volume now exceeds Six Billion Dollars per year as an indication of its importance to the American economy; and

WHEREAS, in the opinion of this group, advertising has not been given the official recognition it richly deserves in the educational institutions of this nation;

BE IT RESOLVED that this body under its various contacts and connections urge wherever possible to all liberal arts colleges and universities, the enlargement of schools of advertising and the establishment of a degree in advertising for those who complete the curriculum.

To aggressively implement the decisions embodied in this Resolution, it is recommended that the President of this organization appoint a committee to properly outline the steps and procedures necessary to bring the full force of this organization to bear upon the accomplishment of the above-mentioned goal.

While the relationship of ADS to the AFA and AAW had been formalized in the presentation of a charter at the 1949 Eugene convention, Burton in the January, 1954 *Linage* put in writing a series of suggestions to maximize the effectiveness of this cooperative venture. His entire statement is presented here and remains an excellent guide for both ADS chapters and Advertising Clubs today.

A very friendly relationship exists between Alpha Delta Sigma and the Advertising Federation of America. The friendship is natural since both organizations aim at betterment of advertising. AFA's president, Elon Borton, has included ADS in AFA's meetings and plans.

Recently the AFA appointed a committee of advertising practitioners, and advertising teachers to evolve a plan for closer, more effective cooperation between advertising clubs and schools.

You will find in the following some specific suggestions for such cooperation. The suggestions include advertising clubs, undergraduate chapters of ADS, and college advertising departments (whether or not they have active ADS chapters).

1. Appoint Advertising Club committees that handle school cooperation as a year-round task and *work at it the whole year, not as an occasional gesture.*
2. Organize a list of Club members who are capable speakers and who will talk cheerfully on their specialties before advertising classes, or before the ADS chapter, or both.
   a. These men will be guided in speech content by the teacher and/or ADS advisor who will indicate what specific questions their talks should cover. This guidance will eliminate 'old-hat' information. It's amazing how little the speakers think the advertising students know about the business.
3. Develop closer cooperation between the Club, its members and the local chapter of ADS.
   a. Let the Chapter provide *intelligent* help in such affairs as as Advertising Week, if the Club has one. "Intelligent" is emphasized here because too often the help consists of putting up cards or performing some other routine job that teaches ADS members nothing about advertising.
   b. If Club meetings need survey or research work done, let the ADS chapter and its advisor (as guide) do the work and pay them the going rate.
4. Set up hard-working job placement committees in clubs that:
   a. Keep a file of job opportunities that will be made available to the school advertising department, and to the ADS chapter.
   b. Keep a file of data sheets submitted by the students of the School's advertising department and/or ADS chapter.

c. Supply summer jobs for advertising majors that will enable students to pick up some job experience before they are graduated.
5. Establish a scholarship for an outstanding student in advertising.
   a. Make the awarding of the yearly scholarship the focal point of a day in which the advertising program of the school is featured—possibly the school can give a presentation of its work, and the scholarship winner can give a short talk. The scholarship should amount to enough to be a real help to the student and to provide incentive for everyone in the school's advertising program whether he is, or is not, a member of ADS.
6. Individual Club members (especially on the retail side) can give projects for advertising students to do—can actually run the advertisements on occasion.
   a. Perhaps performance certificates may be given to winners to provide scrapbook material.
   b. Sometimes small cash awards may be given.
7. Establish an evaluation committee that will determine what it considers acceptable standards for the school advertising program. This committee may perform such functions as:
   a. Making visits to school to examine first-hand how teaching standards are maintained.
   b. Interview students to get their slant and see what kind of advertising knowledge they are acquiring.
   c. Making confidential reports and recommendations to head of school's advertising program.
   d. Making a public report if program head agrees.
   e. Help to obtain needed teaching equipment and materials for school advertising program. Such materials would include:
      • Reference material such as *Standard Rate & Data Service* copies, old copies of Starch Studies, etc.
      • Mechanical equipment that many schools have no money to buy such as film strip projectors, layout tables, etc.

In additions to these few suggestions for closer cooperation between the Advertising Club and schools, some of the broader cooperative aspects that might be considered are:
(1) Assign a permanent academic member to the AFA Board of Directors to act as an educational consultant to the organization. Currently the president of ADS is automatically an ex officio member of the AFA Board of Directors.
(2) Competent speakers from the AFA should be available to debate with economists. English teachers and sociologists since these three groups continually snipe at advertising in print and verbally.
(3) Push harder than ever for wide distribution of films that discuss the place of advertising in the economic system.

(4) Distribute more widely than ever, among the schools, reprints of such articles as that of Otto Kleppner's *Harper's* piece.

Burton tackled the problem of criticism from advertising practitioners who were uninformed of or about the professional advertising programs on many campuses in his March, 1954 President's Corner in *Linage*. He commented:

Eight prominent advertising agency men have contributed answers to a question asked in the February issue of the magazine *Advertising Agency*.

The question: "How do you believe the teaching of advertising in universities can be improved?"

The most interesting aspect of the replies is the uncertainty of the agency men as to what *is* occurring in the teaching of advertising.

One man says frankly, "I don't know how it's being taught now." Another says: "My guess is that the . . . Finally, to hazard a guess." Another says: "Since my personal experience with advertising instruction in university goes back many, many years . . ."

Yet, despite this admitted ignorance most of the respondents indulge in a rather general criticism of advertising instruction as it now exists. Several of the men decry the lack of "practical training." Some point suspiciously at the teachers as men without "practical experience."

Some of the men say away with "how to do it" advertising courses while others say there should be more of them.

Judging from the answers it is hard to believe that more than one or two of the men answering the question has the foggiest idea of what is offered in advertising instruction in the modern universities. How then can these men make worthwhile criticism or suggestions?

One of the men implies that advertising sequences are too trade schoolish—that courses in copy, production and so on should be replaced by additional courses in philosophy, history, English and economics. Apparently he is unaware that in universities offering an advertising major that advertising requirements must be balanced with many hours in the so-called broadening, liberal arts courses. In most schools, indeed, the curriculum forbids the inclusion of an extra-heavy load of vocational subjects.

These men who are worrying about the practical experience of the teaching staff are obviously unaware that universities offering major sequences in advertising almost always require that their teachers have a solid background of actual advertising experience. Check the staffs of these schools and you'll find former agency men, media men, and many others whose advertising experience will command respect. Furthermore, these schools frequently have men from downtown teaching courses. In addition, almost every advertising teacher has outside speakers from the field. Except for schools that minimize advertising, and perhaps offer but one course in the subject, the advertising teacher is likely to be a man of considerable practical background.

Several of the agency men suggested the use of case material. Most advertising sequences emphasize the case approach. Bordens' cases have been used for years in many schools; other case books are used, too. Instructors very often dig up cases of their own, also. This suggestion that cases be used is very often given by men in the field who somehow seem to think that as soon as a man leaves the field and begins to teach advertising that he immediately forgets everything he ever knew—that suddenly he he has become the muddleheaded professor of time-worn jokes.

Perhaps we in ADS can do something to enlighten the men in the field as to just what *is* going on these days in the university classrooms. Possibly we could be more active in inviting the downtowners to visit the schools. Let's not be so passive in nodding our heads when the man in business says "Aw, they can't teach anything about advertising in schools!"

The heck they can't! All over the country people *are* learning about advertising in school. And all over the country employers hiring advertising majors are finding that men with advertising training need lots less instruction and move along much faster. No one in advertising teaching claims that advertising graduates are polished products ready to fit smoothly into advertising jobs the very first day. Advertising teachers *do* know from talking to employers who have hired advertising majors that they'll usually "have more of the same."

The very existence of ADS is indication of the seriousness with which both students, faculty, and some practitioners view the learning of advertising in school. Just from the selfish standpoint, if for no other, ADS members should carry the word to such men as the eight who replied to Advertising Agency's question.

Early in 1955 David Ogilvy, for reasons known only to him proposed a National College of Advertising. His comments, which received much attention in the trade press, implied both directly and indirectly that advertising education in the colleges and universities just was not getting the job done. Burton, as President of ADS, reacted in this manner, according to *Linage*, Vol. 7, Issue 3:

Recently, Mr. David Ogilvy, an agency man who has shown amazing skill in making headlines, proposed a National College of Advertising. Even he must have been surprised by the headline harvest that followed.

The proposal has been discussed, written about, praised, and damned by everyone from agency office boys to advertising managers of large corporations.

While Mr. Ogilvy has displayed a sure instinct for selling Hathaway Shirts, and fizzy mixes for alcoholic beverages, he has failed to sell a whole lot of thinking people that he knows what he's talking about when advertising education is the subject.

A reason for this failure may be found in such Ogilvy quotes as the following:

"Mr. Ogilvy stressed that this type of college would avoid the teaching now being done in advertising courses at ordinary universities which he described as 'sadly useless.'"

When queried in a letter (by me), Mr. Ogilvy admitted that this sweeping charge was based on no investigation or research whatever. In one silly generalization he had condemned the work of more than 800 colleges and universities teaching advertising.

Almost anyone would say after this admission that Mr. Ogilvy had been talking through his homburg. He, it is obvious, knows nothing of what is going on in advertising education at the university level, yet he says it's all bad.

His grandstand play to help in the establishing of a National College of Advertising has the hollow sound of a two-bit piece dropped on a bass drum. Instead of finding out what's going on—instead of using existing facilities and manpower, he wants to establish a super college, manned by retired experts. These experts presumably would bring to the classroom skill gained from years in the field.

Let's consider some aspects of this "ideal" college:

1. It's too narrow. You'd stuff the students like so many olives. It's not good teaching to cram students with one subject. In schools offering advertising majors a balance is made between advertising technique courses and the broad cultural courses. Ogilvy's "ideal" college sounds mighty like a glorified trade school.

2. It is not enough. This school, Ogilvy says, is to supply an elite corps of advertising people. If the training is to be thorough and meaningful, such a school could turn out only a handful of students each year—a pitiful answer to the needs of an eight-billion-dollar industry. And, you can bet that most of these super students from the super university would *still* need further training when they landed a job somewhere.

3. The teaching quality is not assured. Because a man's an expert in a subject doesn't mean he's an expert *teacher*. I remember that the dullest course of my college career was taught by a world-renowned psychologist who simply could not put his subject over. Your advertising expert may be a whiz at putting on a campaign and a ghastly flop at telling someone else how to do it.

What we need in advertising education is more people in the field who will help us strengthen our courses and our teachers. We want to do a better job than we're doing and we'll take all the help we can get to achieve this improvement.

So, Mr. Ogilvy—back to your Hathaway Shirts and your

Schweppes Tonic. Stay with the subjects you know and let us work out our problems with advertising men who stop to think before they make public statements.

Burton's editorial drew comments in most of the trade publications, and to his desk came more than 100 letters from advertising managers, agency presidents, media men, advertising teachers, public relations men, retailers, former students and other interested persons. Paragraphs from a few of these letters are included below. They appeared in the May, 1955 issue of *Linage*:

"I got a big kick out of your advice to Mr. Ogilvy. To my way of thinking, you really got him told." (Advertising Manager)

"I know a lot of other Texas graduates who wouldn't trade their courses under Ernest Sharpe for any part of an 'Advertising Super College'." (Agency Account Executive)

"Blessings on thee for the Ogilvy rebuttal in *Linage*. I recommend the reprinting of this in full by *Printer's Ink*." (Professor).

"I'm impressed by the excellent letter you, as President of ADS, have written to David Ogilvy in defending advertising education and picking Ogilvy up on his 'hollow statements backed up by no research whatsoever.'" (NAEA Executive)

"Your advice to Mr. Ogilvy, as printed in the March issue of *Linage*, was superb. Congratulations and best wishes." (Corporation Publicity Director)

The financial situation of the fraternity had not allowed the National Council to pay anything towards the advisors' expenses for the meeting in Daytona Beach, thus only one-half as many advisors participated in the 1953 convention. Thirty-one chapters were represented by 59 undergraduate delegates. There were 15 representatives of alumni chapters and nine National Council members.

Slightly more than a thousand (1,186) were initiated in the 1953-55 biennium, making the membership in Summer, 1955, a total of 12,274. Of the 1.186 initiates, 1,044 were undergraduate and 142 professional members. Texas initiated one of the largest classes ever, 63, and the City College of New York and the University of Oregon each welcomed 12 new professional members.

Two new chapters at Fordham University and the University of Georgia were installed, becoming the fifty-ninth and sixtieth universities to be granted ADS charters. During the biennium Harold Fellows, president of the National Association of Radio and Television Broadcasters, Washington, D.C., and Thomas L. Yates, president of the agency bearing his name in Fort Worth, Texas, were named to the ADS professional Advisory Board. Russell Z. Eller remained the member representing the western sector in the country.

Clyde Bedell, advertising man, author and consultant, received the Nichols Cup in 1953.

The President's Cup Competition was revised, granting two awards, one for the best commercial campaign and one for the best public service campaign. In 1954 the Cup went to the chapters at Iowa (Public Service) and Roosevelt (Commercial); in 1955 the award went to Penn State (Public Service) and New York University (Commercial).

The selection committee for the AAAN Scholarship felt two recipients to be most deserving, and in 1953 two $250 awards were made to George Frazier, University of Texas and Ellen Ensign, New York University. James P. Wehr of the University of Iowa received the 1954 AAAN Scholarship.

The *Linage* award, going to the chapter with the best newsletter, was given to the Boston University Chapter for the third consecutive year in 1954. In 1955 the City College of New York received the award.

The CCNY chapter was also named winner of two first prizes in the sixth annual Robert J. Murray Memorial Competition sponsored by the Advertising Club of Boston and the ADS chapter at Babson Institute. The awards were presented for the development of an advertising campaign for a consumer product.

On the other coast, the University of Oregon ADS chapter in 1954 and 1955 received the top award for junior advertising groups in the West—the Double A award of the Advertising Association of the West. The award was presented for the chapter's "initiative, thought, and teamwork" in the competition.

1955 *Convention*

While the 1953-55 biennium had reflected ADS' strength and the 1955-57 biennium was to show a 23 percent increase in initiates, some of the internal problems of the organization, particularly difficulties at the chapter level, were becoming of paramount importance to the National Council.

The strength of the fraternity has always been in the hands of its chapters' advisors and there has and always will be an increase and decrease in interest and activity on a particular campus as advisors change, but momentum started in 1947 was to begin to dwindle. Excerpts from a *Linage* article on Burton's Presidential report at the convention showed his concern with some of these problems:

President Philip Ward Burton's report to the 1955 Convention was full of suggestions. These suggestions pointed the way to improving ADS on many fronts.

Elsewhere in this issue of *Linage* you will find that many of these suggestions were adopted by the fraternity.

The need for alumni development was stressed. More alumni chapters are desirable and existing chapters can grow stronger.

The mounting production costs of *Linage* point toward a need for augmenting revenue for the paper. A suggestion that is not new is for the inclusion of advertising in *Linage*.

Travel by national officers is almost impossible because of budgetary restrictions. It is hoped that the upsurge in enrollments will make possible more contact between chapters.

Regional conventions which are held on the even years should be strengthened. Several regions are having successful conventions now.

Associate chapters for schools which do not qualify for ADS charters under present rules was advanced as a possibility.

Associate memberships in existing chapters for underclassmen was suggested to chapters. Some chapters already have freshmen and sophomores attending some meetings and ADS events.

International chapters for ADS are more than just a possibility. Inquiries are on hand from several countries.

ADS should expand with more chapters in schools where the advertising sequence is well developed.

The fraternity needs to stir up competition in the various fraternity contests such as The President's Cup, the AAAN Scholarship and the Linage-Kleppner Award.

The possibility of an ADS nation-wide award for merit in national advertising was presented for consideration.

The convention itself was well planned and executed by the Chicago Alumni and Roosevelt chapters with Stuart Helffrich as General Chairman. It was held in conjunction with the AFA national meetings. Speakers included Fairfax M. Cone, Foote, Cone & Belding, Chicago; Jack S. Petterson, Advertising Manager of the Norge Co., and C. B. Larrabee, Chaiman of the Board of *Printer's Ink*. Larrabee received the Nichols Cup for his series "Thunder on the Right" which appeared in *Printer's Ink* and drew wide acclaim.

For the first time in the history of advertising organization an entire session was devoted to advertising education at the 1955 AFA convention. Advisors participating in the ADS convention attended. Henry Obermeyer, Bozell & Jacobs Vice President, who was then Chairman of the AFA College Cooperation Committee presided. The program was drawn up in *Linage*, Vol. 7, Issue 4:

PANEL I

Moderator: ADS President, Philip Burton, Syracuse University
(1) "How Advertising is Now Taught", Prof. Donald Davis, Pennsylvania State University.
(2) "How the Advertising Industry Can Help the Advertising Teachers", Prof. Royal Ray, Florida State University.

(3) "What Advertising Employers Want of the Graduates They Employ", Gates Ferguson, Director of Advertising and Sales Promotion, Celotex Corporation.

(4) "What Advertising is Now Doing to Help Advertising Teachers", Lester Hafemeister, Advertising Manager, Weyenberg Shoe Manufacturing Co.

PANEL II

Discussion of three recent controversial suggestions: A college of advertising, Special advertising degrees, and examinations and degrees by organized advertising. Moderator: Prof. Charles H. Sandage, University of Illinois. Participants: Robert Kenyon, publisher, *Printer's Ink;* Roger Barton, editor, *Advertising Agency;* Mrs. Bea Johnson, chairman, GAX; Ira DeJernett, president, DeJernett Advertising Agency; Prof. Walter Gaw, CCNY; Prof. C. D. Forrest, Indiana University; Prof. Ellis H. Newsome, University of Iowa.

Twenty-five chapters were officially represented by 49 undergraduates. One alumni chapter sent a delegate, and 25 national officers and advisors participated:

All but two of the members of the National Council were re-elected. They included Burton as President; Gross as executive secretary; Laird as Treasurer (although Canfield served one year of the biennium while Laird was in Europe); Rice, Southwestern Vice President; Joel, Southeastern Vice President; Collier, Western Vice President; and Haverfield as Editor of *Linage.* New Vice Presidents were William Moeckel, Ohio State University and Robert M. Weir, Malden Press, Malden, Mass.

Fellows, Yates and Eller were reappointed to the ADS Professional Advisory Board, but the National Council enlarged the Board to five, naming also Henry G. Little, Campbell-Ewald Co., Detroit, Mich., and Louis F. Gordon, Atlanta, Georgia.

Impressed with how the 1955 convention was handled, President Burton was prompted to comment on the value of the ADS experience in developing leadership in the October, 1955 issue of *Linage.*

Some years of watching ADS men at work has convinced me that membership in the fraternity provides some of the best executive training a college man can have.

This observation is made while memories are still fresh of the national meeting in Chicago. What a sight to see ADS undergraduate members from all over the country get up on their feet to express themselves! Here were poised, confident leaders, ready with ideas and with the force to put over their ideas.

Through ADS these men learn the value of committee work; they learn methods of conducting meetings; they learn to yield gracefully when they find themselves on the minority side of an argument.

On college campuses all over the country these lessons are being taught in ADS chapters. And remember that advertising is looking not just for people who can write copy, do market research, or buy time or space. It is watching for men with ideas and with the executive force to see that the ideas are exploited to the fullest extent.

Every ADS advisor has been gratified to see chapter members develop executive talents. Every advisor has seen that certain new members almost at once demonstrate the fact that they have an instinctive flair for leadership. Others, not endowed with the instinct, have developed it despite themselves.

One of my biggest thrills as an advisor has been the discovering of men who "take over"—who welcome responsibility and who find, in ADS, that they are leaders. Time after time I have seen such men become chapter presidents—and almost to a man I have seen them move rapidly in the advertising business when they left school. While in ADS they developed those qualities that made people say of them: "He's a cinch to get ahead when he leaves school."

As we start a new ADS year you might keep this in mind. Are *you* through your assumption of responsibility and through your leadership qualities going to be the person who'll be named as a "cinch" to get ahead, or are you going to be the run-of-the-mill character who belongs to ADS but never learns the thrill of running it?

During the 1955-57 biennium four new chapters were granted— undergraduate chapters at Long Island University and Manhattan College; alumni chapters were granted for Denver, Colorado and Wichita, Kansas. The number of initiates increased 23 percent over the previous biennium when 1,314 undergraduates and 147 professional members made a total of 1,461 initiates. This brought the total membership in the fraternity to 14,378 by the summer of 1957.

A new prize became available to ADS chapters when Gamma Alpha Chi president Claire Drew Forbes Walker announced the GAX-Advertising Recognition Week Award. The $100 award, to be given for the best Advertising Recognition Week activities, could be won separately or jointly by any ADS and/or GAX chapter. The ADS and GAX at the University of Oregon won the award for both 1956 and 1957.

Competition for the President's Cup was altered in each of the years in the biennium. In 1956 a Cup was presented to the University of Oregon chapter for the best project done in cooperation with the advertising profession and to the University of Arizona for the best chapter activities. In 1957 the two awards were divided into the best activity by a metropolitan and a non-metropolitan chapter. The metropolitan Cup went to Babson Institute and the non-metropolitan Cup to Penn State University.

The AAAN presented its scholarship in 1955 to James Lance of the University of Missouri. In 1956 the committee decided to give two second place awards of $50 each in addition to its $250 scholarship. Fordham University's Robert Patterson was granted $250 and Duncan Osborne, Florida State and James Ulman, Oklahoma, $50 each.

With the acceptance of the financial support given by Otto Kleppner, the previous *Linage* award was renamed the Kleppner-*Linage* award, and the recipient chapter received $50 cash in addition to formal recognition by the fraternity. The award was presented during each of the two years of the biennium, 1956 and 1957, to Fordham University.

1957 Convention

Twenty-nine chapters sent official delegates to the 1957 Dallas convention with Jerry Drake, General Chairman, assisted by Frank Miller and Don Smith, all associated with the Southern Methodist University chapter. Elon Borton received the Nichols Cup and for the first and only time, the National Chapter elected its president *in absentia.*

Gross, Laird and Haverfield were to serve the fraternity again for the coming biennium, and Moeckel and Collier were re-elected as regional vice presidents. New Regional Vice Presidents included: Lawrence E. Bretsch of the University of Rhode Island, Manning Seil of the University of Florida and Jerry Drake of Southern Methodist University. When Moeckel resigned after the first year of the biennium, his successor in the Midwest was Brandel L. Works of Roosevelt University.

During the biennium the fraternity was to continue speaking out on matters of advertising education, to take its stand on the taxation of advertising, to overhaul its national award system, and to attempt stimulation of enthusiasm on the local chapter level.

Within weeks of the end of the 1957 convention, the August 2,.1957 issue of *Printer's Ink* carried an article by Professor Frank M. Dunbaugh of the University of Miami entitled, ''The Pros and Cons of Advertising Education.'' The October, 1957 issue of *Linage* carried reaction to the article by several ADS advisors. Editor Robert W. Haverfield added this Editor's Note: ''Former ADS President Philip Ward Burton urged the Dallas Convention to crusade for advertising education. 'I think we should take a positive stand on things that affect advertising. This is the only way we can attain any real stature. ADS is certainly closely affiliated with advertising education; we should be more of a crusading organization than we have been.' With these thoughts in mind, a third of this issue is devoted to the controversial subject touched off by a recent article in *Printer's Ink.*''

Former ADS national president Philip Ward Burton, head of the advertising department, Syracuse University School of Journalism, spoke as a "Pro" in the Dunbaugh article.

BURTON: *Syracuse*

"People in advertising who keep screaming for liberal-arts training usually imply that advertising graduates lack such background," said Burton.

"In most schools where advertising majors are offered, the students DO devote most of their college credits to liberal-arts courses. Technical advertising courses usually amount to no more than 20 to 30 hours out of a total of 120.

Liberal Arts Included

"Meanwhile, advertising majors are, in addition to acquiring a well-rounded liberal-arts education, learning enough advertising so that they can get off to a much faster start in that first job after college.

"Somehow, advertising seems to have been singled out for the 'trade-school' approach. If the student is given a few specific courses in advertising, shock is expressed. 'We want our children to learn to think, not to take how-to-do-it courses,' they say.

Two Objections Answered

"I have two strong objections to this attitude:

"1. I find nothing incompatible with learning to think and taking advertising courses. The creative thinking students must do in my copy course goes way beyond anything they are required to do in any other course they take, no matter what school gives it.

"2. Advertising is an exacting occupation. It draws upon many skills and facets of knowledge. People are paid well for their skill and knowledge. Why shouldn't they be trained early for this occupation, just as architects, doctors, and engineers are trained? Why are these professions any different? Why aren't courses taken by pre-meds or would-be engineers described as 'trade-schoolish'?"

GROSS: *Missouri*

Says Milton E. Gross, advertising department, Missouri School of Journalism, and National Secretary, ADS:

"I find the most frightening statement in Prof. Dunbaugh's article not among the 'Cons' but in the 'midway' position of Louis N. Brockway of Young and Rubicam, because it reveals what I'm convinced is typical lack of familiarity with advertising education.

"Mr. Brockway said, 'A university course combining liberal-arts training with some of the techniques of advertising MIGHT work out very well, provided it did not slight liberal-arts training too much.'

"The emphasis on 'might' is mine.

Successful Since 1908

"The University of Missouri has offered a major in its school of journalism, combining liberal arts (75 per cent) with journalism and advertising (25 per cent) since 1908.

"Mr. Brockway also believes a liberal-arts education and several years of selling experience 'come close to being the ideal background for the advertising business.

"Advertising students here at Missouri spend two full semesters as local salesmen on the *Columbia Missourian,* a daily of general circulation in Columbia which serves as the school's teaching newspaper. They are exposed to a full curriculum of liberal-arts courses—and in addition receive both theoretical and practical training in advertising techniques.

"My ADS work has familiarized me with advertising training programs in schools throughout the country; in addition, I have served on several accrediting committees for the American Council for Education in Journalism. All of my experience indicates that universities which offer an advertising major in a professional school—either in business or journalism—invariably require at least three hours of liberal arts for each hour of advertising.

"This makes Prof. Dunbaugh's basic question unnecessary (choice between a liberal arts background OR academic training in advertising). But it suggests another question: How are we teachers to educate advertising practitioners to the real facts of advertising education?

EDUCATE AGENCY MEN?

"The agency people obviously need the most 'educating.' Other employers have learned the facts from advertising graduates they have hired; agencies' offers have not been good enough to attract many advertising-trained students.

"Approximately 40 per cent of Missouri journalism graduates are advertising majors, but only about 4 percent of our graduates go into advertising agencies. The others go to large and small dailies, weeklies, business and industry, radio and television stations, magazines and trade journals. And from those groups we hear almost nothing but praise for the training our students receive."

TALBERT : Mississippi

Here are the thoughts of Dr. Samuel S. Talbert, Dept. of Journalism, University of Mississippi:

"Self-made men, especially of the near-genius breed, tend to be snobs. Young Benjamin Franklin, who acquired a superb education without benefit of college, wrote editorials ridiculing the students of Harvard College.

"A more mature Franklin recognized this sneering as a display of vanity—a means of dramatizing his own exceptional talents. Every field of study has had its Franklins.

"Schools of law, pharmacy, education, business administration, journalism, and even engineering have passed through the same purgatory. Successful practitioners in all these fields scoffed at the idea of formal training programs.

Formal Training Economical

"Certainly, a good education in any field, general or specialized, may be obtained outside of college. But formal training is more economical. It assures a quick, thorough, and organized approach to the subject. From this standpoint, education in advertising may be justified as readily as any other university curriculum.

"Advertising education gives a student an opportunity to learn the basic skills of his chosen specialty while he is obtaining a general education. The program of the advertising student is no more specialized than the curricula of majors in history, English, or the social sciences.

"And contrary to the dicta voiced from some high places, training in advertising can be mighty significant with respect to future employment.

Not All Go to Agencies

"Only an insignificant number of college graduates who enter advertising can hope to be employed by the large industries and agencies which have training programs. Most beginners enter advertising through media, small industries, small agencies, and retail stores. They are expected to take on responsible jobs at once. If they have not developed elementary skills, they simply do not get started in advertising.

"I have on my desk twenty notices of advertising job openings. Any of these jobs could be handled by a graduating advertising major. However, none of them would be open to a student who had no training in advertising.

"The jobs require some proof of skill and interest. For this reason the employers contact me instead of the general placement service of the University. For the same reason students continue to enroll in advertising courses in increasing numbers.

"Although advertising education cannot be a complete substitute for experience, it has certain advantages over experience:

"1. As in any professional training, education in advertising makes use of the vast accumulated experience of the best practitioners of the past and present, thereby reducing the expense of trial and error learning.

"2. For many future advertising workers, instructional laboratories provide the only opportunity of a lifetime for receiving systematic guidance and corrective criticism.

"3.During the training period at the university, the student of advertising has an opportunity to experiment and time to think freely and creatively which may never again be available.

"4. Advertising education provides a broad picture of the whole field of advertising and its literature which cannot come from job experience."

ROSS: Houston

Says B. I. Ross, Department of Journalism, University of Houston:

"Seemingly Professor Dunbaugh's article is accurate as far as it goes, however, it does not scratch the surface of the field that is using most of the advertising students who graduate today.

"In nearly every case comments against advertising education were from top level personnel in agency work or personnel work; however, not in one single case was an advertising director or manager of a newspaper asked.

Papers Need These Men

"There are over 35,000 workers in the field of newspaper advertising, and in our case in Texas the small weekly is paying more for our advertising graduate than the agencies.

"In fact, the agencies in most cases are not wanting the boy fresh out of college, but are waiting for him to wear out some leather-soles for a newspaper or radio station.

"For this reason alone the agencies, wanting the cream of the crop, wait until the advertising-educated, weekly-trained, selling-wise young man comes in the door.

"How, then, do the newspaper men feel about the college educated advertising men? Check with the state press associations, advertising directors, check the want ads in Publishers' Auxiliary, and you will find they are in demand."

GAW: City College

Dr. Walter A. Gaw, School of Business Administration, The City College, New York, writes:

"Why is it that the 'cons', despite all that has been said in various conventions and meetings and all that has been written in several periodicals, continue to make liberal arts training and training in advertising mutually exclusive? I know of no college or business where it is an 'either-or' proposition.

"Perhaps the 'cons' should be asked to indicate specific cases to support the broad generalizations that they so freely state as absolute and all inclusive facts.

Voice of Experience

"I wonder where the basis is for the statement that 'the business major is not required to meet the same standard in his electives such as English, as is the liberal arts major.' I have taught in the business schools of two universities and have associates in several others and know that this is not true in any of these cases.

"Incidentally, one cannot but wonder, at times, if a sound training in English might not be a severe handicap to the successful writing of modern advertising copy—much of present day copy has little in common with the grammar I learned in a liberal arts Ivy League University where English is taught *like* it should be.

Greek Literature

" 'Ours,' says one of the 'cons,' 'is an idea business, a problem solving business. I cannot understand how a course in Greek literature, the political theories of Karl Marx, or archeology better fits a student to develop selling ideas or solve advertising problems than an advertising course which has been specifically designed to accomplish just these ends.

"The Fred Whittner Agency has written two articles, one for *Advertising Agency* and one for *Printer's Ink,* in praise of the industrial advertising course here at City College and credits its students with developing some very worthwhile ideas in solving actual advertising problems presented by the Whittner agency.

Shock Treatment

"Our friend, Ogilvy, in my opinion, is employing the 'shock treatment'—'. . . So long as it wasn't advertising'—and as in most of his comments that I have seen on advertising education is so far out in left field as to be unworthy of serious consideration.

"Much of his comments on advertising education has much the same ring as the statements concerning the advertising business that emanate from some of our liberal arts economic departments. Advertising education on the one hand and the advertising business on the other would be the worse off if either were taken seriously.

Who Outstrips Whom?

"Another of the 'cons' says '. . . however, within a few years the liberal-arts graduate with a basic understanding of humankind and its environment would outstrip the advertising major in usefulness and earning power.'

"This, I think, might be difficult to prove statistically, to say nothing of the lack of basis for the implication that the advertising major of necessity lacks a basic understanding of humankind and its environment. It is statements of this very character that the advertising business so bitterly resented from its critics during the 1930's.

Agencies Seek Graduates

"As for giving you some 'pros,' the best I can do is to refer to editorials and articles that have appeared in *Printer's Ink* and elsewhere concerning the effectiveness of advertising training at City College, and to say that many advertising agencies and business firms have sought and continue to seek the services of our advertising majors.

"Most of these graduates have risen rapidly in the firms that employed them. I am sure that our experience is not unique. Other colleges could make similar claims, and so long as this is true, I wonder whether the 'pros' or the 'cons' are the losers.''

DAVIS: Penn State

Donald W. Davis, former ADS national president, and head of the advertising department, School of Journalism, Pennsylvania State University, wraps it up:

"It seems to me that many professional advertising people are somewhat confused as to what constitutes education for advertising, particularly in the training of a university advertising major.

Elective Credits

"For example, the implication by some that advertising instruction cannot be effectively combined with a liberal-arts education is absurd. In my own institution, as in many others, every student who is an advertising major completes precisely the same requirements for a liberal-arts degree as does the liberal-arts student who is not an advertising major. The only difference is in the student's disposal of a limited number of elective credits.

"And, whether the advertising major studies in a journalism school with liberal-arts affiliations or in a business administration school, it should also be remembered that advertising is a business of many facets. For the creative phase of advertising work the strong liberal-arts background is probably favorable; for some of the market research and merchandising phases, more business training might be desirable. Not all advertising graduates need have, nor should have, exactly the same type of university background. The employer can discriminate as to the type of graduate he wants and needs.

Improving Techniques

"By and large, advertising education is doing much to direct many of the better student minds toward advertising work. And the constructive influence of the advertising graduate is unquestionably contributing to the betterment of advertising techniques and standards. His influence is being felt in the advertising departments of media, in retail stores and industry, and in agencies —throughout the land. If a few people on Madison Avenue are failing to sense this influence perhaps they are being blinded by too many eye patches.''

SENGER: *Michigan State*

"The article *Pros and cons of ad education* in the Aug. 2 issue of PI illustrates a couple of things very graphically. One, there is still a broad gap of ignorance between the worlds of advertising and advertising education. And responsibility for this gap lies equally, I'm afraid, on both groups. We still do not do enough to tell the advertising people what we are doing. If we did, then the advertising executives would know that the ad major frequently has as broad a liberal arts background as anyone else, and that only a small percentage of his total credit hours are devoted to specific advertising courses.

"Second, as this article indicates, ad men like many another executive, tend to hire people in their own image. They take the position that it was good enough 25 years ago so it's still good today. This is not the stuff of which progress is made. But as time goes on and more people with advertising education work into responsible positions, this attitude will change."

President Joel, whose trip to Europe prevented his comments from appearing in the October. 1957 issue of *Linage* added his own views, along with a reaction to the October article in his President's Corner in the January, 1958 issue of *Linage*.

Everyone in ADS should feel elated over the October issue of *Linage*. ADS advisors wrote good answers to the attack on advertising education. I've had many favorable comments on this feature and was pleased to see *Printer's Ink* devoted a story to it in the Oct. 18 issue.

I'm sorry we haven't heard from more ADS alumni and undergraduate members on the subject of advertising education.

You can tell us whether you would have been better off taking "anything else in the curriculum but advertising," as some of our detractors assert. You know whether your advertising courses were a farce or a force.

I believe that as the years pass and you who have had college training in advertising succeed to positions of authority in the profession, much of the prejudice and ignorance regarding advertising education will vanish. I'm confident that ADS alumni— more than 14,000 strong—hold the answer to this perplexing problem.

The most ruthless critics are often the least informed. They are, for the most part, men who know nothing about college advertising curricula or the caliber of instruction. Few of them believe in an academic approach to advertising problems, and they look with disdain on those who do.

Most of the critics are men who like to boast that they learned advertising "the hard way" and feel there is little to be learned from teachers, books, or even their own trade publications.

Too bad we don't have more men like Justice Oliver Wendell Holmes who, at 93, said he was still "trying to learn a little more about the law." Or like Clyde Bedell who, at 59, is still studying advertising and believes the academic approach is the most *practical* approach to any business problem.

Although he had no formal college training in advertising and came up "the hard way," Clyde Bedell, in 1955, was awarded the Nichols Cup by ADS for his contribution to advertising education.

His books and lectures on advertising have been internationally acclaimed.

Clyde Bedell is no ordinary ad man. He is a hard-headed salesman with ideals. He is a man who prefers to help one person become a better ad person *and citizen,* than to help three become better ad persons. He is a man who says, "Advertising adolescence can last a lifetime if it is not supplanted by maturity born of wisdom in the big body of advertising's established truth."

This is the man we are honored to have as a professional member of ADS and as guest columnist in this issue of *Linage.*

Bedell, stressing that "It Can Be Done in Schools" commented:

Prominent advertising men are again making nasty remarks about advertising education. It is obvious that a man who says academic advertising training is not good, has never *had* good academic training in advertising. This qualifies him, apparently, to say advertising training is not good.

As foolish as saying that—would be saying "All advertising training is good." It isn't all good.

However, there is a great body of advertising truth that is available to be learned—academically. Indeed, that's the only way much of it can be learned with certainty. Much of America's wasteful and juvenile "big-league" advertising is proof that some of that truth is never learned experientially by some ad creators.

There is no question but that students may be taught to approach white space (or time) respectfully, as something that can be converted into the dynamic economic power called advertising. It is a good idea to have this taught to ad creators before they begin to spend advertising dollars. It can be done in schools.

There are identifiable principles of persuasion that worked in the Garden of Eden. They are used in The Sermon on the Mount. They will be used before the parliament or congress of the world government which will prevail some day. It is well these be taught advertising people early—or they may never learn them, to the great loss of their clients or employers.

Who would speak against liberal arts education? Only frequently it isn't education—it is diversion. Students need to learn a little of the cosmos, and of cosmic plan—of humanity and its goals—of life and its values. Most of this they will learn *after* college. While in school, I believe they should learn how to study, how to discriminate between principles and loose statements, and how to live like men wih a purpose. And if they are to enter the field of advertising they would do well to study it in school— wherever they can find good courses—so they will not be as wasteful and as superficial and as pliant for a buck, as some of their elders.—CLYDE BEDELL

The taxation of advertising by various governments has been of major concern to the industry. This movement toward taxation has increased in recent years. ADS took its stand against the Baltimore, Maryland. tax on advertising passed by the Baltimore city administration in 1957.

President Joel sent the following telegram to Max Bucklew of Van Sant, Dugdale and Company, Baltimore:

"Thousands of Alpha Delta Sigma members throughout the nation protest punitive tax on advertising. Believe measure as unfair and economically unsound as tax on personal salesmanship."

Due to the strong support of the media, advertisers, agencies, and the various advertising organizations this particular tax was retracted.

While the National Council, through pronouncements by the President and publication of *Linage*, continued to provide a concerned and interested leadership in advertising education, participation by individual chapters in the national program left much to be desired. One can conjecture as to the causes, but as has been stated previously, the lack of a dedicated advisor on campus was a primary factor.

For many of the chapters in the major universities, the advertising programs were rapidly gaining academic respectability and as the program matured, more emphasis began to be placed on research and writing. Little if any credit was given the teachers for time spent working with ADS, and a general attitude of "let the students run it, it's their organization" was justification enough for minimal supervision and advising. The result, weak continuity, little enthusiasm, weak programs and often complete inactivity, finally ended in deactivation of many chapters.

When advertising programs were seeking acceptance, when they were striving for recognition, when no other organization concerned itself with advertising education, when teachers were seeking outside help and contact with the advertising practitioner. motivation provided the momentum for a strong chapter.

Aware of the increasing internal weaknesses of ADS, President Joel was to concentrate the majority of his effort during his tenure in providing the necessary enthusiasm to rekindle the ADS' spirit in the campus organization. In the October, 1957 *Linage* Joel verbalized his concern in this maner:

ADS must mean something to its members, and its members must mean something to ADS.

If we are not already doing it, then we must make ADS mean more to a man than the wearing of another key or the displaying of another shingle. An undergraduate member must be made to feel that ADS is the greatest single springboard to his future career. A man does not get this impression when he sees a chapter whose members are apathetic and disinterested. Naturally he is disinclined to associate himself with such a group.

Enthusiasm and willingness to work for the good of a chapter —and the fraternity as a whole—can mean growth and success. If advertising people can't work up enthusiasm for a cause in which they believe, it doesn't augur very well for their future. We, of all people, should know what it takes to put over our cause. Early in our careers—even while we are still in school—we should be able to demonstrate these characteristics and put into use those tools of the trade which make for success.

It goes without saying that *interest* increases with activity. ADS members should keep active. It's good advertising.

We must interest prospective advertising majors in ADS as early as possible. The longer they can participate in fraternity activities, the longer they can associate with advertising practitioners and other students who have a common interest, the more ADS will mean to them. That is the reason I advocate the induction of students into ADS as early as their sophomore year in college.

I find it exceedingly disheartening to see a man initiated into ADS the final semester of his senior year. In such cases, the chapter and the man derive little from the association.

ADS must encourage its members to be leaders and assume responsibility *willingly* when it comes their way. This is invaluable training for the future.

We must lick the lethargy that plagues some of our chapters. Too often there is the tendency to say, "Let John do it!" One never really *belongs* to ADS until he *works* for ADS and experiences the satisfaction of seeing a job well done.

Sooner or later, ADS members will learn that the men who are recommended for jobs in the advertising business—and who get ahead in these jobs—are not the ones who sit back and watch others run the show, but rather those who are in there plugging to keep the show on the road.

The lack of interest and participation in some of the national competitive and scholarship programs produced a major overhauling of the awards program during the biennium. The AAAN dropped its scholarship program after 1957, and National Council discontinued the President's Cup competition in favor of the establishment of a professional competence award, regional scholarships and chapter recognition based on a progress and efficiency report. Joel commented on these changes in his President's Corner in the October, 1958 issue of *Linage*.

A new academic year offers us a new chance.

All the things we didn't accomplish the year before loom back in sight and seem to say—"Well, here we are again. What are you going to do about us?"

Remember back to the fall of '57. Remember your chapter's firm resolve to enter the President's Award competition and the AAAN Scholarship competition. Remember the talk about a chapter news letter and participation in Advertising Week. Remember the high purpose displayed in conversation, but not in action.

Now as we start a new year, our words come back to taunt us—and I hope to prod us. The number of entries for the President's Award reduced the competition to a farce. The number of entries for the AAAN Scholarship prompted the agency men to write off the competition as a flop.

If chapter news letters were published, only three or four put the national president on the mailing list. If chapters contributed to the celebration of Advertising Week, all but a few kept it a well-guarded secret.

True. Chapters had their get-togethers. They initiated new members. Some sponsored lectures and panel discussions, and gave time and energy to money-raising projects. But too many gave the impression they were neither a national nor a professional fraternity—just free-wheeling in their own little orbit.

We added more than 800 names to our rolls during the past year. We did a good selling job. Most of the new men entered ADS with enthusiasm and a desire to make a contribution. How long can we keep them sold if our accomplishments are unfulfilled promises built on "tomorrow's-another-day" policy?

So here we are again face-to-face with tomorrow. It's our new chance. Will we make it any different than yesterday?

Perhaps we can if we start out on the right foot and try to stay in step along the way. The purpose of the new ADS Progress and **Efficiency** Awards is to help every chapter do just that.

The awards will recognize chapters for their professional activity and growth. They are designed to encourage more business-like and efficient practices within the chapters themselves and in their relationship with National. Fundamentally, they should do much to unify the fraternity and put us all on a common footing.

The form of the report which is to be submitted annually by every chapter can in itself serve as a guide-sheet for the year's operations. This new competition is designed to help, not hinder.

It is my hope that it will aid in the development of a well-balanced and efficient program in each chapter. Personally, I have always felt that a chapter's growth and efficiency should be judged on its month-to-month operations, rather than on a single project, sometimes hurriedly thrown together—or more often abandoned in the heat of meeting a deadline.

In what is, admittedly, a loosely organized fraternity, the Progress and Efficiency Awards may help us define our objectives and realize the possibilities that are open to us as a national professional organization.

Perhaps, too, they can mean the difference between excellence and mediocrity. This is most desirable in an era when, according to Charles H. Brower, president of BBD&O, we are always willing to settle for something less than the best.

"This," says Mr. Brower, "is the era of the goof-off, the age of the half-done job. The land from coast to coast has been enjoying a stampede away from responsibility."

Will the year ahead be more of the same?

In ADS, at least, let's stem the tide and pursue achievement for its own sake.

Stewart C. Bird of the University of Georgia received the final $250 AAAN Scholarship. Two Florida State University students, John R. Ray and Pat Starnes were given the $50 awards.

Roosevelt College and Florida State University placed first in the final President's Cup competition in 1958. Roosevelt won the metropolitan division, and Florida State placed first in the non-metropolitan division.

New York University's George Burton Hotchkiss chapter received permanent possession of the President's Cup as a result of its outstanding achievement during the period of the competition. The Cup, awarded on a rotating basis, was given to the NYU chapter for having prepared the best advertising campaigns more frequently than any other undergraduate chapter across the nation. Donated by Ken R. Dyke, 1940-41 President, the trophy had been captured by the NYU chapter in 1941, 1950 and 1955.

It was the second honor to be bestowed on the chapter during the year. In the fall, the chapter was awarded $1 000 by winning first prize in *Playboy* magazine's national collegiate advertising contest. The winning entry included the results of research, a campaign plan, copy, layout, and art work directed to potential advertisers in *Playboy*. Faculty advisor at this time was William L. Doremus.

The Elon Borton chapter at Florida State took both of the newly created awards in 1959 winning the progress and efficiency award based on the submission of a written report on the chapter's activities for the year and the professional competence contest for excellence of an individual promotional event.

Twenty-six chapters submitted P & E reports in 1959. Honorable mention plaques were presented to the chapters at the University of Arizona, the University of Texas, and the University of Illinois. The City College of New York and Texas Tech received honorable mention plaques in the Professional Competence competition.

In the spring of 1959, the National Council announced the first winners of ADS Regional Scholarships. The scholarships were awarded in each of five ADS regions—$100 first prize, $50 second prize. The 1959 winners included:

Eastern Region—Richard C. Roth, Manhattan College ($100); Christ Drakopoulos, Fordham University ($50).

Midwestern Region — Jay I. Wilson, University of Iowa ($100); Steve Hopkins, University of Missouri ($50).

Southeastern Region — Ralph Morgan, Florida State University ($100); Clifford L. Cagle, University of Georgia ($50).

Southwestern Region — James Locklin, University of Houston ($100); Donald B. Alderman, University of Houston ($50).

Western Region — William Youngren, University of Arizona ($100); Anthony Rogers, University of Arizona ($50).

The scholarship entries were judged by the ADS Professional Advisory Board composed of Eller, Yates, Fellows and new members, Fred Black, American Motors, and Lewis Gordon, Pi Sigma Epsilon.

In 1958 the University of Oregon chapter accepted the Gamma Alpha Chi-Advertising Recognition Week Award for the third consecutive time. The chapter received the cup permanently for its 3rd win, although it shared the first place prize with Florida State University.

The Kleppner-*Linage* award for chapter newsletters was presented in 1958 to the City College of New York and in 1959 to the University of Illinois.

In May, 1958 the Cigar Institute of America announced a new contest and project for ADS chapters. The problem was how to sell cigars to young men in the 18 to 30 age bracket. In all, the Institute offered eleven cash prizes amounting to $625, $250 to the top entry and $50 and $25 each to the first and second best entries from each region. Winners also received certificates, a humidor and a supply of cigars.

Winners announced in March, 1959 included first prize to Richard Roth, Manhattan College and regional prizes ($50 winner named first, $25 winner second) to Jay Heyman and Robert William Moore, Long Island University (Eastern); Ralph T. Morgan and William R. Brennan, Florida State University (Southeastern); Robert N. Castner and James B. Locklin, University of Houston (Southwestern); Robert W. Lee Jr., and Donald Dippel, Arizona State University (Western; and Donald E. Rockfield, Ohio State University (Midwest). No second place award was given for the Midwest Region.

In announcing the winners, Stanley Kolker, assistant to the

president of the Cigar Institute commented in the March, 1959 issus of *Linage*:

"We only received 30 entries in the Scholarship Contest, but in the main, the quality of work was top rate. Because of this and because our professional board of judges thought so highly of these papers, we will continue the contest next year and even add $50 to the national prize, making the total $300."

Although only thirty ADS members entered the competition, this represented a doubling of the number of ADS entries for any previous contest.

Fine relationship between ADS and the AFA and the AAW continued and expanded during the 1957-59 biennium. ADS chapters were notified that they might sponsor the AFA high school essay contest in areas where no advertising club sponsored the event. The AAW established a special category in their annual competition for advertising fraternities and college advertising clubs. Entries in the AAW competition took the form of scrapbooks showing chapter or club activities and projects. The AFA established a special five dollar registration fee for ADS members to its 1958 meeting in Dallas and anounced the establishment of the first permanent and continuing educational foundation for the advertising industry. In discussing the Foundation the March, 1958 issue of *Linage* stated:

"'The Advertising Educational Foundation, Inc. has been designated to further education in the field of advertising among the American public and particularly its young people through and with the cooperation of schools, clubs, professional groups, etc.

"The AFA-sponsored organization will be financed by contributions from firms and individuals in the industry.

"Among the aims described for the new organization are research into advertising and marketing curricula; to aid in establishing and carrying out educational programs; to make grants to institutions; to make available funds for scholarships; to publish aids, books and pamphlets; and to provide guidance for the young person desiring to enter advertising."

Individual chapters continued to express in their own way their concern for the professionalization of advertising through education. The University of Texas chapter presented the Texas Journalism library with an Advertising Research Foundation Collection and pledged to underwrite the annual dues for the University's "academic membership" in the ARF for the next ten years. The collection consisted of 97 titles at that date.

"This gift of ARF materials is the finest thing our ADS chapter has ever done in the interest of advertising education," advisor Earnest Sharpe declared. "It carries out one of the primary purposes of Alpha Delta Sigma—to contribute to the improvement of advertising, especially advertising research."

Paul J. Thompson, director of the School of Journalism and

man for whom the Texas chapter was named, in accepting the gift in behalf of the Journalism library, said, "This very fine material makes an important addition to the library. It is wonderful for the students to have access to this research material now."

A special shelf in the library, marked by an appropriate plaque, holds the voluminous array of books and bound research studies of all kinds. The plaque was designed by F. R. Moerke, professional member of the chapter and well-known Texas calligrapher.

Money for the purchase of the collection—an initial payment of $100 to obtain all publications issued by ARF since 1952, pus the annual $50 academic membership fee—was earned by ADS members through the monthly sale of the college magazine on the campus.

The Southern Methodist University chapter cooperated with the Dallas chapter of the National Industrial Advertising Association in the promotion of an educational program to develop more interest and more information concerning industrial advertising. The program consisted of two phases as presented in March, 1959 *Linage*:

(1) Developing a closer relationship between advertising students and the members of NIAA. This is being brought about by special student NIAA meetings.

(2) The holding of a seminar for the advertising faculties of SMU, Texas Christian University and North Texas State College.

The University of Oregon chapter mounted reprints of the "Saturday Review Court of Honor" winning public service advertisments and sponsored a tour of the 25 winners among ADS chapters.

Five new chapters were added during the 1957-59 biennium at Southern Illinois University, Texas Christian University, Texas Tech, Whitworth College and Wichita University. Student initiations totaled 1265, 49 less than during the previous two year period. Professional initiations were up 60 for a total of 207, making the total new members during the biennium 1472, a gain of 11.

Illinois initiated more members during the biennium than any other chapter with 58 students and 7 professional members. Indiana initiated the largest number of students, beating Illinois by one with a total of 59. By July, 1959, 15,850 men had been initiated into the fraternity.

1959 *Convention*

Meeting in August, 1959 at Stanford University, Palo Alto, California, the National chapter enlarged the National Council, made several constitutional changes and elected Walter Guild, President of Guild, Bascom and Bonfigli, San Francisco, Calif.,

National President for the 1959-61 biennium.

Two new vice presidents, one for Students and one for Professional, were created to give the students and the professional chapters better representation on the governing body of ADS. Dale Smith of the University of Illinois was elected the first National Student Vice President; Rol Rider, representing the Los Angeles alumni was appointed to fill the Professional Vice President position.

Regional student vice presidents were elected to serve as an advisory group to the National Student Vice President. The following were elected to this group at Stanford: East—Charles R. Walsh, Fordham; West—Howard W. Smith, Arizona; Southwest—Donald Alderman, Houston; Midwest—Howard Rader, Missouri; and Southeast—Ralph T. Morgan, Florida State.

Gross, Laird and Haverfield retained their positions on the Council. Joel became Chairman of the Council, and Phil Burton was asked to serve as an advisory member. Four regions elected new vice presidents. The Eastern Region selected Bertrand Canfield of Babson Institute, a former national president; the Midwest Region, Frank Senger, Michigan State University; the Southeast Region, Jess Roberts, Executive Secretary of the Atlanta Ad Club; Western Region, Willard "Tommy" Thompson, the University of Oregon; Jerry Drake of Southern Methodist University was re-elected Southwestern Region Vice President. Charles Wolfe, founder and former advisor ADS chapters at Roosevelt and Denver and then advisor at Long Beach State served the second year as Western Region Vice President when Thompson accepted a new position and moved to the midwest.

Constitutional changes made in Stanford in addition to the creation of two new National Council positions included:

a. The number of professional members that a chapter may initiate is unlimited. Former regulations restricted a chapter to six such initiations a year.

b. The Progress and Efficiency reports were made compulsory for all chapters with provisions for suspending chapters not filing the annual report.

c. Newly chartered chapters will serve a probationary period of one year before the charters become permanent.

The Progress and Efficiency Competition started during the Joel administration received considerable discussion at the Palo Alto convention. Delegates agreed that the competition was a good thing, and chapters should be compelled to participate in it in future years. In general, delegates felt that two few chapters submitted reports in 1959.

The convention took the following specific action on the Progress and Efficiency Competition at the convention:

(1) The competition was renamed the Donald . W. Davis

Award after the former president who had died only a few weeks before on June 29.

(2) The competition will continue and is compulsory for all chapters. Satisfactory reports will be due May 20 each year unless permission for delay is granted by the secretary's office. Failure to submit a satisfactory report will result in a probationary status for the chapter, At the end of one year the National Council will either lift the probationary status of the chapter or remove its charter.

(3) If a chapter is reactivated for failure to participate, a $50 reactivation fee must be paid for reinstatement in addition to meeting all other qualifications.

(4) Scores for all chapters are to be published in *Linage* each year commencing with the next submission of reports.

When the necessary constitutional changes were made to place the above rules in effect, it was done so with the recommendation that no chapter could pledge or initiate while on probation, and that no chapter could remain on probation for more than one year.

In the ensuing years the National Council has been most lenient in administrating the above dictate, making every effort to strengthen weak chapters, yet several chapters have been declared inactive. The majority of chapters have accepted the reports in the original spirit, and they have filed them annually. In turn, members of the National Council have given serious attention to their evaluations of the report and suggestions for improvements in individual programs. There is no question that the initiation of the annual report strengthened the program of the fraternity immensely.

The National Council returned to paying part of the expenses of the advisor to the national convention for the 1959 meetings at Stanford. This resulted in seventeen advisors accompanying their delegates to the convention. This was approximately double the number of advisors participating in a convention since the Cape Cod meetings in 1951. Twenty-eight undergraduate chapters sent delegates as did the professional chapters in Los Angeles, Chicago and San Francisco.

Dr. Neil Borden, Harvard University, received the Nichols Cup for his contributions to advertising education. Speakers at the convention included Borden, Walter Guild, Clyde Bedell, Robert Gross, and W. L. Thompson. The initiation fee was increased from $17.50 to $20.00, and the position of executive secretary was changed from an elective position to appointment by the National Council.

Soon after his election as National President, Walter Guild conceived the idea of the "Profession at Work" plan, and he spent much of his tenure as president in helping to put this program into effect. The PAW program called for small groups of students to observe in depth the activities of a firm engaged in advertising.

Under the PAW program, small groups of students, usually accompanied by a professor, sit in on actual discussion, conferences, plan meetings, etc. They observe, but do not participate in the sessions.

The program is based on the premise that one area which is normally closed to the student is the counterpart of the scientific laboratory—a place where he may observe advertising as it is actually planned and created. With the cooperation of the agencies and other firms engaged in advertising, students are provided with these practical experiences.

The program was initiated with the cooperation of the Northern California Alumni Association with the undergraduate chapters at San Jose State College, Stanford University and the University of California, Berkeley. It was followed by groups in Chicago, Los Angeles, St. Louis and New York. Guild commented on that program in his President's Corner in the October, 1960 issue of *Linage*:

Have you ever seen the advertising profession "at work"? Probably not. Doctors-to-be often see surgery performed while still in their pre-medical years, Lawyers-to-be can watch, and listen to, court cases being argued. Students of advertising, however have no easy opportunity of observing the practitioners in action; there is no "gallery" to the Plans Board meeting.

We would like to see if that situation can be changed, to permit students of advertising to look over the shoulders of businessmen as they work on advertising matters. We have started a program called, simply, PAW—Profession at Work. Already tested last year by the alumni in the San Francisco area, this program is being extended to Chicago and elsewhere as fast as is practicable.

The Chicago Alumni Chapter has issued an excellent bulletin describing PAW to its members and to undergraduate chapters in their area. This announcement describes the purpose of PAW —"To ease the transition from education to job . . . a plan aimed at giving students a better insight into the advertising business." It goes on to say that the Chicago alumni will invite selected advertising agencies, advertisers media and similar groups to participate by permitting undergraduate members of ADS to attend specific meetings in these companies as silent observers. Fairfax Cone of Foote, Cone & Belding, Inc., is general chairman for the Chicago PAW program.

How will PAW accomplish its purpose? It will take you behind the scenes of the advertising business. Through the generous cooperation of participating firms, you will be invited, in small groups, to see and hear what transpires in actual meetings, presentations and planning sessions. These will not have been staged for your benefit; their doors will have been opened to you so that you can gain an intimate impression of the "profession at work".

This is our key program for the year in Alpha Delta Sigma. From the San Francisco test we realize that this is not a simple plan to set in operation. It requires the closest kind of cooperation among alumni, advisors and students in each area. Do your part. If you are given the opportunity to share this "laboratory" experience in advertising, take advantage of it. All it costs is your interest in advertising.

While the PAW program benefitted these chapters primarily in or quite near large advertising centers, three fine film, slide and tape presentations by Walter Guild, Chick Collier and Steve Baker of Cunningham and Walsh were made available to all chapters.

On June 10, 1960 the ADS National Council met in Chicago for its first off-year meeting. The Council heard President Guild discuss the PAW program, select Minneapolis as the site for the 1961 convention, asked W. L. Thompson to prepare material on ADS criteria for advertising and took care of a number of organizational matters.

Babson Institute received the Donald W. Davis top chapter award in 1960, and Franklin and Marshall captured the honor in 1961. The National Council abandoned its regional scholarship program in 1960 for three national awards. These were presented to John K. Darling, University of Texas ($500); Joseph V. Angione, Fordham ($300) and Douglas Swail, University of Texas ($200.) The granting of scholarships was discontinued after this as the National Council felt that this need was being taken care of by other means and the fraternity might well invest its funds in another manner.

The professional competence award went to the CCNY chapter in 1960, and to the University of Arizona chapter in 1961. The Illinois chapter received the *Linage* award for the best chapter newsletter for the second year in a row. The 1960 award ended this competition.

Edward Deeb, Michigan State University received first place and $500 in the Cigar Institute of America Scholarship competition in 1960. Second place money ($250) went to Jerry R. Lynn, Southern Illinois University, and the third prize of $100 was won by Patrick Brunnock of Manhattan College. Winners of this competition in 1961 included Frank P. Calabretta of Manhattan College ($500); Jerry Chastain, University of Texas ($250); and Iriving Schlesinger, Arizona State ($100).

This was the final year of this competition. It was canceled because of the small number of entries, a problem that continually plagues almost all such programs sponsored by the national organization. Mr. Eugene L. Raymond, President of the Cigar Institute, noted that the papers of the winning entries were of exceedingly high caliber but added these comments in the September, 1961 issue of *Linage*:

"I am disappointed that so few people entered the contest. From our way of thinking this is a wonderful opportunity for a young man to secure experience, money and recognition . . .

"If a college student is serious about pursuing a career in advertising he must show a prospective employer a record above and beyond excellent grades. A good advertising agency wants a young man who is a self-starter, and can prove, from extra curricular activities, that he is firmly promotional minded."

Raymond cited the example of Dick Roth, then an assistant Account Executive at BBD & O working on the Bristol-Myers account. Dick was offered several positions, and the one major reason for his being sought after was the fact that he had won the contest.

During the biennium the fraternity continued to speak in behalf of advertising education. The following is a reprint of an article from *Western Advertising* which appeared in the October, 1960 issue of *Linage*. It includes comments by Walter Guild and William Dumont, both in behalf of Alpha Delta Sigma.

For some time this publication has been asking advertising people in the West questions of moment—and of the moment. Since this is the time of year when the colleges turn loose their annual crop of young hopefuls, some of whose fancies lightly turn to thoughts of an advertising career, we thought it would be appropriate to pose a query on advertising education.

The question: *Can advertising be effectively taught as a craft in colleges and schools — or should a student major in the humanities and learn the crafts and skills later?*

HAL STEBBINS, Hal Stebbins, Inc., Los Angeles:

Each year I see an endless parade of young men and women who have majored in advertising at college. They have stars in their eyes—ants in their pants. They are "ready" for careers in advertising. But are they?

A graduate is the end product of what he is taught. Now and then we find teachers of advertising who know what it's all about. They are—or have been—practicing clinicians. But all too often they are well intentioned people who know advertising only theoretically.

In any event, they can teach students the *mechanics* of advertising but can they teach its *art?* Can they teach them how to think, how to feel, how to write, how to move people and so move merchandise?

If I had my choice, I would devote my four college years to a liberal arts course. I would get a good background not only in the routine studies but in the philosophies and humanities. For everything is grist for the mill of the advertising mind.

I would follow this by a year in the City Room of a metropolitan daily.

I would top this off by a year or two of selling across the retail counter, or on the road, or door-to-door.

And I would then tackle the job of getting an advertising job.

WALTER GUILD, Guild, Bascom & Bonfigli, and national president of Alpha Delta Sigma.

Having recently returned from a meeting of the National Council of Alpha Delta Sigma, where the topic of advertising education was one of the major subjects of discussion, I can say one thing, and that is that there is a good deal of confusion about advertising education.

The teachers of advertising at the college level feel, with complete justification, that college advertising courses are not given the respect and prestige they deserve. Advertising practitioners, on the other hand, are often either critical of or indifferent to the academic preparations colleges are providing for a career in advertising. This, in spite of the widely expressed need of recruitment of more high-grade talent. Then, too, there is significant and growing opposition from some education "experts" to *any* kind of advertising education being offered in college. This group, which does not snipe at such specialized vocational training as engineering courses, thinks that students should be fed a straight diet of liberal arts, and advertising courses should be eliminated.

As for my own view, I think some practical courses in advertising at the college level are most valuable, if for no other reason than that such course help provide direction for the student. I know at least four of the key people at GB&B would not be in advertising today if it had not been for advertising teachers like Royal Roberts of the University of California, who inspired many able men to follow an advertising career.

GEORGE H. WEBER, vice president, Cole & Weber, Seattle:

For the benefit not only of advertising, but for those who should appreciate it—and that means everyone—something concerning its elements and techniques should be taught both in high school and college.

Students will learn to appreciate what is good in writing—conciseness and clarity. They will learn to recognize what is bad—verbosity and fuzziness. The earlier they learn these things, the better communicators they wi'l be, whether or not they ever become advertising professionals.

Not everyone can become an artist, but everyone can learn to appreciate the pleasing and interesting arrangement of elements that constitutes effective visualization. This too can be taught in high school, to the lasting benefit of every student.

Advertising deserves respect. This respect will come if enough people, early in life, learn how difficult it is to "do advertising."

ROBERT W. DAILEY, vice president, Cunningham & Walsh, San Francisco:

I will advise my son, if he is interested in advertising as a career, to devote his college time to subjects other than advertising.

College, I believe, should help a young person develop his abilities to think, analyze, make decisions, philosophize and to better understand and appreciate the motivations of people and the art of living. He can learn the fundamentals of advertising, marketing and selling during the first years of his business career.

Because he will have a better understanding of himself and others, he should be able to progress more rapidly in becoming proficient in advertising.

WILLIAM DuMONT, former vice president and director Fuller and Smith and Ross; president, Alpha Delta Sigma, San Francisco chapter:

Put me down as middle of the road on teaching advertising in high schools and colleges.

I am for a balance between "doing" and "dreaming." I would pack in all the English, history, languages, psychology and other cultural courses possible—but with a leavening balance of advertising, journalism, public speaking, plus participation in student activities.

Any subject that improves facility for expression and communication as advertising does, belongs in colleges and high schools. Advertising training disciplines students in writing to a point and purpose. Students in my advertising class at Golden Gate College told me they got a lot out of it, which they wished had been mixed in with their "lit" courses while studying for academic degrees.

In the December 1960 issue of *Linage*, Murray Gelman, ADS at NYU in 1951 gave this fine retort:

In *Linage's* October discussion of advertising education, two of the five practitioners quoted stood *against* such training. (Or perhaps I should say they stood *for* liberal arts training exclusively.) One, Hal Stebbins, suggested "a year in the city room of a metropolitan daily," followed by sales work, before starting an ad job hunt.

That sounds good; I agree heartily with the sales idea. But getting into a city room isn't that easy. For one thing, every daily in this country *stays* swamped with job applications. Just-graduateds—even those with journalism degrees and honors—do well to land jobs with papers off in the middle of nowhere. After a year in limbo, they try again for the major leagues; few make it.

Unfortunately, those opposed to advertising training have either forgotten or do not know these simple facts: (1) no college or university offering such training neglects the arts; and (2) no just-graduated has much to offer a prospective employer other than interest, aptitude and hope. If he is an advertising graduate, he can at least prove his interest and aptitude with classroom copy, market studies, layouts, ADS projects, etc. True, they'll be no match for the portfolio he'll assemble after a year in the field; but they'll have helped him get into the field in the first place.

Finally, Mr. Guild's statement that advertising courses at least "help provide direction for the student" is quite correct. Of my fellow ad majors at NYU, almost all entered college with a general interest in advertising; almost all graduated knowing exactly where they wanted to go.

I'm pleased to report that almost all of us are doing what we hoped to and don't regret our advertising training. Nor would I call any of us total clods when the talks turns to world affairs, politics, literature, music theatre, philosophy or—You name it!

In the same issue Walter Guild elaborated in more detail his views of "Why Advertising Education?"

It may be news to you that not all professional advertising people favor college advertising courses as sound preparation for an advertising career. Such people echo the sentiments of many outside of advertising who would abolish these courses from the curriculum. The critic usually happens to favor some one course which he feels is a "must" for the would-be advertising man. such as English, the Arts, Business Administration or even Psychology.

Let me hasten to state that I have nothing against these courses. There's no question but that advertising people must be able to grasp the language, the art forms, business principles and the basics of human behavior. I feel, however, that the critics of advertising courses are 99 percent wrong (after all, no one's perfect). Further, by voicing destructive prejudices, they do a great disservice to those who look forward to a career in advertising, and to advertising itself.

The case for advertising education parallels those for such course as engineering, accounting or journalism. No one in his right mind would suggest that these curricula omit the liberal arts entirely. At the same time, no one is clamoring to strip their undergraduate curricula of specific course in technique.

For proof of the value of advertising education, I don't have to look beyond the staff of our own agency. If it had not been for college courses in advertising (and the interest fostered by ADS), four of our most valued people probably would not be with us or any other advertising enterprise. All four have told me that their interest in an advertising career began as a direct result of their enrollment in advertising classes. They also tell me that their active participation in ADS brought advertising into focus and cinched their decision to seek a career in this field.

Several very successful advertising men outside of our agency have also told me how valuable to them were the fundamentals of advertising they learned in college. Now established in agencies, in media and in representative firms, these men have told me that their ADS membership did, literally, "bridge the gap" from campus to career. They state that ADS gave them insight into advertising, made it possible for them to discuss their potential careers with professionals in advance of graduation and greatly assisted in landing the first job.

I believe that advertising education is not yet fully appreciated by the industry. There is no doubt, however, that through the efforts of Alpha Delta Sigma and such groups as the American Association of Advertising Agencies, advertising education is approaching the status it deserves. Some of the most potent advocates and spokesmen in behalf of continuing and improving advertising education are our own ADS alumni groups. Here are men whose own personal experience in applying their scholastic training to the building of successful careers is certainly testimony which tends to refute the arguments of the critics.

During the biennium three new chapters were installed at Long Beach State College, University of Maryland and at Texas A & M. Chapters initiated 1127 new members, 345 less than the previous biennium when 1472 young men joined the fraternity ranks.

1961 *Convention*

The National Chapter convened in April 1961 at the University of Minnesota where Bill Mindak and the members of the Samuel Gale Chapter, at the request of the National Council, presented a convention headlining more speakers, workshop sessions, and fewer business sessions. Headliners for the event included Harry McMahan, consultant on television commercials; Peter C. Peterson, Executive Vice President of Bell & Howell; Bob Stafford, President of Knox Reeves Advertising Agency; George Sandell, Vice President and Advertising Director of Minnesota Mining and Manufacturing Co.; Jim Fish, Vice President and Advertising Director of General Mills and then President of the Adversiting Federation of America.

While little business was transacted, the convention was a turning point for the fraternity. Since the inception of ADS its home had been the University of Missouri. With few exceptions the executive secretary of the fraternity had been a staff member of the University of Missouri School of Journalism. Milt Gross, who had served ADS most faithfully for 14 years, had asked the National Council in its 1960 Chicago meeting to replace him at the Minnesota convention.

President Walter Guild, indicating the tremendous contribution of Gross, presented him with a plaque at the convention honoring him for his fourteen years of service to ADS as National Secretary.

Rol Rider, who had been elected the fraternity's first National

Professional Vice President in 1959, was elected President for the 1961-63 biennium. Laird and Haverfield were again to serve as Treasurer and Editor of *Linage* respectively. Charles E. Wolfe was the only regional vice president to continue, but most of the men elected to vice presidential positions for the biennium had been associated with the national program of the fraternity in some way.

Richard Joel returned to the post of Southeastern Vice President, a post he held before his election to the presidency in 1957. Hugh Sargent, University of Illinois was elected Midwestern Vice President; Roland Hicks, Pennsylvania State, Eastern Vice President; and John E. McGary, partner in the Robinson-Gerrard-McGary, Inc. advertising agency, Houston, Texas, Southwest Vice President. McGary died during the second year of the biennium, and the Southwest Vice Presidency remained vacant until 1963. The convention selected Tim Alban of the University of Houston as its National Student Vice President and the following members as Student Regional Vice Presidents: Culyar McIlheran, Texas A & M (Southwest); Larry Lee Loose, Franklin and Marshall (East); Gerry Lias, University of Miami (Southeast); Robert Wylie, Southern Illinois University (Midwest); and Joseph De Nardo, Arizona State University (West).

Bill Mindak was elected by the convention to the position of National Professional Vice President and served in this capacity for a year. Soon after the convention adjourned, it was pointed out that the National Professional Vice President should have been elected not by the general convention, but by representatives only of the professional chapters. Thus after serving one year, Mindak resigned and Kent Westrate of Wade Advertising. Chicago was appointed by President Rider with the consent of the professional chapters to serve the remaining year of the biennium in this capacity.

In its first act, the newly-elected National Council appointed Donald G. Hileman, Southern Illinois University as Executive Secretary, and national headquarters of the organization moved to Carbondale, Illinois where it is now located.

Few constitutional changes were made in Minneapolis. Such changes incorporated two basic ideas. The first was a broadening of the base for membership of Alpha Delta Sigma to include public relations and related fields, not just advertising *per se*. The second was to strengthen the regional organizations of the fraternity and to place more responsibility on the Regional Vice Presidents. The constitution was amended to prevent chapters from naming the chapter after its current advisor, thus encouraging the honoring of some advertising practitioner or educator whose relationship to the university and the chapter has been more enduring.

Philip Ward Burton of Syracuse University received the Nichols Cup. It was the first and only time that the award has been granted to a former member of the National Council. Burton served the fraternity as its National President from 1953 through 1957. The Sixth Degree Key was presented to Will G. Grant, president of Will Grant Inc., Dallas, Texas.

The University of Houston received the Donald W. Davis Award as the fraternity's top chapter in 1962, and the University of Georgia claimed the coveted honor in 1963.

Activity of the national chapter during the biennium stressed transition due to the change of national headquarters, and the executive officer of the organization; brought about a review and change of operating policies procedures and produced the planning and preparation for celebration of ADS' fifieth anniversary. President Rider, relying heavily on his experiences in advertising agency management, spearheaded and directed much of this activity.

The drop in new initiates during the 1959-61 biennium to 1127 from 1472 the previous biennium indicated that a thorough study and analysis of the goals and purposes of ADS, as well as it operation policies and procedures, was necessary. Prior to 1961 the National Council considered a chapter active until all evidence of life and interest was gone; thus, according to the chapter roster in the Fall of 1961, 54 of the 70 universities who had been granted charters were considered to have active chapters. During the biennium the programs at all 54 universities were reviewed and nine chapters (Denver, Iowa, Mississippi, Northwestern, Southern California, Syracuse, Temple, Whitworth and Wichita) were declared inactive. Of the remaining 45 chapters another dozen had advisor or organizational problems, leaving 35 chapters fairly strong and meaningful ADS programs.

In the majority of instances where a chapter was declared inactive, the single dominant factor was the lack of an interested and concerned faculty member to serve as advisor. Reasons why such an individual did not exist on these campuses are numerous and varied. Among such reasons are these factors: de-emphasis of advertising education programs; development of other means of contact with industry, reducing the need for ADS; the beginning of the general movement on the part of some students not to become involved in organizations; pressure on the faculty member to devote more time to research and publishing; and general lack of recognition by administration for advising and working with ADS members.

No new charters were granted during the biennium, although the chapter at Boston University was reactivated. The National Council in its off-year meeting in Denver, Colo., in June, 1962 did consider and reject an application from a four year business school. This reflected the organization's position of recommending that professional advertising education must emphasize a strong liberal arts background in addition to professional orientation.

After much discussion and thought concerning the aims and goals of the organization at its Denver meeting the National Council felt no major change was needed at this time; rather, the changes deemed necessary were in operational policies and procedures.

To stress its former decision, the following statement appears in the National Council minutes of the Denver meeting:

It is strongly reaffirmed that the basic purpose of Alpha Delta Sigma is to serve students in bridging the gap from the University advertising education programs to practice in the advertising field. Alumni and Professional chapters are designed for this primary purpose also.

It is agreed that all action taken at this National Council should represent an attitude of growth in Alpha Delta Sigma.

The latter statement was added to emphasize that although certain universities were dropping advertising courses, that certain chapters had become inactive, and that there had been a large reduction in initiates during the previous biennium; the aims and goals of ADS were still as meaningful today as in 1913, its opportunities to serve those universities and students who desire affiliation with and understand the higher purposes of ADS was very real; this could best be done with a positive attitude of growth.

Realizing that if the national organization was to experience the growth reflected in its positive statement of attitude it could not do so with its only paid help being a university teacher who would have only limited time to perform the duties of both the executive administrator and secretary. It seemed it would be necessary to employ a full time office manager in addition to the executive officer to do the detailed work of the organization and to assist the Executive Secretary in implementing policies of the National Council. While this change did not occur in the 1961-63 biennium, a complete revaluation of the financial structure of the organization during the year made this possible in the ensuing biennium.

Steps were taken in the 1961-63 biennium to make the executive officer the communicator for the organization. After a review of *Linage*, the National Council recommended that it become an external organ, and that a newsletter be established for internal communication.

Bob Haverfield, editor of *Linage*, incorporated the suggestions of the National Council in issues during the 1962-63 academic year. Major changes affecting *Linage* had already occurred during the first year of the biennium when two of the four issues were withheld while the financial status of the organization was being reviewed.

Prior to this date, it had been the policy to send *Linage* free to each member. With the membership of the fraternity becoming so large and with no annual dues structure, it was apparent that this policy could not be maintained. In the 1962 Denver National Council meeting, the editor of *Linage* was instructed to contact the membership indicating that publication would no longer be automatically sent to them, but that they could purchase a year's subscription for $1 or 3 years for $2. Distribution of the publication was made on this basis until the 1963 convention when the fraternity voted its first annual dues.

Regional vice presidents were given modest budgets to assist them in conducting regional meetings and the affairs of the regions. *Linage*, in discussing the off-year regional meetings held in 1962 referred to them as the "best ever." The success of these meetings pointed up once again the importance of the regional meetings in accomplishing the aims and goals of ADS.

Most of President Rider's second year was devoted to planning the activities of ADS' 50th Anniversary year, including the 1963 convention in New York City. He appointed William P. Dumont as General Chairman.

Dumont, who headed the Fuller and Smith and Ross West Coast offices at the time of his retirement, was a charter member of ADS at Ohio State. He later served as president of the Northern California Alumni Association.

A series of events were held both on the local and national level from Founder's Day, 1962 to Founder's Day in November, 1963. A special 50th anniversary seal was designed and made available for use by all ADS chapters and its members. A special proclamation was printed on parchment paper and presented by each chapter to key persons in their communities. A copy of the proclamation appears on the opposite page. A special plaque was prepared and presented to the University of Missouri, expressing the thanks of the organization to the university who spawned the mother chapter.

1963 50th *Anniversary Convention*

Two major events highlighted the 50th anniversary activities, the national convention in New York in April and a special Founder's Day celebration in Chicago in November. Attendance records for the number of members participating in a national convention and the number of persons at the convention banquet were set in New York. Fifty-six unofficial delegates registered for the meetings in addition to the thirty official chapter delegates and nineteen advisors. A number of professional advertising men receiving Golden Fifty awards augmented the banquet attendance.

Climax of the convention came with the presentation of the Golden Fifty Awards. The awards were presented to 50 professional advertising men who had made significant contributions to the growth of advertising during the past half-century and to 50 men who had best served ADS since its founding in 1913.

50th Anniversary Proclamation

Be it hereby known to all persons that the twleve months between November 14, 1962, and November 14, 1963 are hereby proclaimed to be the Fiftieth Anniversary Year of the National Professional Advertising Fraternity,

ALPHA DELTA SIGMA

which was founded by seventeen dedicated men at the University of Missouri on November 14, 1913, Columbia, Missouri. In honor to them and to the nearly 18,000 members of the Fraternity this year is commemorated to the ideals of

I Providing an opportunity for college students to achieve a more thorough and accurate understanding of advertising.

II Rendering all possible service towards the improvement of advertising by encouraging ethical and truthful advertising.

III Providing honorary recognition for work done in the field of advertising, by students, professionals, alumni, and educators.

IV Providing an opportunity for the practical application of advertising and for the self-improvement of the individual.

V Encouraging cooperation and understanding between educators and businessmen.

In Honor,
with Truth,
Authority,
and Responsibility,

Rol W. Rider
National President
November 14, 1962

Philip Ward Burton of Syracuse University served as the chairman of the committee making the final selections. Recipients of these awards are given special recognition in another section of this book.

Don Belding, speaking as Benjamin Franklin the patron saint of ADS, gave the major address at the banquet, and Charles H. Sandage, head of the Department of Advertising at the University of Illinois received the Nichols Cup.

Walter Hobbs, president, and members of the New York Professional chapter, served as hosts to the convention. Hobbs and his committee made it possible for delegates of the convention to meet and talk advertising with some of the nation's top practitioners in New York City. Jerry Fields, a specialist in advertising personnel, spoke at the Saturday noon luncheon.

Rex Magee, one of the founders of the fraternity attended the special Founders Day celebration in Chicago in November. His comments, along with a special presentation by Dr. Noel P. Laird, climaxed the evening's festivities. Dr. Laird's amusing but serious take-off on Lincoln's Gettysburg address is presented in part because it reflects the warmth that this "grand ole man" has brought to ADS throughout the years and because of its profound truth.

Practically everything done in the world is the extension of the shadow of a man, a man or a small group of men who inaugurated something in the beginning.

Two score and ten years ago our founding fathers brought forth upon this continent, a new fraternity, conceived in *truth* and dedicated to the proposition that "the truthful man is the only one who will enter the heaven of our profession."

Now we are engaged in a great economic and political conflict, building a universe so that *truth* will in the end triumph over the forces of evil. We are met on a great occasion. We have come together to dedicate our thoughts to those courageous men at the University of Missouri who gave us the foundation for this fraternity.

But in a larger sense we dedicate our thoughts to all the other brave men, living and dead, who struggled since the fraternity was founded to keep it alive, to encourage—*truth, persistence* and *competition*. It is altogether fitting and proper that we also honor our Patron Saint, Benjamin Franklin.

It is for us, the living, to be dedicated to the task of recognizing the great power of advertising, like Benjamin Franklin's electricity, advertising conducts mighty movements of goods from fields, factories and warehouse into stores, homes and nations. It promotes charitable and public service objectives as well as commercial ends.

We here highly resolve that the founders, and our Patron Saint, have not died in vain. It is for us, the living, rather to be dedicated here to the unfinished work which they have, thus far, so nobly advanced, that this nation shall continue to enjoy freedom of communication and that its advertising shall be by the people, for the people, and Alpha Delta Sigma shall not perish from the earth.

With apologies to Abe Lincoln.

Nathan E. Jacobs, a 1924 alumnus of the University of Missouri and then president of Bozell and Jacobs, Chicago, Ill., accepted the plaque presented to the University of Missouri, expressing the fraternity's gratitude to the university for providing the atmosphere in which such an organization could be founded. Fred R. Haviland, Director of Marketing, Joseph Schlitz Brewing Co., Milwaukee, Wisconsin was the speaker for the evening, and Billy I. Ross served as Master of Ceremonies.

Ross, who was completing his doctorate work at Southern Illinois University at the time, but who had been advisor to the award-winning chapter at the University of Houston in 1962, was elected National President at the New York meeting. Noel Laird was re-elected National Treasurer, and Donald Hileman was re-appointed Executive Secretary. Professional chapters re-elected Kent Westrate to serve as Professional Vice President.

Two Regional Vice Presidents, Hugh Sargent and Richard Joel, continued to represent the Midwest and Southeast, respectively, on the National Council. Three men were elected to the Council for the first time—Don Somerville, Boston University (East); Leon Quera, San Jose State (West); and Robert Van Voorhis, Magnussen Advertising Agency, Fort Worth, Texas (Southwest).

Larry Williams of the University of Oregon was elected to the National Student Vice President's post. Students appointed to Regional Vice President positions included: John Burns, Fordham University; Dave Herman, University of Minnesota; Ben Thornal, Florida State University; Jack Moriniere, Texas Christian University; and Craig Mathiesen, University of Oregon.

Lee Fondren, KLZ radio, Denver, Colorado, was appointed Chairman of the Advisory Committee of the National Council, to continue the organization's close ties with the AAW and AFA in particular, and the advertising industry, in general.

The election procedure for the Regional Vice Presidents was changed at the New York convention. The five regional vice presidents elected in New York were to serve for one year. These offices would then be filled for a two year period at the off-year Regional convention. Such a change was made because it was felt such decisions should be made during regional meetings rather than at the national convention, allowing more chapters to participate in the decision.

In another constitutional change Regional student vice presidents serve for one year only and are to be elected at the off-year regional meeting and at the national convention. The convention also made provisions for filling vacancies in the regional vice president and regional student vice president positions between national and regional meetings.

In a move to strengthen the financial base of Alpha Delta Sigma, allowing it to continue to grow and to broaden its base of service to advertising education, the 1963 national convention went on record as approving an annual dues. The National Council later approved the annual fee of two dollars for each active member. A subscription to *Linage* was included in the dues.

Three new Regional Vice Presidents were selected at the 1964 Regional meetings. They were Bill Mindak, University of Minnesota (Midwest); Charles Lewis, vice president of Aylin Advertising, Houston (Southwest) who was initiated into the Texas chapter in 1946; and Glenn Lutat, *Times-Observer*, Los Gatos, California, (West) a member of the Northern California Professional chapter, past president of San Jose State and the first Western Region student vice president. Dick Joel and Don Somerville were re-elected in the Southwest and East.

Regional Student Vice Presidents elected in 1941 included: John Daigle, University of Houston (Southwest); Ron Elbon, University of Colorado (West); Robert Grimes, Babson Institute (East); Jerry Hayes, University of Georgia (Southeast); and Robert Levin, University of Illinois (Midwest).

Bill Ross was re-elected to another two-year term at the Miami convention in 1965 and much that was started in the 1963-65 biennium was to be continued into the 1965-67 era. While an attempt will be made to isolate certain events and activities placing them in chronological order, there will be much overlapping.

Continued study of the aims and purposes of Alpha Delta Sigma during the 1961-63 biennium pointed up that "bridging the gap" was important as ever, but it could no longer be the primary objective for Alpha Delta Sigma. "Bridging the gap" was now totally possible without ADS. Other individuals and organizations in advertising had rallied to the call ADS had pronounced for more than a century.

For example, the American Association of Advertising Agencies joined with and surpassed efforts to assist advertising education that the AFA and AAW had subscribed to many years ago. In the midwest a strong relationship between the agencies in the Central Region of the AAAA and the teachers of advertising in midwest colleges and universities had developed after an exchange of articles in *Advertising Age* in 1951 by Earle Ludgin, president of the agency bearing his name and Dr. Charles H. Sandage of the University of Illinois.

This led to a meeting of Ludgin and Sandage which in turn led to a conference of agency executives and educators in early 1952 for purposes of discussing problems of mutual interest. In the Fall issue of *Linage*, the late Dr. James E. Moyer of the University of Illinois, wrote concerning this meeting and the development of the Central Region 4 A's program:

The outcome of the meeting was the establishment of a permanent committee consisting of representatives from both groups to develop a program to foster better liaison between the agency world and the academic community. It was also decided that this committee could best operate within the existing organizational structure of the 4A's Central Region.

Today, some 13 years later, there is ample evidence to attest to the success of the program. It has received national attention and has been on the discussion agenda of various conferences. Currently it is being investigated by some of the other 4A regions for possible adoption within their respective areas.

Through the years the agency executive serving on the Board of Governors of the Central Region have given their wholehearted support to the Agency-Educator Committee of the 4A's, as it is now called. This committee has been assigned primary responsibility for developing and implementing a program to foster better understanding between educators and agency personnel. The Committee has as co-chairmen an educator and an agency executive . . .

The present program primarily revolves around three principle activities, i.e., agency fellowships (for teachers), agency task force visits to academic institutions, and the annual fall meeting of the 4A's Central Region where educators are the invited guests of the association.

Other advertising organizations on both the national and local levels have followed in developing educational programs to help students "bridge the gap" from the university campus to the practice of advertising.

Thus, ADS had to accept as its aim and goal more than just "bridging the gap". While the individual programs on the campus would remain much the same, performing the "ad club" function of arranging for speakers, tours and participating in money-raising and other activities to gain experience and provide service, it was apparent that as the only university-based advertising organization involving students and as one of three organizations with its major concern being advertising education, the fraternity would have to accept in the future as its primary aim and purpose "the professionalization of advertising through education."

Activities of the national organization of Alpha Delta Sigma since 1963 have centered around the educational function for advertising, both on and off the campus. If advertising is to continue to become "professional" in every sense of the word, it will do so in large part as the result of enlightened education.

Since 1963 ADS has been continually aware of its relationship to its two sister organizations, Gamma Alpha Chi and the American Academy of Advertising.

Gamma Alpha Chi, other than the difference in sex, can be considered identical to the program of Alpha Delta Sigma. There are those who feel that the problems of women in advertising are distinctly different to justify two separate organizations; there are many who feel that such differences are minor and that much could be gained if the two organizations would merge. Since 1963 the National Council has accepted an attitude of complete cooperation with GAX, an attitude which the national representation of Gamma Alpha Chi has generally shared. Specific acts of cooperation have resulted in the past five years, each of which will be discussed later.

The American Academy of Advertising in its decade of existence has made some contributions to advertising education, but it has failed to realize the potential that many advertising educators felt that it had and still does have. Robert Zacher, then National Dean of the Academy, discussed its formation, development and reason for being in the summer, 1964 issue of *Linage*:

The American Academy of Advertising is a professional organization for college and university teachers of advertising and for advertising practitioners who wish to contribute to advertising education at the college level. The Academy was organized by a group of advertising educators who attended the Dallas convention of the Advertising Federation of America.

A major function of the Academy has always been the coordination of efforts to advance avdertising education. Charter members represented two areas in American universities where advertising instruction is most often offered; business administration and marketing on the one hand, and journalism and communications on the other. As the organization has grown, members from the graphic arts and other related areas have been added.

The Academy is the only organization of teachers whose membership encompasses all the instructional areas in which advertising courses are taught. One of the reasons behind its founding was to provide a more satisfactory framework within which all advertising educators might meet and work together. Prior to the formation of the Academy, advertising teachers tended to be segmented, meeting in several separate academic groups in the areas of marketing, journalism or art. The Academy represents an effort to provide closer liaison between all advertising educators; irrespective of the academic discipline in which they may be teaching.

The Academy has spearheaded a national campaign for recognition of the value of professional education in advertising . . . The Academy encourages close relationship between teachers and advertising practitioners . . . The Academy has assisted in the development of internships for teachers.

. . . It is evident from the foregoing that the Academy and Alpha Delta Sigma are working toward many of the same goals. As a professional fraternity, ADS strives toward an increased professionalism in advertising. Much of the work carried on by the two organizations complements that of the other. Just as ADS has long striven to 'bridge the gap' between the classroom and the advertising world for students, so has the Academy sought to strengthen the ties between advertising teachers and practitioners in the advertising industry.

In recent years, there has been a segment of the Academy who feel that the Academy can best serve its members and advertising by emphasizing more its relation to the academic community. As a result the Academy has established a *Journal of Advertising,* encouraging research and publication and acceptance of advertising as an institution in itself and thus worthy of independence status (away from journalism and marketing) as a field of academic study.

Vernon Fryburger of Northwestern University, who was serving the Academy as National Dean in 1965 discussed this particular philosophy and approach in the Winter, 1966 issue of *Linage*:

Seven years ago the American Academy of Advertising was formed to serve seven purposes. These purposes as expressed in the constitution are: (1st) to advance advertising education, (2nd) to appraise advertising performance. (3rd) to promote professional education for advertising, (4th) to study, evaluate and improve advertising education, (5th) to stimulate research and advertising, (6th) to develop closer liaison among academic disciplines relevant to advertising, and (7th) to encourage closer cooperation among teachers of advertising.

I think we all would agree that these are worthy purposes. However, we can only speculate on how well the Academy has served them.

We know we have a going organization. We have 300 members, 16 regional deans, 11 committees, and 4 national officers. Obviously, the Academy has met the need of many educators who wanted to belong to and be identified with a national organization that was solely for advertising; not for advertising as a part of journalism or as a part of marketing, but clearly for advertising.

How has this membership advanced advertising education? Perhaps the satisfaction of belonging is reward enough, and perhaps this inspires confidence and pride that results in better teaching. However, with only 10 percent of the members attending the annual conventions it would seem that the Academy has a great potential that has not been tapped.

Looking to the future, I submit that the Academy will not do much to advance advertising education unless it does more to advance advertising knowledge. Apparently we consider our field of study important enough to warrant a national organization of scholars, but what have we done to define the field, to build the discipline, to provide the incentives and rewards for scholarship? We seek identity and respect in the academic community, but what have we done to earn that respect? The mere fact that advertising is important in our society does not assure its importance in a college curriculum. We know that the vitality of a field of study is measured by its scholarly output, but what are we doing to encourage scholarship?

Advertising knowledge has plenty of room to grow. In its present state it is discursive, generalized, and highly rationalized. It roams from marketing to social institutions to psychology to consumer behavior, to aesthtics, to ethics and so on. It proceeds from many organizing concepts—professional, managerial, functional, vocational, and technical. There is little in it that can be called science. There are no generalizations having universal applicability. There aren't many hypotheses waiting to be tested experimentally.

Our interdisciplinary tradition may be our most significant contribution. However, in looking to other fields for ideas we have neglected to build a central core of advertising ideas. I am not suggesting we turn our backs on outside sources of ideas, but let's shape the course of our own stream. Let's not be diverted by the tributaries.

In brief, I think our most important task as educators is to build an academic discipline that is uniquely advertising, and I think the primary mission of the Academy should be to expedite this kind of constructive work.

To this end I propose a modest 3-point program for the coming year. First, let us clarify the Academy's role. Second, let us reorganize for more effective participation by more members. Third, let us formalize our publishing activity.

Concerning the Academy's role, I have not been at all sure just what the Academy stands for. In the Constitution's statement of objectives we find expressions such as "to coordinate effort," "to encourage cooperation," "to develop closer liaison," "to strive for recognition." This kind of language suggests that the Academy is a fraternal order dedicated to good fellowship and good industry relations.

Too frequently I see evidence that the American Academy of Advertising abdicates its responsibility to the practitioners and turns to them to build the body of advertising knowledge. Clearly, we should *not* look to the practitioners to structure the field, or to contribute substantially to its concent. And certainly we should not ask them to accredit our educational programs. Our practitioner friends are pragmatists seeking immediate answers to immediate questions. If today's students learn only what the practitioners know, tomorrow's problems will be solved with yesterday's mistakes. Bear in mind also, the great majority of practitioners have not had any formal study in advertising. They are not likely to advocate a qualification they themselves do not possess.

I firmly believe that we educators should maintain a healthy independence from practitioner influence and control. How else could we advance knowledge and function as critics of advertising performance?

Don't misunderstand me. I have nothing against practitioners. Some of my best friends are in the business. I admire and respect them. They are intellectually refreshing and are an excellent source of case material. And I see nothing wrong in holding our annual meeting with the Advertising Federation of America. Yet, I think we would do well to meet once in awhile with academic associations in the social and behavioral sciences.

All I am suggesting is that the Academy become more of an "innerdirected" organization. Let us set our own goals, structure our own field, build our own discipline, enhance our own research. Let us plow the long, hard furrow. This is the only way to earn academic respectability.

The Academy has done a splendid job of recruiting members, electing officers, and appointing committees. Yet, at these annual meetings we usually have only about 10 per cent of the members present, and those who do attend are mostly the same people year after year. We have 16 regional deans. The idea of having a grass roots organization supplementing the national organization is a good one. But what is happening at the grass roots level? We have 11 committees. Some are functioning. Some are not. The responsibilities of at least 2 special committees, the one on Educational Materials and Methods and the one on Advertising Age's Creative Workshop are not clearly defined.

I have nothing against deans, but perhaps we have too many of them. If we are going to have regional officers let's consider some reapportionment so that they will approximate the distribution of advertising educators, not geographic areas. In some regions we have a regional dean who apparently represents one educator—himself.

We've had no guidelines for budgeting funds. We follow no clearcut policy in jointly sponsoring publications of Bill Ross' study. We've had a vote to amend the constitution with only 25 members voting. And what they were voting on was not made clear.

In the year ahead I propose that we re-examine the entire organizational structure with a view toward broadening member participation, clarifying committee assignments, and establishing operating policies that are so essential to a strong, responsible and continuing organization.

Publish or perish is a popular admonition to scholars. I suspect it applies even more to academic organizations. The best way to serve all of our members and to demonstrate our vitality to the industry, as well as the academic community at large, is to publish thoughtful papers such as those presented at this meeting. The opportunity to publish in itself is a strong incentive to scholarship. The Academy should provide this opportunity. We have a plan for publishing occasional papers as a first step toward publishing a journal. We will put this plan in effect this year.

These then are the three proposals for progess: let's clarify the Academy's goal, reorganize for more effective action, and get our publishing underway.

Our large membership reflects the hope of many advertising educators that some day somehow they will have one, single national organization that clearly serves their interests. I assure you your officers this year will do their best to make the Academy that organization.

If the direction of the Academy continues as Fryburger suggests, this may be reason enough for its existence alone; however, there are professional advertising educators who feel that the aims and purposes of the Academy, are so similar that each organization and the total effort would be strengthened by closer cooperation between the groups, perhaps even a combining of forces in operation and management. To date, officers of the Academy have not considered seriously any proposals for more direct cooperation with ADS and GAX.

An ADS Roundup began in 1963 to contact as many members of ADS as possible. Concerning this program, President Ross wrote in the Winter, 1964 issue of *Linage*:

As a result of the ADS Roundup, many of you are receiving information from ADS National for the first time in many years. Welcome back and in the future let's keep in closer touch.

Many of you asked in your letters, just why do you want to hear from me after all of these years? It is a good question and I want to answer it for you in this column.

First of all, we have plans to publish a book during this our Golden Anniversary Year. In it we hope to carry the names of the members of the fraternity . . .

Secondly, we want to bring you up to date on what the fraternity is doing and ask your help when it is needed . . .

Third we want you to become more active in the fraternity—work with the alumni-professional groups, help us form new chapters both on and off campus. . .

Fourth, we hope you will help ADS, other practitioner groups, and colleges and universities in continuing to help elevate advertising to professional status . . .

Fifth, be a supporter of advertising education by talking with interested high school and college groups. Many schools have eliminated advertising education programs and many others are in the process of reducing advertising offerings. Follow with interest the happenings at your campus. Where advertising education is eliminated or reduced, professionalization of advertising is dealt a deadly blow.

I think you can see why you should stand up and be counted.

It was ironic that the professional advertising educators on the university campus, most of whom were involved with ADS during its first half century, did not recognize the value of continued contact with ADS alumni. Advertising educators had long felt that many practitioners did not understand or care to know what was being taught in advertising courses on college campuses, but the same educators failed to see the help that ADS alumni and professionals could provide in this necessary educational process.

Prior to 1963 the general attitude that prevailed among the majority of ADS members was that it was a campus organization, designed for students, and that once one left the campus we severed all responsibilites and ties to the organization. Later, during the 1965-67 biennium, Robert Bryson of the University of Oklahoma who served as Southwest Regional Vice President from 1966 to 1968 prepared a suggested pledging statement which was to stress "the continued relationship of ADS," indicating that after graduation the relationship changed from one of "receiving to one of "giving."

For a number of years the national office has sent each undergraduate upon completion of his degree a letter of congratulations, telling him about the professional chapters, encouraging him to become associated with one if he locates in a city where there is a chapter. The letter continues with an expression of hope that the ADS experience on the campus has been of benefit to him and has helped him to understand the higher purposes of ADS; that he will now give of his interest, time and money to assist his own chapter and university and its students and faculties in the continual development of the advertising education program. It is only through such a continuing program that a professional level of advertising can be realized.

It is difficult to know how many of the new initiates accept this philosophy. All communications from national headquarters continually emphasize this point of view, but the advisors and officers of the local chapters remain the key individuals in its communication and acceptance by the membership.

The ADS Roundup resulted in an ADS directory being printed and distributed which listed initiates up through and including July, 1966. Jim Fish of General Mills Co., Minneapolis served as General Chairman for the project which was officially begun with the presentation of a branding iron to Fish at the National Founders Day dinner held in Chicago in March 1963.

Kent Westrate has proved to be a most enthusiastic Professional

Vice President, and he has continually sought to express the National Council's interest and concern in the professional chapters. In spite of Westrate's and the Council's efforts only a few cities have developed good and continuing programs. Chapters in Chicago, Memphis, Miami, New York and Northern California have had meaningful programs on a continued basis for more than a decade which would indicate that they have developed a degree of permanence and stability.

Chapters in Dallas, Houston, Los Angeles, Milwaukee, Minneapolis, Seattle, Washington, D.C., and New Jersey have operated off and on with various degrees of success. Atlanta, Georgia formed the most recent professional chapter. .

Historically, the national organization has provided little guidance to the professional chapters. These chapters have never had to file annual reports and they have been allowed to operate as they wished. The Miami and the Northern California professional chapters seem to have functioned more nearly to the ideals of the national fraternity—that is, service to advertising education, in particular to the universities and colleges near them. Northern California long worked with the chapters at Stanford and more recently with San Jose State and San Francisco State. The advertising programs at the two former schools have all but been dropped as both institutions moved primarily to graduate education. Neither Stanford nor California have active ADS chapters today.

The Miami Professional chapter struggled in recent years to keep the ADS program at the University of Miami as the de-emphasis of advertising courses in the School of Business threatened to eliminate the chapter.

In the view of Bob Harris, past president of the Miami Professional chapter and the current Vice President of the Southeast Region, "with the lack of strong advertising orientation in marketing programs that have reduced or de-emphasized their advertising offerings, it is even more important that the ADS chapter provide this kind of background." Representatives of the Miami Professional chapter were convincing enough that the campus chapter at the University of Miami has once again become active. The degree of interest of the Miami Professional chapter in advertising education is also shown in its effort to change the ADS constitution to admit Junior Colleges. The rapid growth of Miami Dade Junior College accounted for their interest, and this will be discussed later in connection with ADS and the Junior College movement.

The Chicago chapter throughout the years has worked with Northwestern, De Paul and Roosevelt universities, although such cooperation has been primarily the responsibility of one or two members and has been an auxiliary activity rather than as a major function of the organization. Much the same situation has been true with the New York Professional chapter, but even to a lesser degree.

The Memphis chapter, one of the most active over the years, started out as an alumni group, and its program has become primarily social. When a charter was granted to Memphis State University in 1967, the professional chapter took an active part and has maintained a continued interest. Prior to this the chapter gave assistance to the program at the University of Mississippi until it became inactive.

Executive Secretary, Donald Hileman, attempted to assess the role of the professional chapter and the professional alumni member in an article in the Spring, 1965 issue of *Linage*. It is printed here in its entirety, because it is important that the questions it raises be considered by persons concerned with the future of ADS.

ALPHA DELTA SIGMA is for the undergraduate. This has been a basic premise in the operation of the fraternity since its inception. It is still the foundation of the fraternity today. This is the prime difference between ADS and other advertising organizations. This basic premise should continue to be the primary goal of the fraternity in the future.

Few, if any, persons vitally concerned with ADS, advertising and advertising education will find disagreement with the thoughts expressed in the opening paragraph. Yet, many can, will and should raise questions which reflect on the implications of these statements—which reflect on ADS and its nearly 20,000 members. They are questions which the fraternity should consider.

It has also been suggested that our alumni and professional chapters be called professional chapters dropping "alumni." There is much to be said for this suggestion. For the sake of editorial simplicity and clarity, in this article, at least, henceforth the alumni and professional chapters will be referred to as professional chapters.

Today, we list a dozen professional chapters across the country. What about them? What are the specific purposes of these chapters? What is the role of the alumni who has left the university campus? What obligations and responsibilities and what benefits are associated with the practitioner who joins the fraternity as a professional member? Should ADS be more than it is? If not, why? If so, what? and how?

In reality, for the majority of members initiated as undergraduates, their association with ADS, for all practical purposes, ceased once they left the campus. Perhaps this is well and good. The fraternity provided each member a vehicle for associating with professionals, it set before him lofty goals and ideals and in most instances it literally helped him to "bridge the gap" between the campus and the job. Upon successful completion of his academic program the graduate usually gets married, finds a job and develops new interests and associations. He feels his need for ADS is limited, if at all.

In addition, he soon becomes acqainted with other advertising organizations. In most advertising centers there are advertising clubs; if not, junior advertising clubs. There are media and copy groups and countless other specialized advertising organizations for the professional. Certainly, the existence of so many fine advertising groups for the professional is one of the primary reasons ADS has never developed the strength in professional chapters as has, for instance, Sigma Delta Chi. Perhaps this is as it should be, but there is a segment of the fraternity who feel this is not enough, that ADS should give more thought and attention to its relationship with the alumni, with the professional.

OBSERVATIONS ON ALUMNI GROUPS

One such person is Charles Lewis, Vice President of the Southwest Region, who recently made these observations on the subject:

A. *Most alumni groups lack purpose. They drift . . . lose contact with each other.*

B. *Where groups are active, they are usually revitalized by a fresh group of newly graduated members and usually members that know each other because they went to the same school.*

C. *Members are more interested in being active in alumni chapters of Alpha Delta Sigma the first and second year after graduation. In about the third year, the member has found a home in his profession and no longer relies on the fraternity as a transitional prop.*

D. *Alumni chapters do not have access to a list of incoming graduates. The graduate finds it difficult to become associated with the alumni chapter.*

E. *Newly graduated students have a strong desire to cling together and find solutions to their career-making problems.*

F. *Most alumni members would like to participate in programs, but don't know how or have failed to find an alumni group program satisfactory to everyone.*

We're sure you won't find complete agreement with all of these observations. Lewis, in making them, recognized that his experience, as is all of ours in ADS, is limited. These are generalizations, applying in part to some professional chapters and not to others, but what is important is that the generalizations are close enough to reality to cause thought and concern.

FROM CAMPUS TO JOB

It seems necessary at this time to describe the present procedure used by the national office for the transition (at least on the record) from the campus to the job. On the initiation form appears a proposed graduation date. In the processing procedures for each applicant, an envelope is addressed to the member at his permanent home. This is placed in a file according to the date of graduation.

Shortly after this date, the member is sent a congratulatory letter asking him to fill in a form, giving his new address when he accepts his first position. *Linage* is sent to him for a year. Thereafter, he is subject to the $2 annual dues assessment which includes *Linage*. It is then the member's responsibility to keep the national office informed of changes in address.

A list of current presidents of the professional chapters, giving their addresses, is included in the mailing. Graduates are encouraged to contact the president, if they locate in a city where we have a professional chapter. Often, the national office has sent to the presidents, the names of individuals moving into their community. A systematic procedure has not been set up to insure this action. It can be. Henceforth, the follow through leading to active participation in a professional chapter is up to the individual and the chapter.

How many undergraduates moving to a city with a professional chapter actually make contact with that chapter? Very few. Why? We really don't know. We need to study this matter. Perhaps it is as mentioned earlier, there just isn't a need, or at least few ADS members recognize the need, if it does exist. It is to be expected that there will always be a large number, even a larger majority of ADS members who will prefer not to be associated with a professional chapter. This is their privilege. However, some members of the fraternity feel that there are a significantly large enough group of members who would profit by such association to encourage our considering the matter further.

Granted, much of the lack of interest in the professional chapter lies with the individual ADS member, but have the professional chapters met their responsibilities in the situation? Not as much as they could or should. Why then haven't they?

There are many possible reasons. Some may apply to one chapter and not to another, but here are a few possibilities to think about. Few of our professional chapters are *real* ADS chapters; rather they are a group of professionals meeting together, in the name of ADS, with little genuine interest or concern for the primary goals of the fraternity. They are essentially "other" advertising clubs. There are exceptions, but they are few.

We will not conjecture why this is, but certainly one reason is the "loose" nature of the operation of these chapters with the national fraternity. They are not required to make annual reports, we have never provided them with a *real* sense of purpose or direction. Thus, the fact that the professional chapters are not *real* ADS chapters is as much the responsibility of the national chapter and the national council as it is the local professional chapters responsibility.

The previous remarks do not imply that the present program of the majority of professional chapters is wrong, or that they should not be doing what they are doing; rather, it is a matter of emphasis, of what they should be doing that they aren't. A good professional chapter of ADS will and should engage in many of the activities of that of an advertising club or any other good advertising organization, but will be done in order to increase this professionalization of members as well as the members of the undergraduate chapters in the area.

Does the young professional, in his first two or three years on the job, following graduation from the university, have needs not now being taken care of by existing advertising organizations? Again, the answers to this many-pronged question are not readily available. Perhaps the junior advertising clubs, in cities where they exist, come the closest to meeting these needs. Certainly, any study of the problem would have to consider the programs of the junior advertising clubs.

SUGGESTED ACTIVITIES

Thus, the national organization must develop policy if it is to provide guidance for future development of the professional chapter. As a start, Lewis suggests some of the things that the professional chapter should be doing. They are as follows:

A. *Help and encourage students to pursue a career in advertising.*

B. *Help advertising students adjust to professional life after college life.*

C. *Counsel newly graduated students on the job situation by market and by job categories.*

D. *Compile and furnish basic job market information each year.*

E. *Expose newly graduated members face-to-face with experienced professionals, giving them an opportunity to meet with, talk to people, ask questions and seek advice.*

F. *Arrange private, specialized counseling meetings for specific job areas.*

G. *Advise on methods for job seeking.*

Lewis feels that ADS has never fully exploited its affiliation with the Advertising Federation of America and the Advertising Association of the West. There is much to support this point of view. From his background as a member of the ADS national council and as president of the Houston Advertising Club, he currently holds, Lewis offers certain proposals for action. Again, it is necessary to comment that these proposals are submitted only as "in the formative stage." Each member should consider them thoroughly. The proposals are:

A. *Work through National to set up at least one sort of formal alumni activity per year in each major market city area, preferably in June. The meeting to be a sort of combined adver-*

*tising "barmitzvah" and "orientation" program. A mixer
followed by individually arranged conferences. It would be
designed specifically to help fulfill the function of "Bridging
the Gap."*

B. *Specialized job counseling would be offered in such things as
copy, art, layout, media, agency work, sales, production, print,
broadcast, etc., all keyed to that local situation.*

C. *Ask ad clubs or AFA and AAW to sponsor the graduating
students and provide the mixer party and the necessary coun-
selors—particularly important where alumni group is weak.
The Alpha Delta Sigma alumni group would be asked to set
up the program and run it where they have the interest and
manpower.*

D. *The AFA and AAW would be encouraged to appoint coordina-
tors with the view of providing continuity to the alumni group
and to assure the continuation of the program.*

E. *Students would be asked to register for the program in advance of graduation. Registration opportunity would be available at all undergraduate chapters. Students could select
market city.*

F. *Interested students from other cities would have to pay their
own way to the offering market city.*

G. *Graduating students should be given an alumni packet which
will include a directory of current, national and regional officers, campus advisors, alumni chapters, AFA and AAW
clubs, etc. The packet should also include at least a couple of
business reply cards, addressed to National, for use in reg-
istering the newly graduated member at his new address. The
information after being recorded at National is made available
to the alumni group in that area for local contact.*

H. *Questionnaires should be mailed to the students six months
and one year after graduation to determine:*

1. *Any address changes.*

2. *A report on success in job hunting.*

3. *To gauge the level and value of the alumni programs in
their area.*

I. *Alumni groups should be given a model program to follow.
It should include:*

|1. *Recommendations for activities.*

2. *Suggestions for contacting and handling incoming students.*

3. *Should encourage the appointment of a "college coordinator" for each school in the district. This coordinator would
be delegated with the responsibility of establishing contact
with students graduating from his particular school each
spring.*

J. Alumni chapters should be designed to attract and rely on members one and two years out of college. The first-year graduates should be given committee assignment . . . jobs which would give them opportunity for further orientation to the market area. The second year after graduation members should be given the organization jobs—jobs which provide the necessary continuity. Students three years out of college should become eligible for the Advisory Board and should hold office only if second-year graduates are not available.

The concern of the fraternity for the professional chapter was expressed in 1959 at the Palo Alto convention with the establishment of the position of Alumni and Professional Vice President on the National Council. During the past two years, Kent Westrate, has gien new meaning to this position. He has provided fine leadership, yet he would be the first to admit that the definition of the role of the professional chapter, as well as the relationship of the fraternity to its alumni and professional members is a bit hazy.

PHILOSOPHY OF MEMBERSHIP

Recently, Westrate consolidated his thinking into concrete words which he expressed in a new brochure being printed for potential professional members of ADS. It would seem the philosophy expressed in these statements would be just as meaningful for the undergraduate turned professional upon graduation. We quote in part from the brochure:

How to get more out of advertising? or . . . how ADS serves you by service to advertising.

Who can benefit? *Young trainees or an old pro, you can benefit from a professional membership in ADS. It can enrich your tomorrows, whatever your job is today. If you're actively interested in the advertising aspects of marketing or communications or related fields, ADS is the professional group for you.*

What does ADS offer? *In ADS you have a chance to learn more while you serve others. Learn from the leaders. Debate with contemporaries. Teach the youngsters .Work on that pet project you just can't finish at the office. Earn your reward by your own unique contribution. Or simply socialize with old pals.*

Why you should join ADS? *If you are beginning your career, you owe it to yourself. If you are a supervisor or executive, you owe it to your company to keep in touch with prospective employees. And if advertising has been good to you, you should be good to it by encouraging brighter students to study more and better advertising in college.*

What's ahead for the ADS alumni and professional? for the professional chapter?

The national chapter meetings in Miami and Houston and the National Council meetings in St. Louis and Denver in 1966 and 1968 respectively have not provided the answers. Perhaps the fact that nothing major has been done to advance the professional program of ADS is an answer in itself.

Hileman and Ross attempted to provide one answer when they established a professional chapter at the university level. Southern Illinois University became the first and only such chapter. The idea was promoted through *Linage,* and the internal house organ, *Body Copy,* was started in the Fall of 1963.

The idea as executed by the S.I.U. chapter was to hold two annual meetings, once in the Fall during homecoming and once in the Spring on Advertising Day during the Department of Journalism's J-Week activities. The S.I.U. chapter had its foundation during Journalism Week in 1964.

Thus, members of the Professional Chapter (graduates automatically become members upon graduation) are more directly associated with the university undergraduate chapter. The development of the professional chapter places responsibility on and provides an opportunity for the alumni and professional members to see that the undergraduate chapter achieves a maximum ADS experience. It should add continuity and permanence to ADS on the campus.

It is the responsibility of the Professional chapter president to assist the undergraduate chapter advisor and president in any and every way possible. He will call on other members of the professional chapter when their services are needed.

The S.I.U. chapter established a $5 annual dues—$2 of which would be sent to national for the member's national dues and $3 of which would go into a Scholarship and Loan fund at Southern Illinois University to provide financial assistance to S.I.U. chapter members.

Membership in the professional chapter of a university need not interfere with membership in a professional chapter in an advertising center. Not only was such dual membership compatible; it was encouraged.

During the 1963-65 biennium the number of initiates bounced back to near the level of the 1957-59 biennium when the largest number of members were initiated into the fraternity. A record number of professional initiates (52) combined with 1,312 undergraduates to make a total of 1,364 new ADS members for the 1963-65 period. This was an increase of 217 over the previous two year period. Much of the credit for the increased membership in the biennium can be given to the establishment and promotion of Membership Awards—a gold plaque to each chapter initiating a minimum of five new professional members between July 1, 1963 and July 1, 1964.

Twenty chapters received their awards at the 1965 national

convention in Miami. Chapters at Colorado, City College of New York, Florida State, Ilinois, Oklahoma and Southern Illinois received both awards, and chapters at De Pauw, Florida, Franklin and Marshall, Georgia. Houston, Indiana, Kansas, Long Island, Marquette. Michigan State. Minnesota, New York, Oregon, and Texas received the gold award only.

As of Fall, 1963 the National Roster listed 45 active chapters. During the biennium new charters were granted to Drake, Fairleigh Dickinson, Ferris State and West Virginia and the University of Mississippi reactivated their chapters. The National Council declared the chapters at Long Beach State, Ohio State and Wisconsin inactive, leaving 47 active chapters in the Fall of 1965. a net gain of two during the two year period.

Southern Illinois University received the Donald W. Davis Award in 1964 and Florida State won in 1965, becoming the first chapter to repeat since 1959 when the chapter won both the Davis Award and the Professional Competence Award.

The National Council, in its meeting in New York City in 1963 established certificate awards to be presented each year to the top chapter in each of the other regions. In 1964 chapters at Franklin and Marshall, Georgia, Houston and San Jose State received this award; in 1965 they were granted to chapters at Babson Institute, Southern Illinois, Texas Christian and San Jose State.

Two changes proposed and discussed during the 1961-63 biennium, particularly at the National Council meeting in Denver in 1962, became effective during the 1963-65 biennium. Mrs. Glenn (Betty) Paulsgrove, wife of a soil conservationist and mother of three, became the ADS office manager effective January 1, 1964, the first full-time person to be employed by the fraternity. Mrs. Paulsgrove remained in this position for more than two years and did much to establish sound business procedures in the operation of the fraternity.

In an effort to centralize all communications of the fraternity and to make its executive officer the communications officer, Don Hileman was named Editor of *Linage*, effective with the Fall, 1963 issue. The National Council in its November, 1963 meeting in Chicago, expressed appreciation to Robert Haverfield for his 14 years service to ADS as Editor of *Linage*.

Other actions taken at the November, 1963 National Council meeting in Chicago included: requirement of both the president's and advisor's signature on the annual reports, holders of sixth degree keys to determine future recipients of this award, establishment of a screening committee to speed up the process for considering new chapters, and the presentation of a plaque with a gavel to all past and future national presidents.

The tendency to de-emphasize professional advertising education in favor of strictly liberal arts education was a matter of greet concern for the National Council in its Chicago meeting. The situation had been briefly discussed at the New York national convention when the following proclamation from the Miami Alumni Chapter was presented:

At the recent Southeastern Regional meeting in Miami a local and national trend in educational circles was discussed. This was the trend away from specialization and toward liberalized education — particularly in fields of advertising, public relations and marketing.

The Greater Miami Professional and Alumni Chapter is deeply concerned regarding this trend, as it feels that it is detrimental to the future interests of advertising.

On March 20, 1963 our Board of Directors went on record as affirming the importance of specialized education in American colleges to combat the swing toward "liberalized education"; and requested that their convention delegate bring this matter before the convention now assembled.

The matter did not receive adequate attention in New York and even with much discussion in Chicago no specific action was taken. The National Council did urge all ADS members to give serious though to the problem, and the Editor of *Linage* was encouraged to present enlightening statements on the subject in the future issues.

In consideration of the de-emphasis of professional advertising education on some campuses and upon the recommendation of a special study committee headed by Hugh Sargent, Midwestern Vice President, the National Council in its Chicago meeting did make this specific statement to guide the screening committee in the consideration of new chapters:

Charters should be granted to those universities and colleges whose advertising and/or marketing courses are taught with the purpose of preparing a student for a career in advertising and related fields and where the attitude of administrators and faculty are sympathetic to the philosophy and aims of Alpha Delta Sigma.

1965 *Convention*

The national meeting in Miami, Florida, in April, 1965 was significant in many ways. The facilities, arrangements and hospitality of the Miami Professional Chapters were excellent; the interest and concern of the student delegates in some of the larger problems facing ADS and advertising education in general was remarkable to behold.

Delegates had nothing but praise for the work done by Ed Grout, Dave Bowers, Nick Cestrai, and L. L. "Duke" Zimmerman, heads of the convention arrangements committees. "Welcome ADS" signs greeted delegates driving into Miami. One sign, the largest moving letters in the United States (larger than those on Times Square in New York City), flashed a welcome on the Gulf

American Building at Biscayne Blvd. and 79th Street.

A special group of University of Miami ADS'ers greeted guests at the registration desk in the Carillon Hotel where they could make arrangements to see the city, received a "Lucky Bag" of gifts and information, and were given a special welcome from Miami Beach's Golden Girl.

Speakers at the convention included Howard H. Bell, now President of the American Advertising Federation and then Director of the National Association of Broadcasting's Code Authority; Larry Huckle, Eastern Advertising Manager of the *National Observer*, one of the Dow Jones publications; and John Cain of *McCall's* magazine. Cain accepted a special award given by ADS to *McCall's* for its excellent series on "Questions and Answers about Advertising."

Biggest gripe of delegates, and well justified was "no sun." As one delegate commented, "We might just as well be in Anchorage," and he was so right. President Ross, who engineered a series of long and extended, but constructive business sessions in spite of numerous difficulties, was the first to agree, and he praised the delegates "for their sincere interest in the real problems facing the fraternity."

The meetings in Miami indicated that students today are as concerned about the problems of advertising and advertising education as are educators and practitioners. Those who wish to treat ADS as another college fraternity, collecting individuals primarily interested in advertising in a group for social purposes, are wrong. Granted, far too many of the members and chapters fall into this category, but it was apparent in Miami that the leadership of most of the chapters, at least, rests with concerned young men, vitally interested in the welfare of their chosen profession. The national meeting in Houston in 1967 further substantiated this conclusion.

Four issues of major importance received attention in Miami: the general reduction in advertising courses in some universities, the growth of advertising courses in junior colleges, the role of women and ADS and the relationship with Gamma Alpha Chi, and the role of the professional member and the professional chapter in ADS.

The matter of ADS and its relation to GAX and the fairer sex was pretty well resolved once again in somewhat definite fashion. Delegates wished to encourage all the cooperation between ADS and GAX both on the local and national level, short of merging the two organizations, short of taking women into ADS.

Few definites resulted from the convention in the organization's continuing attempt to define the role of the professional member and the professional chapter in ADS. One specific action in Miami was to henceforth refer to all alumni and alumni chapters as "professionals," dropping the use of the word "alumni" entirely.

Discussed in Miami was the establishment of a National Professional Chapter at large, the Washington, D.C., Professional chapter's assistance in the development of a catalog of ADS merchandise, and the New York Professional chapter's establishment of a "Better Jobs Foundation" to assist recent ADS graduates in job hunting.

Via a mail ballot taken shortly after the convention (made necessary when time ran out in Miami) the fraternity did authorize the establishment of a National Professional Chapter at large, which would allow persons not directly near or related to any undergraduate or professional chapter to become associated with the organization.

As a result of yeoman-like work on the part of Charles Anderson, who was initiated at the University of Maryland and who was instrumental in the establishment of the Washington, D.C., professional chapter, a merchandising program was accepted by the National Council during the biennium, offering to members such items as mugs, paddles, and decals. The program was dropped by the National Council at its Denver, 1968 meeting when two years of experience with the project created more problems than was worth. Orders had been small, and problems with the suppliers fulfilling requests as indicated were primary reasons given for dropping the activity.

Ernie Baldwin spearheaded the New York Professional Chapter's attempt to help graduates locate positions through the establishment of the Better Jobs Foundation. In the Winter, 1966 issue of *Linage* Baldwin gave this report on the first year of activity:

The year 1965 saw the conception and continued development of a non-profit, nationwide clearing house of information on job openings and persons seeking jobs in advertising, marketing and public relations—a unique service known as the Better Jobs Foundation, a division of Alpha Delta Sigma.

The period from May until December saw some 175 applicants registered with the BJF. Of this number, 78 persons were known to have been helped in finding jobs. BJF has found jobs for its applicants in the folowing cities: Chicago, Pittsburgh, Atlanta, Philadelphia, Buffalo, Albany, Rochester, Pittsfield, Boston, Providence, and, of course, the Metropolitan New York area which includes New Jersey, Long Island, Westchester and lower Connecticut.

Of the 78 persons aided in finding employment—17 were women and 61 were men. Sixteen were ADS members. In addition to the above number, six persons found jobs through our efforts during the first week of January, in spite of the city-wide subway and bus strike that paralyzed nearly all business and industry.

The Better Jobs Foundation was founded for the sole purpose of: (1) Serving business firms and advertising agencies in their search for creative talent; (2) assisting the professional advertising, marketing and public relations executive to find a better job; and (3) aiding the graduate student to "bridge the gap" between college and a career in advertising.

BJF is *not* an employment agency. There are no placement fees to either the employer or applicant. Our work is made possible only by voluntary contributions from its sponsor members composed of associations, business firms and advertising agencies.

Much discussion occurred at the convention concerning what could be done to prevent the continued reduction in advertising courses and programs at some universities. Such erosion of courses and programs seemed to be taking place in the extreme eastern and western half of the country and primarily in marketing departments rather than in journalism departments. For example, San Jose State University, during the early years of the 1960's was the only school with a major professional advertising program of any size in the entire state of California.

There is an indication today that several of the other state schools in the state are re-emphasising advertising education. One of the schools with an expanding program, San Francisco State, was granted an ADS charter in 1966.

It was obvious that this issue as well as the teaching of advertising at the Junior College level involved more than just ADS. In reality, they are matters which should be of vital concern to such organizations as the American Academy of Advertising, Association for Education in Journalism and the American Marketing Association. To a lesser extent such practitioner organizations as the American Advertising Federation and the American Association of Advertising Agencies should be interested in these matters.

The National Council, in its meeting following the Miami convention, voted to endorse the following statement submitted to the Council by Daniel Pliskin, advisor to the Fairleigh Dickinson chapter:

That Alpha Delta Sigma take an active part in preventing the kind of erosion that is developing in programs of advertising, marketing and journalism in colleges and universities throughout the country and that a special committee be organized to inform heads of colleges and universities involved in teaching these disciplines of their importance and growth in the national scene.

In the Fall of 1965 letters were sent to administrators telling them of the work of the ADS advisor on their campus and reminding them of the value of advertising education programs. Shortly thereafter the joint commission of the Advertising Federation of America and the Advertising Association of the West made a statement calling "for an industry-wide effort to raise the standards for the advertising curriculum offered in colleges and universities." The Commission added that the American Academy of Advertising was the logical organization to propose industry-wide action for improvement of education for advertising. The issue which was to receive the most attention in Miami and again in Houston in 1967 was the subject of the growing number of junior colleges offering advertising courses. ADS became involved directly when the Miami Professional chapter proposed a constitutional change to allow chapters at junior colleges.

Linage had attempted to present the issue to the ADS membership in an article by Robert Rice, advertising teacher at Miami Dade Junior College, in the Fall, 1964 issue and a statement by David Bowers, President of the Miami Professional chapter, in the Spring, 1966 issue.

A response came before the convention in Miami in the form of a statement by Professor Milton E. Gross, Assistant Dean of the School of Journalism at the University of Missouri, a member of the accrediting committee of the Association for Education in Journalism and long-time Executive Secretary of ADS. His statement indicated that he felt to admit junior colleges into ADS would be a move to lower the professional standards ADS has long encouraged for advertising.

The motion to change the constitution to admit junior colleges received a majority vote, but did not receive the two-thirds majority necessary to change the constitution. The general consensus of delegates seemed to be that Robert Rice and his colleagues were doing a fine job in advertising instruction at Miami Dade Junior College, that we would want to encourage the Miami Professional chapter to assist Rice and Miami Dade in every way possible—short of the establishment of an ADS chapter at the school.

James Webb Young received the Nichols Cup and Rol Rider the Sixth Degree Key at the Miami convention. President Ross presented gold and silver Membership Awards to the winning chapters and Scott Ellington, president of the Florida State chapter, presented awards to winners in the FSU Creative Sweepstakes.

Sponsorship of the Creative Sweepstakes speaks well of the young men at Florida State, as well as its advisor, Dick Joel. The purpose of the sweepstakes was to discover the creativity of the ADS undergraduate members. The work of the entrants also got good exposure at the national convention in Miami Beach where finalists' entries were viewed by professional ad men and fellow ADS members.

To obtain funds for administering the sweepstakes and the cash prizes that were awarded, Florida State sent a direct mail piece explaining the project to the alumni of the FSU chapter.

They were neither asked for any specific amount nor told how much was needed. A response of nearly 20 per cent was far above the average return for direct mailings for product sales.

The total entires in all categories was 72, with ten chapters participating. The Charles H. Sandage chapter at Southern Illinois University won the award for most entries, followed closely by the chapters at New York University, West Virginia, Texas Tech, Texas and Fairleigh Dickinson.

Rick Harvey of Texas Tech, who took home $65 in prize money, received the Grand Sweepstakes Award for the best entry. Winners of the five media categories included: Harvey (newspaper); Cam Sharpe, Washington (radio); Ronald Geskey, Southern Illinois (television); Jack Kendrick, Texas (Direct Mail) and Peter A. Pignetti, West Virginia (magazine).

Ross, Laird and Westrate were all re-elected to another two-year term in Miami, and Hileman was reappointed Executive Secretary and Editor of *Linage*. Vice Presidents, elected at meetings in 1964, had another year to go on the Council. There was one change when Bill Mindak, who was going abroad for the year, resigned. Robert Haverfield, long-time Editor of *Linage,* was elected to fill the Midwest Vice President position.

Delegates elected William Flavin of Ferris State as their National Student Vice President and the following for Regional Student Vice Presidents: Tim Martien, Babson Institute; Donald Morris, University of Missouri; Franklyn Tauzel, West Virginia University; Larry Wood, University of Texas; and Lewis Abramson, University of Oregon.

Several constitutional changes resulted from discussion in Miami. Actual ratification came as a result of a mail ballot to chapters in the Fall of 1965. The replacement of the word "professional" for "alumni" and the establishment of a National Professional Chapter has already been mentioned. Other changes included: making the president also the chairman of the board when he is elected to a second two-year term; requiring the reg ional vice presidents to submit a financial report to the collegiate chapters in his region; changing the word "secret" to "prescribed" as it applied to the initiation ritual; and adding a penalty clause for failure of chapters whose members do not pay the annual dues.

Three new regional vice presidents were elected during the regional meetings in 1966. Robert Bryson of the University of Oklahoma, became the Southwestern Vice President; David Little, Advertising Manager of Sicks' Brewery, Seattle, Washington, the Western Vice President; and Alfred R. Manduley of Manhattan College, the Eastern Vice President. Joel and Haverfield were both re-elected.

Delegates at the 1966 regional meetings elected the following Regional Student Vice Presidents: Michael E. O'Connor, Manhattan College; Clay Jennings, University of Georgia; Mike Houtchens, University of Missouri; Marv Feldman, University of Oklahoma; and John Blanchard, University of Washington.

Members of the National Council met in St. Louis, Missouri, in July of 1966. The Council voted to recommend a constitutional change at the national convention in Houston during the Spring of 1967 to redistrict the regions, placing Colorado in the Midwestern Region and West Virginia in the Eastern area. They had been in the Western and Southeastern regions respectively. The change also agreed that if Youngstown University wanted to be in the Eastern Region, recommendation would be made to change Ohio from the Midwest to the East.

The Council took the first step leading to closer cooperation with Gamma Alpha Chi when it asked President Ross to present the following proposal to the national convention of Gamma Alpha Chi which was to meet that Fall:

That ADS chapters located on campuses without Gamma Alpha Chi chapters, be given the power to initiate women into Gamma Alpha Chi (should GAX wish to do so); and that when these GAX members on that campus reaches ten, that a separate GAX chapter be formed.

Should Gamma Alpha Chi accept the above proposal, the National Council of ADS would recommend at the Houston convention the following proposal:

That ADS give Gamma Alpha Chi chapters permission to initiate ADS members on campuses where there are GAX chapters, but no ADS chapter, with the ADS member being affiliated with the GAX chapters and that once there are ten ADS members that a separate ADS chapter be formed.

Other subjects discussed during the St. Louis National Council meeting included: ADS relationship to the Junior Colleges; ADS relationship to the merging AFA-AAW organization; a proposed Advertising Executive Program which would bring top advertising practitioners to the university campus for a week; possible establishment of a FAA (Future Advertisers of America) organization at the high school level, patterned after the FFA program in agriculture; a closer working relationship of the professional and undergraduate chapters in an immediate area; greater stress on the continued role of the ADS members in *the professionalization of advertising through education,* particularly with newly initiated members; ways of reaching more freshmen and sophomores on the university campus, as well as potential members in programs related to advertising, but outside the marketing and journalism departments; and a possible joint award with Gamma Alpha Chi for Advertising Recognition Week Activities.

Some of these areas were to receive further attention in Houston; others remain as possible areas for future development by

ADS. Where specific action was taken, the subject will be discussed in more detail.

The subject of lack of Negros in advertising and in ADS has been discussed by the National Council on several occasions. The general concensus always seemed to be that ADS has never consciously excluded Negroes from the fraternity; in fact, never has there been a mention of race on the official forms used by the fraternity. To find out just how many Negroes there were in the organization, Executive Secretary Don Hileman sent a questionnaire to chapters inquiring about such initiates in the Fall of 1964. His findings were reported in this manner in the Winter, 1965 issue of *Linage*:

Alpha Delta Sigma is highly segregated—meaning only as this term is predominantly used these days, primarily white. Has this been by design or happenstance? While the proportion of lesign to happenstance differs within each chapter, as well as)etween chapters, it probably has been the result of both.

One thing seems certain, Alpha Delta Sigma need not feel the guilt of discrimination any more than most organizations, but neither can it shed completely the responsibility for the lack of opportunity for the Negro in advertising.

Why the discussion of the subject? Why this article? It is most necessary at this time if the fraternity is to relate to reality, adjust to the times. While the national office has not been swamped with letters concerning the Negro in advertising, in the advertising programs in our universities, and more specifically in ADS, it has received enough expression and concern to merit some thought and consideration of the Negro and ADS.

A query to all chapters resulted in knowledge that six chapters have initiated a total of seven Negroes. None are currently active on the university campus at this time. The undergraduate chapters of Arizona, Fordham, Long Beach, and Washington and the Chicago Professional chapter have one member each. Roosevelt University of Chicago, two.

That the small number of Negroes in ADS can be attributed primarily to happenstance is exemplified in the statement of one advisor, who commented:

"In my years at this institution I don't believe I have had more than 2 Negroes in class and they were not in courses which would have qualified them for membership in ADS. The Negro matter has never been a problem, one way or the other."

This gentleman, and he very much is that, was quite sincere in stating that the problem didn't exist, but of course, what he really implied is that the problem never had to be faced—and by and large this has been the situation in most chapters. While some individuals in some chapters may have excluded Negroes by design, or would have if the situation had arisen, the truth is that for most chapters the problem just didn't arise, since there were few, if any, Negroes studying advertising in our colleges and universities.

John Johnson, publisher of *Ebony*, when asked why we didn't have more Negroes studying advertising, replied that the primary reason was that it would be of little consequence since few, if any, job opportunities existed in advertising for the Negro.

In recent years many advertisers, media and advertising agencies have consciously sought out Negroes with the necessary educational and talent requirement. Such a movement has been treated in the normal course of events, with relatively little fanfare or attention.

Therefore, as job opportunities in advertising continue to increase, we can expect more Negroes to seek out the professional advertising programs in our universities and of course, more Negroes will become eligible for Alpha Delta Sigma.

Race has never been a qualification for membership in ADS and the records in the national office do not make this distinction. White or black (or any other color, race or religion), dedication to the principles of ADS, academic excellence, and professional competence will always be the prime criteria for membership.

While the degree of enthusiasm for accepting the Negro will vary from chapter to chapter, and among individuals in each chapter, there is every indication that many universities and ADS chapters are quite eager to accept Negro students. One queried, "How do we go about encouraging Negroes into our program?"

There are ways—scholarships, being one. Another is to make the opportunities known. Perhaps a reprinting of this article in your university newspaper, along with a statement of your own chapter's policy, might be very much in order. One thing is most important; whatever you do, treat the event as if it were another every day occurrence. It isn't of course, and some awkwardness will result, but the importance of the event makes it most worthwhile.

One last note of reality. While the advertising industry is making much progress in providing equal opportunity for the Negro, there will not be a sudden rush of jobs available. While we want to welcome the Negro into our programs, we must help him to realize that his success in advertising is not assured—but then again, it isn't for any of us; however, with our interest and concern, his road will be a little easier.

Of course, much has happened in the civil rights movement since this article appeared. ADS, while seriously never discouraging Negroes in advertising, has done nothing, at least on the national level to see that more Negroes are provided an opportunity to work in advertising. This could well be an area where ADS can and will make a major contribution in the future.

Membership in the fraternity continued to grow during the 1965-67 biennium. A total of 1,417 members were initiated, representing a 4 per cent gain over the 1,364 initiated during the 1963-65 period. The Herbert Hall Palmer chapter at Rhode Island University initiated Dr. Jagjit Singh as the fraternity's 20,000th member in 1966. Dr. Singh exemplifies the increasing international flavor of both advertising and ADS. He was initiated at Rhode Island where he held a teaching position at the time. He is now employed by Esso Standard Eastern in Bombay, India as a marketing researcher.

Three new charters were granted to Little Rock University, Memphis State and San Francisco State; the chapters at Fordham and Franklin and Marshall became inactive. The result was a net gain of one chapter with the roster at convention time, 1967, listing 48 active chapters. When Dr. Noel P. Laird retired from Franklin and Marshall, the college discontinued all advertising offerings and the advertising courses at Fordham have all but been eliminated.

In 1966 the Samuel C. Dobbs chapter of ADS became the first chapter to score 100 points in the Donald W. Davis competition. Three members of the National Council—Robert Bryson, Oklahoma; Robert Haverfield, Missouri; and Treasurer, Noel Laird in reviewing Georgia's annual report individually and without consultation all said this chapter participated in every activity and met every requirement for a real ADS experience. Thus Georgia joined its sister Southeastern University at Florida State in winning the coveted Davis award twice since 1959. Carlos L. Zellner served as president during this outstanding year, and Professor Alan D. Fletcher as advisor.

Southern Illinois and San Jose continued their domination of the top chapter award in their regions. Texas Tech and Rhode Island won the award for the Southwestern and Eastern regions respectively. It is interesting to note that Rhode Island, whose chapter is located in a marketing department with a limited number of advertising courses, demonstrates the success that can be obtained with an ADS chapter in a university without strong academic offerings in advertising.

Texas Tech climbed from a chapter whose charter was about to be dropped in 1964 to win the Davis award in 1967. Georgia, San Jose State, and Southern Illinois repeated as top chapters in their respective areas and CCNY, ranking as the second best chapter in the nation, received the Eastern Region top chapter award.

Chapter 7

The Present

Delegates at the 1967 convention of Alpha Delta Sigma held in Houston, Texas, in April of that year took action on two matters the fraternity had been discussing for several years. The National Chapter voted to embark on a closer working relationship with Gamma Alpha Chi and with the junior colleges.

The constitutional change concerning the relationship of ADS and GAX was the exact proposal recommended to the delegates by the National Council at its St. Louis meeting. GAX could initiate ADS members on campuses where there was not and ADS chapter and vice versa. Thus far, the action has proved highly successful for both organizations. GAX members on the campus of New York University have been the only ones to initiate men into ADS, but their interest and help has made it possible for six young men to become active in a professional program on the campus which we feel confident, will someday lead to complete reactivation of the ADS chapter at NYU.

The benefit to GAX has been even more apparent. More than a half dozen ADS chapters have initiated GAX members; already this has led to the development of a GAX chapter on several of these campuses. The move seems to be a workable compromise. Neither ADS nor GAX loses its identity, but it opens new avenues for closer cooperation on the national and regional level, and yet leaves the local university to do nearly as it wishes. Many chapters have indicated that they will run their respective organizations essentially as one, and at the other extreme they will maintain separate officers and organizations and cooperate in a limited number of activities.

On the regional level, the Southwest Region has held joint ADS-GAX meetings for several years with outstanding success. There is indication that other regions will follow this pattern in the future.

On the National level, *Linage* became the official publication for both organizations effective with the Fall, 1967 issue. Near the masthead of this first joint issue appeared this statement:

With this issue of *Linage*, history is being made for both Alpha Delta Sigma and Gamma Alpha Chi. It reflects the first major step of these two organizations to cooperate extensively on a national level.

On the university campus, the two groups have long worked together with effective results. There is no reason why the national programs of the two organizations should not work together equally well. Our goals are essentially the same. Our primary difference is sex.

The editors pledge that *Linage* shall become an effective spokesman for each organization and for advertising education.

Bari Bodden, Service Coordinator, Foote, Cone & Belding, Houston, Texas, became the second Associate Editor of the publication and was assigned the primary responsibility of collecting and editing GAX news. C. Dennis Schick, who joined the staff of the Department of Journalism at Southern Illinois University to teach advertising and work on his doctorate, was appointed an Associate Editor of *Linage* in the Fall of 1966. Both organizations expressed extreme satisfaction with the new *Linage*.

The implementation of the workings of the two organizations has been left primarily to the two executive officers of the organizations—Mary Helen Montgomery of the University of Oklahoma and Don Hileman. Cooperation in office operations and procedures have been and are being considered to eliminate duplication and to reduce expenses. For example, the two organizations now share a membership form and an attempt is being made to parallel such things as dues, regions, initiation forms, and jewelry. Such cooperation can be expected to continue. Some members of both organizations feel that at some future date. the two organizations might have one office, one executive officer; that such an office might include the American Academy of Advertising, bringing under one roof the primary record keeping operations of the three organizations directly and primarily concerned with advertising education. Such considerations may be in the immediate future.

The officers of the two organizations have been meeting together. Ross, Hileman and Bryson met with Montgomery and

Lou Letts, Vice President and President-elect in Oklahoma in January, 1967 to discuss the National Council proposal made in St. Louis in June, 1966. This proposal was later adopted by GAX at Arizona State University in November of that year and by ADS in Houston in April, 1967.

Montgomery and Letts attended the National Council meeting of ADS in Denver in 1968 and Ross, Hileman, and Lee Fondren (elected President in Houston), will participate in GAX meetings at the University of Oklahoma in November 1968.

In Denver, the National Council of ADS went on record as encouraging joint national meetings of the two organizations and agreed to postpone its 1969 convention scheduled for San Francisco in the Spring to hold a joint ADS-GAX national meeting in November of 1969 in the midwest.

After a number of years of considering what should be the relationship of ADS to junior colleges, the following addition to the constitution was accepted in Houston:

Associate chapters may be established in junior colleges which may have been fully accredited by the official accreditation bodies of the region wherein the school is located and which offer an adequate group of courses in advertising and related subjects. Members in associate chapters will be granted all the rights and privileges of the fraternity.

Linage, in an attempt to present both sides of this controversial subject, asked Richard Joel and Milton E. Gross to present the alternative positions in answering the question: Should ADS chapters be chartered at Junior Colleges? These distinguished advertising educators did such an admirable job and the issue is so important to advertising education and ADS that we present both statements here.

A past national president, Joel was vice president of the Southeast Region at the time his statement was made, and it is in this Region that there was pressure to charter ADS chapters at junior colleges. He said "Yes" and supported his position in the Fall, 1965 issue of *Linage:*

Everything in Article I of our Constitution substantiates my reasons for urging the fraternity to amend the Constitution and establish undergraduate chapters of Alpha Delta Sigma at junior colleges.

Charters, of course, would be granted only to those junior colleges which are fully accredited by the official accrediting bodies of the region in which they are located, and which offer an adequate curriculum in advertising and related subjects. I would want the further assurance that the size of the school, the caliber of the faculty, and the number of students interested in advertising would warrant a chapter.

Our Constitution states we exist "to provide an organization for male *college* students who are interested in advertising and related fields.''

When the Constitution was written, the junior college movement in this country was all but unknown. Certainly the framers of our Constitution did not anticipate the growth in number and importance of this development in American education.

John Gardner, U.S. Secretary of Health, Education, and Welfare, said recently: ''We must accept the idea that the junior college is an acceptable part of our educational system.''

Many students throughout the nation are getting good educations in junior colleges. We find impressive curricula in many disciplines in a growing number of these colleges. A few of them already outdistance some four-year colleges in the number and scope of their offerings in advertising and related subjects. These are the schools I envision as sponsoring new chapters of Alpha Delta Sigma.

Our Constitution states explicitly in Article I that ADS exists ''to provide an opportunity for the undergraduate to achieve a more thorough and accurate understanding of the field of advertising.''

And I say, ''The sooner the better.''

I believe students should have this opportunity as early as possible in their college careers. But I also believe this accurate understanding can come only from qualified teachers—men dedicated to the point of view that advertising is necessary to a free society. This requirement should be met before any college—junior or senior—is granted an ADS charter.

Our Constitution also states that ADS exists ''to render all possible service towards the improvement of advertising by encouraging ethical and truthful advertising.''

I look upon the admission of junior college students to our ranks as an enviable opportunity for our professional fraternity to improve advertising's image not only among future advertising men, but also among the entire college public.

Our Constitution says ADS exists ''to provide an organization for the practical application of advertising and the self-improvement of the individual.''

Again I say, ''The sooner the better.'' An active ADS chapter on a junior college campus would give students with a common interest an opportunity to band together, to further develop their communicative skills, and to feel more confident about the job that lies ahead, be it in a senior university or in the business world.

Furthermore, our Constitution states that ADS exists ''to encourage cooperation and understanding between education and business.''

We know of practitioners who are eager to support Alpha

Delta Sigma at the junior college level and who feel cooperation between business and education can get a head start here. They are anxious to help interested young men, some of whom may never have a chance to go to a senior college and become ADS members, but who want a career in advertising and can make the grade with their two-year junior college training.

I look upon the admission of qualified junior college students into our ranks as one of the finest challenges we face. Very selfishly, I also look upon the granting of charters to junior colleges as the stimulus this fraternity needs to move us forward in undergraduate membership and renewed professional enthusiasm.

It is no coincidence that during the period 1963-65, twenty or more chapters of ADS—all at four-year colleges—recorded fewer initiations than in 1961-63. ADS can thrive only in an environment that encourages academic training in advertising. And this is the exception rather than the rule today. On university campuses throughout the land, administrators are restricting rather than expanding offerings in advertising.

It is heartening, therefore, to see a number of junior colleges devoting their attention to a field of study neglected, even ignored by their older sisters. It is equally heartening to hear of an increasing number of students in these colleges showing an interest in advertising as a career. And to know their interest is being stimulated by faculty and courses which in number and, in some cases, in quality, exceed those found in senior institutions whose interest in advertising is often matched by their interest in animal husbandry.

I feel Alpha Delta Sigma should judge an educational institution not so much by its liberal arts offerings (every reputable junior college stresses these today), but by its genuine interest in building a meaningful advertising curriculum, by the dedication of its faculty, and by the number and caliber of students choosing advertising courses.

Many junior college graduates go on to senior universities; some do not. In either case, ADS can help and will be helped. If a man enters a senior college in which there is an ADS chapter he goes as a more knowledgeable and useful member. If he goes into the business world from junior college, he takes with him a more professional attitude toward advertising and a desire to work with ADS professional members.

Kent Westrate, professional vice president of ADS, says he believes the overwhelming majority of professional members favor the admission of qualified junior colleges. The six professional chapters in attendance at the National Convention in Miami gave unanimous support to junior colleges.

Our National Treasurer Dr. Noel Laird points out that the Society for Advancement of Management is now looking to the junior colleges for membership. In fact, Dr. Laird recently was instrumental in establishing a SAM chapter at the junior college he now serves.

The objectives of the Society for Advancement of Management are much the same as ours. They, too, seek to bring together business executives and students; they, too, seek to give students an opportunity to participate in professional activities; they, too, are dedicated to the promotion and advancement of their field. Is there any reason why Alpha Delta Sigma should not follow SAM's enlightened policy toward junior colleges?

Let's not be blinded by academic requirements or hidebound by fraternity tradition. Let's fear less the infiltration of the two-year preparation, and welcome more the transfusion of enthusiasm and professional interest. Let's be more concerned about what we can contribute than what we can gain.

All of us need to give more thought and planning to the non-academic side of student life. It is an element in the educational process that has much to do with whether a student achieves any solid belief in himself and in worthwhile values. As education becomes a series of routines for faculty and students who have no genuine sense of community, the role played by a group like ADS becomes increasingly important.

If we can help an intelligent promising junior college student find something a little more real, a little more personal, a little more related to the world, it will be worth any risk that the adherents to the status quo feel we might be taking.

As a past national president and a long-time worker in ADS, I would be the last person to advocate anything that would lessen the prestige or usefulness of this fraternity. But I will be the first to oppose academic snobbishness which closes the door on the opportunity we have to encourage interested students to enter advertising and to add strength to ADS.

Gross, Assistant Dean at the University of Missouri, and former Executive Secretary of ADS (who at the time of his statement was Chairman of the American Council for Education in Journalism (ACEJ), the national accrediting body for professional programs in journalism, said "No" for the reasons printed in the Fall, 1965 issue of *Linage*.

I was much distressed to read in the Spring 1965 issue of *Linage* the opinion of Dave Bowers of Miami that Junior Colleges should be admitted to Alpha Delta Sigma.

The present ADS constitutional requirement of a four-year college was put in about 15 years ago because the National Council at that time believed that professional education for advertising required at least fulfillment of requirements for a baccalaureate degree with professional courses in advertising, marketing and/or journalism backed up by broad and thorough coverage of the liberal arts and social sciences.

That was, let me point out, some ten years before the Carnegie and Ford Foundation reports criticized education for business on the grounds that too much of it was too specialized. Alpha Delta Sigma not only anticipated that criticism; it refused to grant charters in schools which did not meet the standards of the accrediting bodies. I have been saddened, in the last year or two, to see an ADS charter granted to one unaccredited school which had previously been rejected by the fraternity—because a student could get a degree with less than 25 per cent of his work in liberal arts and sciences.

I believe there are few more than half a dozen ADS chapters in schools which are not accredited either by the American Association of Schools and Colleges of Business or by the American Council on Education for Jouranlism, and probably none in schools which are not accredited by one of the regional associations.

If ADS is to achieve its goals of improvement of advertising and cooperation and understanding between education and business, then surely the last thing it should consider would be watering down the standards of education for advertising.

A junior college may be able to teach some superficial skills which a graduate could take with his certificate in advertising into the advertising business. A junior college could also teach a student to tie sutures—but who would be satisfied with a doctor —or lawyer, or an architect or an engineer—who had only a junior college education?

Of course the junior college is here to stay. It is no ideal answer to the educational needs imposed by the population explosion, but it may be that it will develop into a satisfactory solution, at least for some students. For students who plan to transfer and work for a bachelor's degree, the junior college can offer the basics, the survey courses, in the various arts and sciences which students will explore in greater depth as upperclassmen. For students without the ability or desire for a complete college education, the junior college can offer technical training in various skills.

But advertising demands more than superficial skills and in my opinion the junior college which offers eleven courses in advertising and related fields must be depriving students in other, more important areas.

That student is being cheated who does not receive the best possible choice of curriculum, highest quality instruction and wisest advisement his school can provide.

Many advertising men scoff at professional education for advertising even at upperclass levels. Some offer it a little more sympathy if the discussion is in terms of graduate education. If ADS wishes to take the position that all the education one needs for the advertising business is two years beyond high school, then why not go whole hog and put ADS chapters into high schools?

Acceptance of associate chapters at junior colleges seemed to be a workable compromise of divergent points of view expressed on this subject over the years. It now allows the fraternity to work officially with those junior colleges in communities where they already are providing many young men for advertising positions, to give counsel and guidance and to express ADS' continued concern for excellence in all educational programs.

Yet, the designation of associate chapters still distinguishes the two year program from the four. It appeared to be the common consensus of most in attendance at the Houston convention that ADS wants to scrutinize all applications for associate chapters most thoroughly; that ADS still stands firmly behind the encouragement of all ADS members to seek a four year education if at all possible. To date, the National Council has not received a petition for an associate chapter.

In another constitutional change accepted in Houston, three chapters chose to become associated with chapters in different regions. Colorado left the Western Region for the Midwest; Youngstown left the Midwest for the East; and West Virginia changed from the Southeast to the East. The constitutional change reads as follows:

Any chapter located on the geographic border of a region that wishes to be transferred to a neighboring region may apply to the National Council for approval of the transfer.

In an effort to provide the national chapter with more funds to finance an expanding program, delegates voted to make the jewelry optional. The national initiation fee remained at $20, and an official certificate and membership card will be included. New members then have the option of purchasing whatever piece of jewelry they choose. The change became effective June 1, 1967.

The National Council in its meeting immediately following the convention in Miami had voted to add an extra day in Houston. The change proved most beneficial in many ways. Throughout the convention, the new spirit of ADS, "professionalization of advertising through education" permeated the thinking of all involved. It resulted in the passage of the following resolution:

Whereas, we hold beyond contest that there now exists an organized body of knowledge related to advertising, and

Whereas, the advertising industry is highly aware of the need for greater professionalism, which goal demands the establishment of certain standards, and

Whereas, we hold that the primary purpose of Alpha Delta

Sigma is to aid in professionalization of advertising through education, and

Whereas, we hold that renewed efforts must be made to achieve greater recognition and respect for advertising as a profession

Now, therefore be it resolved that the 1967 Convention of Alpha Delta Sigma go on record as urging that professional academic education be an important concern of all advertising practitioners

And, be it further resolved that this convention publicly commend and support those advertising organizations which seek to encourage professional advertising educational standards through such action as:

Establishing endowed chairs in advertising education;

Providing advertising scholarships;

Underwriting advertising research; etc.

And, be it further resolved that Alpha Delta Sigma take the initiative in securing support for these objectives from all related advertising groups, associations and practitioners.

Concerning the implementation of this resolution, David Little, Western Vice President made this statement in the Spring, 1967 issue of *Linage*:

Conversations in Houston regarding the Resolution on Advertising Education pointed up the fact that we have merely saluted motherhood and the flag unless specific steps are taken at the local level. I think it is wise to remember that we do have an avenue of approach available to us . . . the local business community. In the final analysis, I believe our appeal can best be made to the selfish interests of advertisers and agencies alike. Surely, there is ample precedent for this approach since every successful campaign in history has provided a meaningful answer to the question of "What's in it for me?"

Publicly financed schools rely on state legislatures for budget approval. Legislators are generally responsive to the wishes of industry leaders since industry pays a big chunk of the taxes that support schools. Therefore, if it pointed out to businessmen that it is the job of schools to train the people needed by industry— advertising people as well as economists, chemists, accountants, etc.—it seems logical that we should be able to enlist the aid of business groups in our efforts to bring PROFESSIONAL STANDARDS TO ADVERTISING EDUCATION.

I firmly believe that ADS undergraduate chapters can do a great deal toward the implementation of the Resolution. In those areas where a professional chapter exists, immediate steps should be taken to inform that chapter of the nature and intent of the Resolution. Where there is no professional chapter, a direct approach should be made to the local Advertising, Marketing or Sales

Club. A request should be made to have an ADS day scheduled as a regular meeting program. This is an excellent way to explain our activities *and* request the support outlined in the Resolution.

Be ready to provide tangible guidelines for any support that may be offered. Examples:

- Establishing endowed chairs in advertising education
- Providing advertising scholarships
- Underwriting advertising research
- Participating in student internship programs
- Providing guest lecturers for the various advertising courses on both the college and high school level
- Formation of Professional ADS Chapters
- Expression of interest in the advertising sequence—by letter or personal visit—to college administrators, legislators, city/county school boards, etc.
- Letters of appreciaton to college administrators saluting good work by teachers or students of the advertising sequence when appropriate

These are just a few examples of the things that can be done. To repeat an earlier statement, the key to any successful program is "What's in it for me?" And don't forget to ask *yourself* that question. The answer is more and better job opportunities through greater understanding and appreciation of the role of advertising in the American economy!

I think the incentive is sufficient; let's get to work.

In Houston, delegates and advisors were urged to stress the longtime responsibilities and opportunities of membership in ADS, to make certain in their pledging and initiation ceremonies to stress the importance of "giving back" of interest, time, and money to the universities and their advertising educational programs through the years.

Lee Fondren, Station Manager and Director of Sales of KLZ, Denver, Colorado, who had served during the previous four years as Chairman of the Advisory Council, took over the reins of the fraternity for the 1967-69 biennium. Ross became Chairman of the Board. Delegates, in electing Fondren, felt that with his wide background in other advertising associations and his intimate understanding of ADS that he was the logical person to further the goal of "professionalization of advertising through education." He is the only man to ever serve as president of both the Advertising Federation of America and the Advertising Association of the West. He was Chairman of the joint commission which resulted in these two organizations joining forces as the American Advertising Federation; and he was the first recipient of the AAF's "Advertising Man of the Year" award presented in 1967.

Laird and Westrate were re-elected to their positions of Treasurer and Professional Vice President, respectively. Hileman was reappointed Executive Secretary. When Joel took a leave of absence to teach at the University of Wisconsin and Little left his position with Sicks' brewery to enter graduate school at the University of Oregon, Bob Harris, WFUN Radio and past president of the Miami Professional chapter and Jerry Lynn, San Jose State College, were elected to one year terms as Vice Presidents of the Southeastern and Western Regions.

Delegates to the Houston convention resoundingly disagreed with the National Council's recommendation to abolish the National Student Vice President's position and elected Ray Dryden, Texas Christian University, to serve during the 1967-69 biennium. The various regions elected these members to the Regional Student Vice President's positions for the 1967-68 academic year: Tom Dellarmo, City College of New York; Ober Tyus, University of Georgia; John Turk, Marquette University; Fred Koenig, Texas Tech; and Ken Becker, San Jose State College.

Charles W. "Chick" Collier, President and Executive Director of the new American Advertising Federation, received the Fraternity's G. D. Crain, Jr. Award for service to advertising education. The award, formerly known as the Nichols Cup, was changed this year when the G. D. Crain, Jr. Foundation accepted sponsorship of the award. Crain is the founder and Chairman of the Board of Advertising Publications, publishers of *Advertising Age* as well as other publications in the marketing field.

Sid Bernstein, publisher of *Advertising Age,* accepted a special citation to that publication for its contribution to advertising education. Collier, Bernstein and president-elect Fondren all presented major speeches at the convention.

Ross received the Sixth Degree Key, and his chapter at Texas Tech learned that they were winners of the new ADS-GAX Advertising Recognition Week Award. Presentation of the award was made at the ADS-GAX breakfast during the AAF meeting in Houston in June.

Richard Joel, advisor to the Florida State chapter, presented two students from the University of Georgia and Southern Illinois University special awards for their entries in the chapter's national Creative Sweepstakes. The chapter ended the competition with these awards because of the limited number of entries by chapters and their members. Joel did announce that he had arranged special awards for ADS members in a contest sponsored by the Coca Cola Company for its product, Sprite.

A total of 38 chapters were represented at the Houston meetings. This included 32 undergraduate chapters and six professional chapters (Atlanta, Chicago, Miami, Houston, Northern California and Puget Sound). Twenty-four advisors participated in the convention. A resolution commending Richard Brien, advisor; and Lee Stepelton, president of the host University of Houston chapter, passed unanimously. Entertainment at the convention included a trip to NASA and a visit to the Astrodome.

In their meeting following the National chapter sessions in Houston, the National Council created the Sidney R. Bernstein Advisor's Award to be given bi-annually in the off-year of the national meetings. In 1968, Dr. Ernest Alonzo Sharpe of the University of Texas became the first recipient of the award.

In other action, the National Council created the Aid to Advertising Education Award, hereafter referred to as the AIDE Award. The AIDE Award can be given annually by each of the local chapters to someone who has made a special contribution to the advertising education program at his university. The recipients of the fraternity's bi-annual G. D. Crain Award have given real stature to this award. Members of the fraternity compare this national citation to the Gold Medal Award that *Marketing Communications* (formerly *Printers' Ink*) and the American Advertising Federation (formerly AFA) gave annually to a person making an outstanding contribution to the field of advertising. These two organizations provide a Silver Medal Award for each Advertising Club in the AAF to present to someone in their local community who has made such a contribution to advertising. It is hoped the AIDE Award for advertising education will be accepted with the same honor the Silver Medal Awards have been received in the local communities.

During his tenure as president, Fondren provided an ingredient in the national program of ADS that had been lacking since the days of Donald W. Davis—the personal visitation of the organization's top officer to local campus chapters. Fondren's positon with KLZ radio takes him all over the country on business, and where such visits take him to cities near campuses with ADS and GAX chapters, he would often visit the campus itself or will arrange their invitation to attend and participate in Ad Club meetings where he might be speaking. Insufficient funds prevented the fraternity itself from providing the president with such travel funds. In addition Fondren has been able to tell the ADS story and present its program to many of the other professional crganizations with which he has had contact.

During the 1967-68 academic year, the National Office instigated a new service which had modest success. In attempt to provide those ADS members wishing summer positions in advertising, they contacted members of the AAF, AAAA and ANA for positions they might have available. In turn they asked each ADS member interested in a summer position to send in an information sheet which was then sent to each prospective employer. While this clearing house operation resulted in few summer positions this year, there is indication that it can be helpful in the future.

One reason for its limited success this year was that students who wanted jobs wanted them in areas where jobs were not available, and firms offering the positions were not in the areas where the students were located. One thing is apparent—since students desire summer jobs in their local areas, the local chapters and universities are going to have to take a more active role, or students and companies must reconsider their limitations on geographical considerations.

Four new Vice Presidents were elected at the regional meeting held in the spring of 1968. Two, Roland Hicks of Ferris State and Bill Mindak of the University of Texas had previously served on the Council. They were elected in the Midwest and Southwest Regions respectively. The Western Region selected Jack Tenge of San Francisco State, and the Eastern Region selected Joe Pisani of the University of Maryland.

Student Regional Vice Presidents elected for the 1968-69 academic year included Tom Dellarmo, Manhattan College, Eastern region; Kinton E. Hall, University of Florida, Southeastern region; Paul D. Ritter, Ferris State, Midwestern region; Ken Becker, San Jose State, Western region; and Mike E. Skaggs, Texas Tech, Southwestern region.

The National Council met in Denver in June of 1968 with all eleven members present. The long range goals, and objectives of ADS its changing emphasis, its relevancy to its membership to the advertising industry itself, received much of the attention during the two day meetings. Fondren appointed Ross as Chairman of a committee with Hicks and Mindak as members to consider all of the points mentioned during the discussion at Denver and to draft a policy statement on the long range goals and objectives at the 1969 national chapter meeting.

Perhaps reflective of the continued change in the national program of ADS were two other actions of the Council. The first was the establishment of a committee to study the positions and titles of members of the National Council with recommendations for any changes being made at the 1969 convention. Mindak was appointed chairman of this committee with Ross and Tenge as members. One recommendaton given to this committee by the Council was serious consideration of eliminating all references in the ·constitution and in all communications to the word "fraternity," replacing it with "society." Such a change would reflect the organization's growing preoccupation with the "professional" nature of the organization away from the image associated with fraternities on a college campus.

The second action was to change the title of "Executive Secretary" to "Executive Director", which reflects more accurately the position of the person directing the activities of the national headquarters. Such a move parallels changes recently made by other advertising organizations such as the American Association of Advertising Agencies and the American Advertising Federation.

As a means of establishing a closer relationship between the campus chapters and its professional members, and as a means of strengthening the financial base of both the local undergraduate and professional chapters, the National Council established a $5 dues for all professional members, effective June 1, 1968. If payment is made directly to the chapter, the local chapter keeps $3 for its own operation and submits $2 to national headquarters. If payment is made directly to the chapter, the local chapter keeps understood that it is the wish of the member that the entire $5 goes to support the national program of ADS.

The ramifications of this change can benefit all levels of the ADS program. It continues to place greater responsibility of support for the program, financially and otherwise, on the professional members and less on the undergraduates. Not only will it provide a sound financial basis for the university chapter, but it will also be an incentive to keep files of graduates up-to-date. Once this contact is established, it is hoped that the chapters will make greater use of professional members and as each professional member pays his annual dues it will serve as a reminder of his responsibility to the generation of young advertising men coming.

Undergraduate members of a chapter will continue to pay only the $2 national dues.

Upon the recommendation of National Student Vice President Ray Dryden, the National Council voted to start a new program for its members during the 1968-69 academic year—a program of increased assistance to its members who desire to locate positions in areas other than their own. It was generally accepted that each year more companies, media and agencies, were coming to the campus; but that these were still limited in many instances to regional organizations. To implement this program the Council accepted the following procedures:

(1) President Fondren is to contact each of the Ad Clubs in the AAF asking them to select three persons to serve as contacts for ADS and GAX people desiring to locate in their community. The names of these persons will apear in the winter issue of *Linage*.

(2) That the Winter issue of *Linage* each year be designated as "Job Market" issue and that in addition to the carrying of the names referred to above that the issue carry articles on such subjects as "How to Interview", "How to Get the Job" etc.

(3) That this issue be mailed specifically to personnel people in the AAAA, AFA, ANA, AIA, NAEA etc.

(4) That this issue be used to solicit advertising for *Linage*.

(5) That the issue be sent to placement services of universities with ADS and GAX chapters.

Other actions taken in Denver, 1968 included: encouragement of Professional Vice President Westrate to explore the possibility of more University-based professional chapters patterned after the S.I.U. professional chapter; acceptance of any advertising recognition project done at any time of the year as being eligible for the joint ADS-GAX Advertising Recognition Award; presentation of the ADS lapel pin to each new initiate effective, Sept. 1, 1968; appointment of a committee (Hicks, Chairman; Pisani, Laird), to review the present jewelry and to recommend two pieces of jewelry to be accepted as official jewelry for the organization; appointment of Dryden and Westrate to consider revision of the ritual; appointment of a committee including Harris, Dryden, Westrate to study, recommend and work at the establishment of new undergraduate chapters and members; and nomination of John Crichton, James Fish, and Mel Hattwick as candidates for the G. D. Crain Jr. Award to be presented at the 1969 national convention.

In another move emphasizing the "professional" rather than the "fraternity" goals of ADS, the National Council suggested that the jewelry committee keep the lapel pin for general distribution and consider seriously a tie-tack as the second piece. The Council felt the key to be obsolete.

Revision of the ritual was proposed again to bring it more in line with the "professional" rather than "fraternity" orientation. Fondren submitted an abbreviated ritual used in initiating outstanding members of the advertising community at the AAF, ADS-GAX breakfasts. It was recommended to the committee for study and possible acceptance.

Texas Tech again walked off with the ADS-GAX Advertising Recognition Award in 1968. Its International theme brought to the campus speakers from various parts of the world, and the professionalism demonstrated during the week and in its presentation brought praises from the judges. ADS and GAX chapters at Southern Illinois University and the University of Oklahoma won second and third place in the competition respectively.

Past President Ross and current President Fondren have continued to stress the importance of this activity. Ross commented in the January, 1967 issue of *Body Copy*:

As many of you know, the promotion of an Ad Recognition Week (ARW) program is a pet project of mine. True, I push this activity more than any other one activity by an ADS chapter and my reasons are many. In this column I'd like to give you a few thoughts on ARW and then urge you to try promoting such a program on your campus this year to see if it does not do many things for you, your chapter, and your school.

IT EXPLAINS ADVERTISING — Through an effective ARW program you can bring to your campus competent practitioners to explain just how advertising helps our capitalistic system. The national theme of this year's AAF-ARW program is "Truth in Advertising" which leaves many avenues open to your participants. Three audiences should be considered as primary: fellow students on your campus; faculty and staff members; and citizens of your locale. An understanding of advertising is important to each group. Particularly, college professors have been criticized by practitioners because they often speak out against advertising without having the benefit of valid information—this is your opportunity to give them the valid information.

IT PROMOTES ADVERTISING EDUCATION — In many schools advertising education needs all the help it can get from any and all corners. Programs have been reduced in some schools and eliminated in others. Through an effective ARW program you can call attention to your program, the students in the program, the future of the program etc. Very seldom will you see an administration reduce or minimize an academic area that is vocal and active. Activity alone indicates the interest that many administrators use as a yardstick of importance of that program on a campus.

Don't overlook the fact that by exploiting advertising education you may be helping to recruit more and better students for a major in advertising. At our school we invite area high schools to take part in our ARW program and use it more-or-less as a student recruiting program.

EXPLOITING YOUR ADS CHAPTER — I would think that little need be said about this area. You should immediately realize what a promotion such as this could mean to the members of your chapter. A well publicized program should bring you recognition from students, faculty, staff, practitioners, and citizens of your community. A professor of mine used to say, "He who tooteth not his own bazoo, the same shall not be tooteth."

OTHER BENEFITS — There are many fringe benefits from an effective ARW program. As an example, this can be an event in which you can urge visitors to come to your campus. Advertising practitioners are aware of the week and should be willing to make a special effort to attend.

Those chapters in an area with a local advertising club may find it helpful to work with them for the program. All advertising clubs are urged to participate in an ARW program.

Freddie Koenig who was co-chairman of the award-winning ARW week at Texas Tech did an excellent job in describing the details of organization and work in the Tech program in a Fall, 1967 article of *Linage*. It reflects the kind of real ADS experience that can be achieved on a campus where there are interested and concerned advisors and students. For this reason Koenig's remarks are printed in their entirety:

At Texas Tech we think the Advertising Recognition Week program is so important that we have two vice-presidents in our ADS and GAX chapters—one for programs and one for ARW. In other words, it is a year-around job with our chapter. The purposes of ARW for our community are these:

1. To better acquaint the people of Lubbock and the South Plains with advertising's place in the economy;

2. To give Tech's advertising students and local advertising personnel current information on trends, statistics and methods of promotion;

3. To give advertising students experience in the organization and coordination of such a promotion campaign;

4. Promote advertising education for in many schools advertising education needs all the help it can get from any and all corners.

5. To recruit more and better students for a major in advertising.

These are the purposes set up for our school, and, of course, at different schools you can find other purposes. But, the important point is to set up goals and purposes you want to accomplish with your ARW program. With these goals in mind, the task will be easier. Now with the added incentive of the ADS-GAX Award for the best ARW program held on a college campus, it could mean special recognition for your school. Now that you have something to shoot for, start aiming.

ARW is not something to start work on the week before the program is to be held. If anything needs to be stressed, it is to plan your program early, as early as possible. At Tech, for the ARW program in February, we start in October! Our chapter advisor even sends letters before this time to invite prospective speakers. We aim at the very top men in advertising, and to assure their acceptance it is important to contact them early.

At one of our joint ADS-GAX meetings, early in November, a roster is completed listing all ADS-GAX members and their address and telephone numbers. The two co-chairmen of ARW, vice-presidents of ADS and GAX, then form the following committees:

Publicity Committee, Invitations Committee, Miss Advertising Committee, Display Committee, Ticket Committee, Physical Arrangements Committee, Billboard Committee (under the Publicity Committee), Scrapbook Committee

The important thing is to assign competent members as chairman for each committee. This done, equal number of members both ADS-GAX are put on these committees. Our committee roster then lists more than 30 members from each organization.

1967 *Award-Winning Program*

Last year, joining together in a team effort, the Lubbock Ad Club, the J. Culver Hill Chapter of Alpha Delta Sigma, the Alpha Lambda Chapter of Gamma Alpha Chi, and the American Women in Radio and Television chapter of Lubbock presented "The Truth in Advertising," February 12-18, 1967. A blueprint of the planning and actual execution of the week can be seen by examining each committee's work.

Publicity: This committee can make or break your ARW, so it is very important to include people who are somewhat familiar with PR and the different media in your area. They were assigned the job of informing the various media of our plans for ARW and drawing up a plan of operations for each meeting. The local radio and TV stations were called upon to help us in the public service announcements. The newspapers, local marquee display companies, billboard companies, ministerial organizations, the Junior Chamber of Commerce, Lions Clubs and other civic clubs in the area were all contacted. Each committee member was assigned certain radio stations, TV stations, newspapers, etc. in order that the people who were responsible for getting the information to the media would learn the special needs for that medium.

We hoped to establish some personal relationship with these media people, and were successful. The media were then supplied with a pre-release sheet explaining ARW, its purposes and the proposed program and speakers. The radio stations were given spot announcements or teasers, and during the month of February, ran a number of announcements. Personalities from ADS and GAX were scheduled for appearances to explain ARW. Our Miss Advertising and two vice-presidents made almost daily appearances on three of the radio stations the week prior to ARW.

The *billboard committee,* a sub-committee, obtained the use of four billboards located in heavily traveled areas, use of one traveling trailer board and the cooperation of several marquee companies.

The newspapers were furnished with reports of all speakers as we received them, and they furnished us advertising space. The *University Daily,* Tech school paper, was of great benefit with its continuous news stories and advertisements—at no cost.

A direct mail campaign was used as a reminder to members and advertising alumni. Mail pieces were sent to the Lubbock Ad Club and each advertising student with agenda information for each week.

During the week itself, the publicity committee followed

through with continuous news releases and PR work, making sure both print and visual media were on hand to record the happenings. Of great assistance was the Public Relations Office at Tech, who put out news releases at every turn of interest.

Display: Their duties were to prepare and post announcement *ON* the Tech campus. This area included the buildings and entry activity billboards located on primary campus entrances. Using the "Truth in Advertising" symbol, the committee cut silk screen stencils and ran off 25 posters, 15 by 20'', to be posted in the buildings. Following the same format as the indoor posters, 4' x 5' billboards were painted and posted a week prior to the actual ARW. Students in art were helpful in this area and gave them experience in both art work and clearing the channels through the school administration for use of the entry boards.

Invitation: The invitation committee was responsible for inviting civic leaders, department heads and instructors, and keeping a list of acceptance. Personal invitations were handwritten and personally delivered to all concerned. 1,300 of these invitations were mailed to the entire membership of the Lubbock Chamber of Commerce, with another 300 being sent to the memberships of the four sponsoring groups, including Congressmen and other interested individuals who had been suggested to receive the invitations.

Included in these invitations was a preliminary program of the events.

The design of a program was also a function of this committee. Place cards were made for all seated at the Head Table for the Awards dinner, as well as the special guests who had received special invitations and complimentary tickets.

Miss Advertising: Sponsoring organizations felt that the selection of a "Miss Advertising" would stimulate interest within the organizations and would create an outside awareness of the organizations and some of their activities.

The committee set up the rules for candidates and brought in the screening committee. In order to be eligible, a girl must have been either a GAX member or eligible for membership. The finalists were presented in a joint ADS-GAX meeting where they were voted on by members after they had mixed informally and been interviewed formally.

Tickets: The ticket committee decided on possible sizes of the tickets, price range and door prizes, and a design. By the end of January, the design was completed on paper master for printing, tickets were cut to size and numbered for the door prizes. Tickets were sold individually and in packets. The individual tickets were categorized according to sessions as follows:

1. morning session 10-11

2. morning session 11-12
3. luncheon
4. afternoon session 1-2
5. Silver Awards Dinner 6-8

The five individual tickets were grouped into a book for the complete day. Student books sold for $3.75 and Ad Club books sold for $5.00. The price to students was less expensive because all sessions were free to students with the exception of lunch and dinner. Tickets were made available at key points on the campus, and 200 were sent to the Ad Club for distribution. Several complimentary tickets were distributed among the administration and faculty.

Physical Arrangements: This committee did the actual manual labor during the week itself. Setting up speakers chairs, presentation materials as slides, films, replacing bulbs, etc. This group is also important. Nothing leaves a bad taste in a speaker's mouth more than to have the bulb in the projector blow! These men are life-savers.

Scrapbook: This year an award will be given to the chapter with the best scrapbook, and this incentive alone should merit active participation. Not only does it show other schools what you have done, but provides helpful assistance in the future for refreshing old ideas. Main points are keeping a complete file on the activites and pictures to supplement them.

The chairmen met once a month in the beginning with the general committee chairmen while the committees met as often as necessary, usually once a month at the start and more often as the week drew near.

The search for speakers began in July to allow enough time for acceptance. Plans called for a full week of activities in February and these plans were set in October and November with new events being added as they developed. The week concluded with the Silver Medal Award Dinner.

Before the dinner, a style show by Catalina of California was presented. This presentation was brought to our campus with the help of a local merchant. To bring this closer to the campus Tech beauties were picked to model the 1967 merchandise, which had not been released to the public. At the dinner, awards were presented to worthy practitioners, students who had given outstanding service, and the profession as a whole. The students' awards were presented by professional members which strengthened the bond between professional and students interests. This event is where our chapter usually brings in the top names in advertising. This year, Don Belding, one of the founders of Foote, Cone & Belding Advertising Agency, was the featured speaker. This event is the highlight and climax of a week of activities and should be treated as such.

The following SEVEN STEPS TO SUCCESS are suggested in preparing a presentation similar to this program:

1. Start the search for a speaker early and start at the top.

2. Special guest and dignitaries should be invited early enough so that they may plan to attend.

3. Both student and professional groups should work more closely together and meet often to iron out problems.

4. The student chairmen should be elected officers of the chapter.

5. Don't try to, but INCLUDE every member of the sponsoring organizations in the planning and the work.

6. There should be an inter-change and progress report between the sponsoring groups often. Especially when plans are changed.

7. Appeals should be made for attendance by persons both on and off the campus. Program sessions should be scheduled so that they coincide with times students would be changing classes for easier attendance.

BUT, ADVERTISING RECOGNITION WEEK still depends upon you, for it is only as successful as the enthusiasm and the work of the members!

Chapter 8

The Future

Much of the future of Alpha Delta Sigma depends on an understanding and acceptance of its new and broader role of "professionalization of advertising through education." "Bridging the Gap" was an appropriate function fifty years ago. It is not viable today.

"Bridging the Gap" refers to "the ad club" function of ADS and, while very important, it can be performed on any campus without any association with a national organization or movement.

Alpha Delta Sigma, along with GAX and other such advertising organizations as AAF and AAAA, has been so successful in fulfilling this need that no formal structure is now necessary to perform the function.

The "ad club" function helped students "bridge the gap" from the campus to the advertising field by bringing speakers to the campus, arranging for field trips, participating in money-making and service projects. Today, the teacher of advertising is not only accepted by the various advertising organizations, but very often welcomed by them. Any teacher who wishes to provide his students with the opportunities discussed above as "ad club" functions can do so most easily.

The "fraternity" concept has become less attractive to students, and it is for this reason that the National Council will recommend in 1969 that the organization be called a "society", with even stronger emphasis on "professional".

Thanks to affluence, television and many other factors, the student is more mature and sophisticated today than in the past. His concern and preoccupation with the possibility of military service, in a war he does not fully understand makes him a little less concerned with a job after graduation. The emphasis currently is on the individual and individual freedom, not on group effort and the acceptance of collective responsibility.

When the student seems less interested, it is easy for the advertising educator to justify not being an advisor of an ADS chapter. Much too often, he receives little, if any recognition for the time he devotes to ADS. Seldom is his position as advisor considered in his promotion, salary increases, or assignment of time. Not only is he not recognized for his effort, the time he devotes to ADS could well be spent doing research and writing articles for publications—activities that are rewarded handsomely.

Yet, the "ad club" function is still a primary part of the ADS program on a campus. As Past Presidents Burton and Joel pointed out that the experiences in planning, organizing and executing the program can be most beneficial to the ADS member.

It is obvious, then, from the previous discussion that in the future ADS must mean more than what is involved in the "ad club" function of a chapter. From the "ad club" function the undergraduate member acquires both knowledge and experience beyond the classroom; he is made aware of the interest others in advertising have for him and his welfare as a potential employee in advertising; he may receive assistance in getting either a summer job or a permanent position; and he is made aware of the sense of "professionalism" that should permeate all the activity of the chapter and the university advertising program.

The above experience is meaningful where the advertising educator has accepted the broader goal of "professionalization of advertising through education." Each of the specific activities and the philosophy of the undergraduate program results from this overriding concern and devotion to advertising education and to the student.

Where the advisor has accepted and understood this broader goal of ADS, the likelihood of the members of his chapter understanding and accepting it are much greater. The more the graduates understand and accept this philosophy, the greater is the probability that they will continue their interest in the advertising program at the university. Greater also, is the likelihood that they will continue to support the program through scholarships, visits to the campus, student recruitment.

As one advisor put it, "It is easier to see that as ADS aids advertising education, it aids our total program, which in turn aids our faculty, which in turn aids the students." It should be added that it also helps advertising in general.

All associations and organizations have membership problems, and the field of advertising is no different. Thus, it would seem that if ADS can be successful in getting students to accept this higher purpose of ADS, such individuals upon graduation would understand better the aims and goals of such organizations as the AAF, AAAA, ABP, ANA.

The acceptance of such an attitude by lawyers, doctors, teachers and ministers is a prime ingredient in their being considered members of a profession. Such an acceptance by students, teachers and practitioners of advertising is vital to its being accepted as a profession.

Once ADS accepts this higher goal, what can it do in the future to speed up the progress toward professionalization in advertising? The Education Commission of the National Education Association lists these six criteria for professional stature:

1. A profession is based on a body of specialized knowledge

2. A profession seeks competence in membership

3. A profession serves the needs of its members

4. A profession has ethical standards

5. A profession influences public policy in its field

6. A profession has group solidarity.

An examination of where advertising stands today on these points, as well as a review of where ADS is already aiding and where it can aid, will give insight to the professionalization of advertising.

A PROFESSION IS BASED ON A BODY OF SPECIALIZED KNOWLEDGE. Few challenge the fact that advertising today is based on a specialized knowledge. Libraries have set up divisions for the many books written on and about advertising. It is interesting to note the number of advertising books written by advertising educators, who in most cases have been advertising practitioners. Not to be forgotten is that advertising education programs in schools are built around this body of knowledge.

As Vernon Fryburger pointed out in his article on the role of the American Academy of Advertising, the development of a specific body of knowledge related to advertising should be one of its prime functions.

ADS has contributed little directly to this area, and its contribution in the future can be seen in the following: a continuance to stress excellence in studies; encouragement of more promising graduate students; and development of a positive academic climate resulting in the support of the Academy, the AAAA Educational Foundation, and other organizations more directly concerned with furthering advertising education.

A PROFESSION SEEKS COMPETENCE IN MEMBER-SHIP. In general one cannot say that advertising has a membership standard that all of its workers must fulfill before entry. Yet, this is not to say that advertising is without any membership requirements in practice. The many organizations of advertising that do require standards certainly offer proof that advertising is moving into this direction. Alpha Delta Sigma, as an advertising organization, has entrance requirements, yet one cannot consider this enough for a defense on competence in membership. While there has not been a formalization of educational requirements in the field, most positions do seek and prefer a college graduate.

A PROFESSION SERVES THE NEEDS OF ITS MEMBERS. Advertising, in the broad sense, does not necessarily serve all of those who perform advertising tasks, yet the many organizations of advertising very definitely serve their members and in turn serve all of advertising. To name a few: American Advertising Federation, American Business Press, Association of Industrial Advertisers, Association of National Advertisers, Alpha Delta Sigma, etc.

A PROFESSION HAS ETHICAL STANDARDS. In a recent move by the American Advertising Federation and the Better Business Bureau, a code of advertising ethics was prepared and distributed nationally. Not all who have copies of the code are practicing all of the points on the code, yet many advertisers are and encouraging others to do likewise. Some organizations have adopted ethical standards that are followed by the members or the members are asked to resign or are dropped.

Alpha Delta Sigma endorses the code of the AAF and BBB.

A PROFESSION INFLUENCES PUBLIC POLICY IN ITS FIELD. In this area the organizations of advertising have again come to the front. Legislators have turned to these groups to aid them in understanding the functions of advertising and in evaluating the needs. Two advertising organizations, AAAA and AAF, now have Washington offices to aid in this function. Yet, all organizations including ADS do influence public policy in advertising. In many cases it has been the result of adverse criticisms about advertising that has brought the advertising organizations to the front to defend its position. An example of this can be seen by reviewing the clippings about the ''consumer protection'' drive by many housewives groups. The advertising organizations came to the defense of the many businesses that had been depicted as villains.

A PROFESSION HAS GROUP SOLIDARITY. Today more than at any other time in the history of the U.S. there is solidarity within advertising, but it still cannot be called group solidarity. There is a certain amount of solidarity within each

1—TRUTH . . . Advertising shall tell the truth, and shall reveal significant facts, the concealment of which would mislead the public. 2—RESPONSIBILITY . . . Advertising agencies and advertisers shall be willing to provide substantiation of claims made. 3—TASTE AND DECENCY . . . Advertising shall be free of statements, illustrations or implications which are offensive to good taste or public decency. 4—DISPARAGEMENT... Advertising shall offer merchandise or service on its merits, and refrain from attacking competitors unfairly or disparaging their products, services or methods of doing business. 5—BAIT ADVERTISING . . . Advertising shall offer only merchandise or services which are readily available for purchase at the advertised price. 6—GUARANTEES AND WARRANTIES . . . Advertising of guarantees and warranties shall be explicit. Advertising of any guarantee or warranty shall clearly and conspicuously disclose its nature and extent, the manner in which the guarantor or warrantor will perform and the identity of the guarantor or warrantor. 7—PRICE CLAIMS . . . Advertising shall avoid price or savings claims which are false or misleading, or which do not offer provable bargains or savings. 8—UNPROVABLE CLAIMS . . . Advertising shall avoid the use of exaggerated or unprovable claims. 9—TESTIMONIALS . . . Advertising containing testimonials shall be limited to those of competent witnesses who are reflecting a real and honest choice.

separate group of advertising, although not in advertising in general. It is also true that there is more and more solidarity between groups. The American Advertising Federation serves as a federation of advertising organizations.

At the national level of Alpha Delta Sigma there has been more group solidarity in recent years. In years to come there will be more still if the goal of professionalization of advertising through advertising education is followed.

No, advertising is not a profession in every sense of the word, but the industry is progressing in each of the six criteria areas. The direction of advertising is toward professionalization. Those who doubt this need only to take a review of the actions of the advertising organizations, including ADS, that are currently working in this direction.

One of the strong supporters of advertising education, Theodore S. Repplier, past president of the Advertising Council, told the members of the American Academy of Advertising: ''Why should not the universities be working on the problems of advertising? Why should not we in advertising apply the principle which works so brilliantly for American science whereby the colleges and the universities channel a great river of new information, new principles and practical applications into our national defense and industries? It is this togetherness which has produced today's breathtaking pace of science—so rapid that by the time a scientific concept is grasped by the layman it is probably already obsolete. We in advertising do not need to go as far as setting up a Rand corporation to put the university's social scientists to work at reducing some of our unknowns, but the point is to begin. There are so many things we do not know.''

In a speech to members of the Western Region of ADS in 1964 Walter Terry, current chairman of the American Advertising Federation, told the audience that ADS must be concerned with the total cause of advertising. He said that the whole advertising industry had to be involved in the many attacks on the ''over-commercialization through advertising. We must educate the people.'' He stressed the need for teaching economics and advertising principles. He aslo pointed out that the advertising student is in the noncommercial atmosphere and is close to other students in other fields. He urged that ADS'ers must be so organized that they will be able to speak with strength on the subject. He suggested debates with other majors and a formal ADS stand on a national level. Community advertising recognition should be an ADS goal. He closed by saying that, ''We must rise to the challenge of the industry today.''

These men and many others have seen the role of Alpha Delta Sigma as being one far more reaching than to merely ''bridge the gap.'' The direction of ADS was changed as a result of such thinking during recent years.

THE FUTURE OF ADS

W. F. G. Thacher, former national ADS president 1942-47, was asked what he thought about the future of the organization. He said:

"Who can predict? Certainly not I. Too long have I been out of the main stream of its activities to play the oracle. This much is impressed upon me, however: The old *mystique* of the fraternity—whether social or professional—has lost much of its glow and glamor. The Greeks on the campus are no longer a dominant group. No longer does the right to wear a piece of jewelled hardware constitute a sufficient motive for membership. Now and more insistently will the prospective candidate ask, "What is there in it for me?""

He continued that the success of ADS will depend on academic offerings and the attraction of students of superior dynamism and personality.

Another dedcated former national officer, Milton E. Gross, spoke out on the subject to the Midwest Regional convention in 1966. His talk, "Is ADS Really Necessary?" brought out many of the things that had been questioned by many. He said that ADS has not outlived its usefulness. "I think it can continue to be useful if you direct its efforts toward three important goals. First, the local chapters, and the national organization, must do everything possible to maintain the present standard of advertising education and to keep up with continuing improvements in advertising education."

In supporting this point he said that the campus is different from what it was 30 years ago. The courses are much tougher. Advertising is more than a technique, and it requires more than a technical education. He continued: "I believe that ADS should be most wary of accepting petitions for charters for new chapters in schools which are not accredited by one of those agencies (American Council on Education for Journalism and the American Association of Collegiate Schools of Business). I think that is the best way ADS can help improve advertising education."

His last two points pertained to the concentration on the undergraduate members and the acceptance of women into ADS.

Dr. Ernest A. Sharpe, national president of ADS in 1953, was asked, "As national president of Alpha Delta Sigma, what would you say about advertising in America, and education for advertising, in 1953, to an audience assembled in 2052?"

"My first thought," he said, "was to wonder whether ADS would still be in existence in 2053. I wonder because of the approaching climax in the struggle of the United States and its free-world allies against Russia and its communist satellites. A communist world would abolish ADS, because ADS believes in truth, in a just God, in free private enterprise, to mention three beliefs intolerable to communism. But I don't believe there will be a communist world in 2053. On the contrary, I believe the US will be a greater nation in a freer world than ever before, and will be operating largely by the same Constitutional policies as we know them today. Therefore, I think the environment during the next hundred years will be favorable for the continued development of ADS.''

He added that he thought ADS would be very alive in 2053 and ''will be considerably larger, more professional in attitude, and more influential in the field of advertising. In the free world of 2053, the scope of ADS will be world-wide. Think on that!''

WHAT IS BEING DONE?

Many things have already been taking place to aid in the future development of Alpha Delta Sigma. The starting point would have to be the acceptance of the primary goal, ''TO AID IN THE PROFESSIONALIZATION OF ADVERTISING THROUGH ADVERTISING EDUCATION,'' by the 1967 national convention.

The movement of *Linage* from being an internal ADS publication to its present role as a spokesman for advertising education, Alpha Delta Sigma and Gamma Alpha Chi, has played an important part in fulfilling the goal. Favorable comments have been received from advertising practitioners on the editorial quality of the current publication.

The closer relationship of Alpha Delta Sigma with the many other advertising organizations has been beneficial to all involved. President Lee Fondren, a former national president of both Advertising Federation of America and Advertising Association of the West, has provided most of the groundwork for this development.

The cooperating efforts between Gamma Alpha Chi and Alpha Delta Sigma have resulted in easier operations and less confusion among chapters. A cross-initiation agreement was reached two years ago on campuses where one of the organizations existed and the other did not. The existing organization could initiate members into the other organization. This has been beneficial to both organizations and has resulted in the establishment of new chapters in some cases. Cooperating efforts are being made in many other areas.

A more thorough examination of the advertising curriculum of schools requesting ADS charters has to improve in the calibre of incoming chapters. Schools without a specific program in advertising are no longer considered for chapters.

The recently installed Aide to Advertising Education Award (AIDE), where local chapters may honor the persons who have aided the advertising educational program at their schools, is helping to fulfill the goal of ADS.

In an effort to aid advertising, advertising education, and the local chapter, the national organizations of ADS and Gamma Alpha Chi have encouraged the participation in Advertising Recognition Week programs. An award has been offered by the two groups.

The initiation of professional members who are prominent today in advertising, but who did not have an opportunity to become a member when in school, has been an effective program in obtaining the support needed from the advertising industry. President Lee Fondren has developed this program more than anyone else.

The very fact that Alpha Delta Sigma is now taking definite stands on advertising and advertising education issues has placed the organization into a position of respect by the industry.

ADVERTISING EDUCATION RESOLUTION

It may be said that the new direction of ADS began when this complete resolution was passed by the delegates to the National Convention at Houston, April 9, 1967:

WHEREAS, we hold beyond contest that there now exists an organized body of knowledge related to advertising, and

WHEREAS, the advertising industry is highly aware of the need for greater professionalism, which goal demands the establishment of certain standards, and

WHEREAS, we hold that the primary purpose of Alpha Delta Sigma is to aid in the professionalization of advertising through advertising education, and

WHEREAS, we hold that renewed efforts must be made to achieve greater recognition and respect for advertising as a profession.

NOW, THEREFORE BE IT RESOLVED that the 1967 Convention of Alpha Delta Sigma go on record as urging that professional academic education be an important concern of all advertising practitioners

AND BE IT FURTHER RESOLVED that this convention publicly commend and support those advertising organizations which seek to encourage professional advertising educational standards through such actions as:

Establishing endowed chairs in advertising education;

Providing advertising scholarships;

Underwriting advertising research; etc ......

and

BE IT FURTHER RESOLVED THAT ALPHA DELTA

SIGMA take the initiative in securing support for these objectives from all related advertising groups, associations and practitioners.

Resolution Committee

David Little, Chairman

True, the passing of a resolution alone does not assure a prosperous future, but with the continued aid of the members, advisors, the national officers, the chances of a bright future are far better.

SECTION II
APPENDIXES

APPENDIX A

Founding Dates of All Alpha Delta Sigma Chapters

Chapter No.	Institution	Founding Date
1.	University of Missouri	1913
2.	University of Illinois	1914
3.	University of Kentucky	1914
4.	Georgetown University	1920
5.	Dartmouth University	1922
6.	University of Michigan	1923
7.	University of Washington	1923
8.	Georgia Tech	1924
9.	Columbia University	1924
10.	University of Oregon	1924
11.	University of Oklahoma	1924
12.	Boston University	1925
13.	University of Kansas	1925
14.	University of Minnesota	1925
15.	Syracuse University	1925
16.	Washington University	1926
17.	Oregon State University	1926
18.	University of Alabama	1927
19.	University of California	1927
20.	Washington State University	1928
21.	University of Southern California	1928
22.	University of Nebraska	1928
23.	Ohio University	1928
24.	University of Texas	1928
25.	University College of Los Angeles	1929
26.	University of Wisconsin	1929
27.	De Pauw University	1930
28.	Butler University	1931
29.	Indiana University	1932
30.	New York University	1933
31.	Temple University	1933
32.	Pennsylvania State University	1933
33.	Franklin and Marshall College	1937
34.	City College of New York	1938
35.	Stanford University	1940
36.	San Jose State College	1940
37.	Northwestern University	1940
38.	Babson Institution	1941
39.	State University of Iowa	1946
40.	Roosevelt University	1947
41.	Baylor University	1948
42.	De Paul University	1948

43.	Wayne State University	1948
44.	Emory University	1949
45.	Michigan State University	1949
46.	University of Miami	1949
47.	University of Colorado	1949
48.	Rhode Island University	1949
49.	University of Florida	1949
50.	Ohio State University	1949
51.	University of Arizona	1950
52.	University of Denver	1950
53.	Southern Methodist University	1950
54.	University of Houston	1951
55.	University of Mississippi	1952
56.	Arizona State University	1953
57.	Marquette University	1953
58.	Florida State University	1953
59.	Fordham University	1954
60.	University of Georgia	1954
61.	Long Island University	1956
62.	Manhattan University	1957
63.	Whitworth College	1958
64.	University of Wichita	1958
65.	Texas Tech College	1958
66.	Texas Christian University	1958
67.	Southern Illinois University	1959
68.	Long Beach State College	1959
69.	University of Maryland	1960
70.	Texas A & M University	1960
71.	Drake University	1964
72.	Fairleigh Dickinson College	1964
73.	Ferris State College	1964
74.	West Virginia University	1964
75.	Youngstown University	1965
76.	San Francisco State College	1966
77.	Little Rock University	1967
78.	Memphis State University	1967
79.	Western Michigan University	1968
80.	University of South Carolina	1968

Robert W. Jones
President 1929-1931

Herbert Hall Palmer
President 1931-1933

E. H. McReynolds
President 1937

Don E. Gilman
President 1938

Howard Willoughby
President 1938-1939

W. F. G. Thacher
President 1942-1947

Donald W. Davis
President 1947-1949

B. R. Canfield
President 1949-1951
Treasurer 1947-1949

Ernest A. Sharpe
President 1951-1953

Philip W. Burton
President 1953-1957

Richard E. Joel
President 1957-1959

Walter Guild
President 1959-1961

Rol W. Rider, Jr.
President 1961-1963

Billy I. Ross
President 1963-1967

Lee Fondren
President 1967-

Eric J. Smith
Secretary 1939-1940
Treasurer 1940-1943

Milton E. Gross
Executive Secretary 1947-1961

Donald G. Hileman
Executive Secretary 1961-
(Title changed to Executive Director)
Editor, LINAGE 1963-

Robert W. Haverfield
Editor, LINAGE 1950-1963

Noel P. Laird
Treasurer 1951-

APPENDIX B

National Presidents

1913-20   John B. Powell — Instructor at the University of Missouri, later editor of Chinese newspaper. Considered Founder of ADS. (ADS was not a national organization during this six-year period.)

1920-26   Oliver N. Gingrich — Instructor at the University of Missouri

1926-28   E. K. Johnston — Professor at the University of Missouri

1928-29   Charles Fernald — Professor at the University of Illinois

1929-31   Robert W. Jones — Professor at the University of Washington

1931-33   Herbert Hall Palmer — Professor at Syracuse University

1934   Bruce Barton — Chairman of the Board, Batten, Barton, Durstine & Osborn

1935   Paoli A. Smith — Sparrow Advertising Agency, Birmingham, Alabama

1936   Charles C. Younggreen — Reincke-Ellis-Younggreen & Finn, Chicago, Illinois

1937   E. H. McReynolds — James Mulligan Printing and Publishing Co., St. Louis, Missouri

1937   Chester H. Lang — Vice President, General Electric Co., Schenectady, New York. (Took over after death of E. H. McReynolds)

1938   Don E. Gilmer — Vice President, American Broadcasting Company, Los Angeles, California

1938   Howard Willoughby — Director of the Lane Magazine and Book Company, Menlo Park, California. (Took over as president during the 1938 Los Angeles Convention)

1939   Charles C. Younggreen — Reincke-Ellis-Younggreen & Finn, Chicago, Illinois.

1940   Ken R. Dyke — Senior Vice President, Hardy Jones, Smith Dingwall Associates, New York

1941   Lou E. Townsend — Bank of America, San Francisco, California

1942-47   W. F. G. Thacher — Professor at the University of Oregon

1947-49   Donald W. Davis — Professor at Pennsylvania State University

1949-51   B. R. Canfield — Professor at Babson Institute

1951-53   Ernest A. Sharpe — Professor at the University of Texas

1953-57	Philip W. Burton — Professor at Syracuse University
1957-59	Richard E. Joel — Professor at Florida State University
1959-61	Walter Guild — Guild, Bascom & Bonfigli, Inc., San Francisco, California
1961-63	Rol Rider — Professor at California Polytechnic College
1963-67	Billy I. Ross — Professor at Texas Technological College
1967-	Lee Fondren — Station Manager and Director of Sales, Time-Life Broadcast, KLZ Radio, Denver, Colorado

National Secretaries

1920-26	Herbert Graham — University of Kentucky
1926-38	Arthur Hallam — University of Oklahoma
1938-39	William Clinton Billig — University of Southern California
1939-40	Eric J. Smith — Smith & Hemmings, Los Angeles, California
1940-47	E. K. Johnston — University of Missouri
1947-61	Milton E. Gross — University of Missouri
1961-	Donald G. Hileman — Southern Illinois University

National Treasurers

1920-26	Myron McCurry — Georgetown College
1926-28	Walter B. Cole — De Pauw University
1928-29	Arthur Hallam — (Served as secretary-treasurer)
1929-40	James S. Shropshire — University of Kentucky (Did not serve consecutive terms of office.)
1940-43	Eric J. Smith — Smith & Hemmings, Los Angeles, California
1943-43	John Eggers
1943-47	Edward E. Keeler — University of Southern California
1947-49	B. R. Canfield — Babson Institute
1949-51	Carl C. Webb — University of Oregon
1951-	Noel P. Laird — Franklin & Marshall College

Editors of "Linage"

1948-49	George K. Morgan — University of Missouri
1950-63	Robert W. Haverfield — University of Missouri
1963-	Donald G. Hileman — Southern Illinois University

APPENDIX C

GOLDEN FIFTY AWARD RECIPIENTS

Practitioners

Fred Adams, President, G. M. Basford Company.

Thomas B. Adams, President, Campbell-Ewald Company.

R. E. Allen, President, Fuller & Smith & Ross Incorporated.

Bruce Barton, Chairman of the Board, BBDO.

Don Belding, professional member Alpha Delta Sigma and former member of Professional Advisory Board; retired executive Foote, Cone & Belding Company.

Louis N. Brockway, President, Young & Rubicam, Inc., New York.

Elon G. Borton, professional member Alpha Delta Sigma, former President and General Manager, Advertising Federation of America.

Charles H. Brower, President and Chairman, Executive Committee, Batten, Barton, Durstine & Osborn.

Robert B. Brown, former member Professional Advisory Board, Alpha Delta Sigma, Executive Vice President, Bristol-Myers Co.

R. M. Budd, Director of Advertising, Campbell Soup Company.

John W. Burgard, Vice President in Charge of Advertising, Brown & Williamson Tobacco Corp.

Leo Burnett, Chairman of the Board, Leo Burnett Company, Inc.

Ralph Starr Butler, Retired Vice President, General Foods Corp.

Ernest Elmo Calkins.

H. E. Cassidy, President, The McCarthy Company.

Fairfax M. Cone, Chairman, Executive Committee, Foote, Cone & Belding, Inc.

Charles W. Collier, Regional Vice President, Alpha Delta Sigma, Executive Vice President, Advertising Association of the West.

John H. Crichton, AAAA, New York, New York.

John P. Cunningham, Executive Vice President, Cunningham & Walsh, Inc., New York.

Thomas D'Arcy Brophy, Retired Board Chairman, Kenyon & Eckhardt, Inc.

Fred Decker, Publisher, *Printers' Ink.*

Ben Duffy, BBDO, New York.

Roy S. Durstine, Secretary and Treasurer, Batten, Barton, Durstine & Osborn, Inc., New York.

Clarence E. Eldridge, Consultant, International Paper Company.

Robert Feemster, *Wall Street Journal*, New York.

James Fish, General Mills, Minneapolis, Minnesota.

Lee Fondren, Radio Station KLZ, Denver, Colorado, Chairman, Coordinating Committee, AFA-AAW.

Donald Frost, Executive Vice President, Bristol-Myers Company.

Samuel Gale.

Frederic Gamble, AAAA, New York, New York.

Budd Gore.

Will C. Grant, professional member, Alpha Delta Sigma, Chairman of the Board, Grant Advertising, Incorporated.

George H. Gribbin, Chairman, Young & Rubicam, Inc.

John E. Grimm III, Vice President, Director of Marketing, Household Products Division, Colgate Palmolive Co.

Walter Guild, Guild, Bascom, and Bonfigli, San Francisco, California.

Marion Harper, Jr., Chairman of the Board and President, Interpublic Inc.

Claude Clarence Hopkins.

G. B. Hotchkiss.

Hurnard J. Kenner, professional member of Alpha Delta Sigma, former General Manager, Better Business Bureau of New York City.

Otto Kleppner, professional member Alpha Delta Sigma, President, Kleppner Company.

Sigurd S. Larmon, President, Young & Rubicam, Inc., New York.

Carrol B. Larrabee, Former Publisher of *Printers' Ink*.

Al Lasker.

Ernest John, MacManus, John and Adams, Detroit, Michigan.

Neil H. McElroy, Chairman of the Board, Procter & Gamble.

William A. Marsteller, Chairman of the Board, Marsteller Inc.

Charles G. Mortimer, President, General Foods Corporation.

Wesey I. Nunn, former professional member, Alpha Delta Sigma, former Advertising Director, Standard Oil Company of Indiana.

David Ogilvy, Chairman of the Board, Ogilvy, Benson & Mather, Inc.

Stuart Peabody, Former Assistant Vice President, The Borden Company, now a consultant.

James Proud, formerly AFA, New York, New York.

Rosser Reeves, Chairman of the Board, Ted Bates & Co., Inc.

Stanley Resor, President, J. Walter Thompson Company, New York.

Theodore S. Repplier, professional Alpha Delta Sigma member, President of the Advertising Council.

J. S. Roberts, former Regional Vice President, Alpha Delta Sigma, Executive Secretary, Atlanta Advertising Club, retired advertising director of Retail Credit Company, Atlanta, Ga. of Advertising, California Packing Company, San Francisco.

Raymond Rubicam, Chairman, Young & Rubicam, Inc., New York.

Everett M. Runyan, member Alpha Delta Sigma, former Director of Advertising, California Packing Co., San Francisco.

Horace Scott, member Greater Miami Professional Chapter, Alpha Delta Sigma, retired.

Warner S. Shelby, President and Chief Executive Officer, N. W. Ayer & Son, Inc.

Hal Stebbins, President, Hal Stebbins, Inc.

Frank Stanton, President, CBS.

Albert R. Stevens, Advertising Manager, The American Tobacco Co.

Norman H. Strouse, President, J. Walter Thompson Company.

Hugh W. Thomas, professional member Alpha Delta Sigma, former Vice President, McCann-Erickson, Inc., San Francisco.

Lou E. Townsend, former National President of Alpha Delta Sigma, Past President of Advertising Association of the West, former Advertising Manager of Bank of America.

Julian Tuthill, professional member Alpha Delta Sigma, President, Tuthill Public Relations, Tucson, Arizona.

James Webb Young, former Vice President, J. Walter Thompson Company, professional member Alpha Dela Sigma.

Walter Weir, Chairman, Executive Committee, Donahue & Coe, Inc.

Paul West.

Fred Wittner, President, Fred Wittner Co., Inc.

Howard Willoughby, former National President, Alpha Delta Sigma, Executive Vice President, *Sunset Magazine.*

John Orr Young, A Co-Founder of Young & Rubicam, Inc., now a consultant

L. L. Zimmerman, professional member Greater Miami Alumni Chapter, Alpha Delta Sigma, Account Executive Radio Station WCKR, Miami, Florida.

Educators

Bedell, Clyde, professional member Alpha Delta Sigma, Advertising Consultant.

Borden, Neil H., Professor of Advertising, Harvard University.

Bretsch, Lawrence, posthumously, Regional Vice President of Alpha Delta Sigma, Professor of Advertising, Rhode Island University.

Brewster, Arthur J., posthumously, long-time advisor to Arthur J. Brewster chapter of Alpha Delta Sigma, Syracuse University, Advertising Manager, Smith-Corona Typewriter Company.

Burton, Philip Ward, two terms as National President of Alpha Delta Sigma, Professor of Journalism and Advertising, Syracuse University.

Canfield, B. R., former National President, Alpha Delta Sigma, Professor at Babson Institute, Wellseley, Massachusetts.

Davis, Donald W., posthumous award, former National President of Alpha Delta Sigma, Advertising Hall of Fame, one-time professor at Pennsylvania State University.

Drake, Jerry, former ADS Regional Vice President, Professor at Southern Methodist University.

English, Earl F., professional member of Alpha Delta Sigma, Dean of the School of Journalism, University of Missouri.

Gross, Milton E., Professor of Journalism, University of Missouri, and National Secretary of Alpha Delta Sigma, 1949-1961.

Haverfield, Robert, Editor of *Linage* for many years, Professor of Advertising, University of Missouri.

Hileman, Donald G., National Secretary, Alpha Delta Sigma, Professor of Advertising, Southern Illinios University.

Hoffman, Carl, Professor Emeritus of Advertising, San Jose College, San Jose, California.

Joel, Richard, Former National President of Alpha Delta Sigma, Professor of Advertising, Florida State University.

Laird, Noel, National Treasurer of Alpha Delta Sigma, 1953-1963, Professor, Franklin & Marshall College, Lancaster, Pennsylvania.

Palmer, Herbert Hall, founder of Herbert Hall Palmer Alpha Delta Sigma chapter, Rhode Island University, retired professor of advertising at Rhode Island University.

Rice, Leslie, former National Treasurer, Alpha Delta Sigma, Professor of Advertising, University of Oklahoma.

Rider, Rol, National President, Alpha Delta Sigma, formerly with Young & Rubicam Company, now teaching at California Polytechnic College.

Sandage, Charles H., Chairman, Professor of Advertising, University of Illinois.

Sargent, Hugh, Regional Vice President, Alpha Delta Sigma, Professor of Advertising, University of Illinois.

Senger, Frank W., Regional Vice President of Alpha Delta Sigma, Professor of Advertising, Michigan State University.

Sharpe, Ernest, School of Journalism, University of Texas, former National President, Alpha Delta Sigma.

Thacher, W. F. G., Professor Emeritus, University of Oregon, former National President of Alpha Delta Sigma, life-time member of National Council.

Thompson, Willard, Assistant to President, University of Minnesota, former Advertising Professor, University of Oregon.

Washburn, Roger, former Regional Vice President, Alpha Delta Sigma, Professor of Advertising, Boston University.

Webb, Carl, former National Treasurer, Alpha Delta Sigma, executive of Oregon Press Association.

Wolff, Charles E., Regional Vice President, Alpha Delta Sigma, Professor, Long Beach State College.

Wood, Elwin G., Chapter Advisor of Elwin G. Wood Chapter, Alpha Delta Sigma, Professor of Advertising, University of Arizona.

APPENDIX D

Sidney R. Bernstein Advisor Award

The Sidney R. Bernstein Advisor Award is the most recent national award. It was approved by the National Council at the 1967 national convention in Houston. The cash award is made biannually to the advisor who is chosen by the National Council from nominations submitted by the local chapters.

The initial award was given in 1968 to Dr. Ernest A. Sharpe, University of Texas advisor.

The award is sponsored by the G. D. Crain, Jr. Foundation, Chicago, and is named after Sidney R. Bernstein.

A friend of advertising education, Sidney R. Bernstein is publisher of *Advertising Age* and president of Advertising Publications Inc., which also publishes *Advertising & Sales Promotion, Industrial Marketing, Marketing Insights* and other publications.

He has been with *Advertising Age* since its inception in 1930, and was made managing editor in 1932 and editor in 1938. In 1958 he became editorial director of that publication, as well as of the two associated publications. He was named executive vice president and general manager of the publishing company in 1961 and president in 1964.

Mr. Bernstein is a former Vice President for Marketing Management and a member of the Executive Advisory Council of the American Marketing Association, and has served as a director of the association, and chairman of its marketing statistics committee, as well as president of the association's Chicago chapter; and as vice president of the National Conference of Business Paper Editors and the Society of Business Magazine Editors. He has conducted a special course on creative advertising at the University of Chicago, was a visiting lecturer at the College of Communication Arts of Michigan State University, and is a member of the College of Commerce advisory committee at Roosevelt University. He has just been named a member of the new National Marketing Advisory Committee of the U. S. Department of Comerce.

Mr. Bernstein is a native Chicagoan; attended the University of Illinois, and holds an MBA degree from the University of Chicago. He is active in a variety of advertising, selling and marketing organizations, and is a member of the Professional Advisory Board of Alpha Delta Sigma. He is a member of Sigma Delta Chi (journalism), Beta Gamma Sigma (scholastic honorary); the National Press Club, Washington, D.C., and the Chicago Press Club, among other organizations. He is also a member of the National Advisory Council, Boston Conference on Distribution. He was chosen "Advertising Man of the Year" for 1957 by American Legion Post 170, and again in 1961 by the

Chicago Federated Advertising Club, when he was one of nine persons elected to the 1961 Distribution Hall of Fame by the Boston Conference on Distribution. That same year the Chicago Junior Association of Commerce & Industry named him "The Outstanding Local Citizen in the Field of Communications" for 1961.

First recipient of the Sidney R. Bernstein Advisor Award in 1968, was Dr. Ernest Alonzo Sharpe, University of Texas.

The achievements of Dr. Sharpe include: Professor of Journalism; advisor to Paul J. Thompson Chapter of ADS since 1947; Phi Beta Kappa; Graduate Advisor and Director of Graduate Curriculum; past national president of ADS; past president of Austin Advertising Club; author of *G. B. Dealey* of *The Dallas Morning News*; *Printer's Ink* Silver Medal; American Vice-Counsul to Portugal during World War II; and positions with McCann-Erickson and the *Bryan Daily Eagle*. His degrees are: B.J., Texas, 1939; B.A. (in English), Texas, 1940; M.J. Texas, 1941; Ph.D., Wisconsin, 1964.

APPENDIX E

The Sixth Degree Key

The Sixth Degree Key, the highest award in Alpha Delta Sigma, is presented only when the National Chapter is in convention, to a member of the fraternity who has performed signal service for Alpha Delta Sigma. The members of the National Council are responsible for the nominations and selections for the award.

Following are the names of the men who have received this award:

1931—Robert W. Jones, University of Washington. An outstanding advertising educator who served as national president of ADS from 1929 to 1931.

1933—Bruce Barton, member through Boston University chapter. One of the founding fathers of Batten, Barton, Durstine, and Osborn Advertising Agency, for whom the Boston University chapter is named. He served as ADS national president in 1934.

1939—George Burton Hotchkiss, New York University. An early pioneer in advertising education, as well as author of many advertising books.

1939—Don Gilman, member through the University of California chapter. An advertising practitioner who served as ADS national president in 1938.

1939—Howard Willoughby, member through Stanford University chapter. Well-known vice president and general manager of *Sunset* magazine for many years who served as ADS national president in 1939.

1939—Frank A. Nagley, member through the University of Southern California chapter. He served for many years on the marketing faculty of the University of Southern California.

1940—E. K. Johnston, University of Missouri. National president of ADS from 1926 to 1928, who was an outstanding advertising teacher at the University of Missouri.

1941—W. F. G. Thacher, University of Oregon. He was the wartime president of ADS (1942-1947) and one of the early pioneers in advertising education.

1947—Edward E. Keeler, University of Southern California. He served as national secretary and treasurer of ADS during the early 1940's.

1949—Donald W. Davis, Pennsylvania State University. Advertising educator and author, who was national president of ADS from 1947 to 1949.

1951—B. R. Canfield, Babson Institute. He served as national president of ADS from 1949 to 1951.

1953—Milton E. Gross, University of Missouri. Advertising educator who served as national secretary longer than any other officer (1947 to 1961).

1953—Roger D. Washburn, Boston University. Educator at Boston University who also served as ADS advisor.

1953—Ernest A. Sharpe, University of Texas. Advertising educator who served as national president from 1951 to 1953.

1954—Herbert Hall Palmer, Syracuse University. Pioneer advertising educator who served as ADS national president in 1931.

1955—Noel P. Laird, Franklin and Marshall College. Long-time ADS national treasurer who was advisor of the Franklin and Marshall chapter.

1957—Philip Ward Burton, Syracuse University. Advertising educator and author who served as ADS national president from 1953 to 1957.

1959—Richard Joel, Florida State University. National president of ADS from 1957 to 1959 while teaching advertising at Florida State.

1959—Robert W. Haverfield, University of Missouri. Advertising educator who edited the official ADS magazine, *Linage,* for many years during the 1950's and early 1960's.

1959—Lou Townsend, professional member through the Northern California chapter. Advertising practitioner who was national president of ADS in 1942.

1961—Will C. Grant, member through Southern Methodist University chapter. Well known advertising practitioner for whom the S.M.U. chapter is named.

1965—Rol Rider, California Polytechnical Institute. Advertising practitioner who turned educator and was national president of ADS from 1961 to 1963.

1967—Billy I. Ross, Texas Technological College. Advertising educator who served as national president of ADS from 1963 to 1967.

APPENDIX F

The G. D. Crain Jr. Advertising Education Award

(Formerly called The Nichols Cup)

The award, first given in 1951, goes to "an advertising man who has rendered outstanding service to advertising education." Selection of the winner has been by undergraduate chapters of ADS, based on nominations made by the ADS National Council. The award is given bi-annually at the national convention.

Until 1966 the award was known as The Nichols Cup in honor of Charles G. Nichols. Mr. Nichols was the first president of the Boston University chapter of ADS. At the time of his death, a few years ago, he was president of the George M. McKelvey Company, Youngstown, Ohio.

In the fall of 1966 the G. D. Crain Jr. Foundation of Chicago announced that it had accepted the sponsorship of the award. The National Council recommended that the award be named after Mr. Crain, which was accepted by the Foundation.

G. D. Crain, Jr. could well have been a recipient of the award. A founder and chairman of Advertising Publications, Inc., he is a native Kentuckian. Following graduation from Centre College he was city editor of the old *Louisville Herald* and a columnist for the *Louisville Courier-Journal*.

After leaving Kentucky he established *Industrial Marketing, Advertising Age,* and *Advertising & Sales Promotion,* which serve all aspects of advertising and marketing in the United States and internationally.

Mr. Crain was one of the founders of the Association of Industrial Advertisers, of which he is an honorary life member. He is a past president of the National Conference of Business Papers Editors and a past president of the Chicago Business Publications Association. The latter organization named him as one of those who have contributed most to business publishing on the occasion of its 75th anniversary in 1960.

The Chicago Federated Advertising Club presented him a citation for contributions to advertising on the twenty-fifth anniversary of the establishment of *Advertising Age.*

Long active in the promotion of international advertising, Mr. Crain has been honored in Tokyo by the Dentsu Advertising agency for his work in this field.

He was named the first chairman of the executive committee for the James Webb Young Fund for Education in Advertising.

As with any award, the stature is determined by the recipients, and on this basis the G. D. Crain, Jr. Advertising Education Award presented by Alpha Delta Sigma ranks among the finest in the industry. Information about the recipients of the award and the year in which the award was made follows.

1951—Otto Kleppner

1953—Clyde Bedell

1955—Carroll B. Larrabee

1957—Elon G. Borton

1959—Neil H. Borden

1961—Philip Ward Burton

1963—C. H. Sandage 1965—James Webb Young

1967—Charles W. "Chick" Collier

1951—Otto Kleppner. Up to his last semester in high school, Otto Kleppner had prepared for engineering, but at that moment he came upon a book that changed his life's plans; after reading and rereading that work, he knew that advertising was the field for him. Instead of going on to an engineering school for which his application already was in, he enrolled at New York University, School of Commerce, to study under the man whose advertising text so influenced him—Professor George Burton Hotchkiss. After attending N.Y.U. for six years at night, Otto Kleppner was awarded his Master's degree. Meanwhile, he got his early jobs in advertising, and became advertising manger of Prentice-Hall. He left that job to go into the agency business, founding The Kleppner Company of which he is still the very active President.

While at Prentice-Hall, he spent his nights and weekends working on a book called *Advertising Procedure* which now is in its forty-fifth printing, Fifth edition (1967) with more than 300,000 copies sold—the largest selling text on advertising ever published. The book is dedicated to Professor Hotchkiss.

Otto Kleppner also has been active in the affairs of the 4A's, serving as a governor of the New York Council, chairman of its Committee on Government, Public and Educator Relations, and as a director and member of its Operations Committee. He is the author of the 4A booklet, "Careers in Advertising" (fourth edition) which has been widely distributed.

In speaking of *Advertising Procedure*, Otto Kleppner said, "The time to write your first book is when you are very young. You may not know much, but then you have lots of time and few doubts. As you get older, you know more but you have less time and many doubts." His writings on advertising have also appeared in *Harper's Magazine* and have been published abroad in eight languages.

He is the father of two sons and a daughter: Dr. Adam Kleppner, associate professor of Mathematics at the University of Maryland, Dr. Daniel Kleppner, associate professor of physics at Massachusetts Institute of Technology, and Mrs. David H. Folkman of Houston, Texas.

1953—Clyde Bedell. His career began with an agency in Dallas where he had helped two clients compile an amazing growth story. Subsequently, he had agency experience in Chicago and San Francisco, where he became involved with copy research.

He served with Butler Brothers in Chicago for eight years. As Director of Sales and Advertising, he headed an advertising department of over 500 people and a sales force of over 250. He served with the N. W. Ayer Agency on the Ford Motor account, designing a sales training program that helped Ford enjoy the one year in ten before World War II that they exceeded Chevrolet in sales.

Bedell also served with consultant James O. McKinsey, and since 1939 has served as an independent consultant—with the exception of two years at the Fair Store in Chicago. He served as chairman of Chicago's State Street Promotion Managers and was chosen by them to write Chicago's major war bond selling ads.

Bedell's works include *The Seven Keys to Retail Profits, How to Write Advertising That Sells, Let's Talk Retailing,* and *Department Store Way of Life.* He lectured at Northwestern University for five years. He was the first person named to the Retail Advertising Hall of Fame, and was named a member of the Golden Fifty by ADS in 1963. George Nichols, long-time editor of *Printer's Ink,* called Clyde Bedell one of the top ten copywriters in the U.S. and "nowhere near the bottom of that list."

Bedell served for six years on the Board of Chicago's Metropolitan Council of Social Agencies, twice as President of the Friends of the Public Library, for four years as president of Chicago's Northwestern University Settlement, and twice as president of the largest PTA in Illinois.

An enthusiastic newspaper promotion man on the East Coast once wrote that "Clyde Bedell has done more for retailing than premiums have done for cereals."

1955—Carroll B. Larrabee. Larrabee was born in 1896 in Coudersport, Pennsylvania. He graduated from Peddie School in 1914 and Brown University in 1920. He attended University College in London in 1919. He began his career as a reporter for the Bradford, Pennsylvania, *Daily Era* in 1920. In late 1920 he served on the staff of *Printer's Ink* as an editorial writer. From then until 1955, he served the publication as associate editor, managing editor, president, publisher, and chairman of the board.

In 1955 Larrabee became Director of Publications, Applied Publications, for the American Chemical Society in Washington until he retired in 1962. He served in the Army during 1917-1919, when he was awarded the Purple Heart. He is a recipient of the medal for special services to journalism from the University of Missouri School of Journalism (1953).

He received the ADS Golden Fifty Award in 1963, and in 1965 was given an Alumni Citation for distinguished service in the field of Communications by the Peddie School.

Larrabee served as director of the Magazine Publishers Association during 1942-1955, and on the National Committee for Education of Alcoholism during 1948-1954. He was the president of the Peddie Alumni Association for 1927-1928. He is author of numerous books on advertising and merchandising subjects. Larrabee is a member of the Advertising Club of New York, and of the Cosmos and National Press Clubs of Washington. Since his retirement, Larrabee has been living in Annandale, Virginia.

1957—Elon G. Borton. Borton was born on a farm near Flint, Michigan. He worked his way through school, and graduated from Greenville College in Illinois. He has had some law and post-graduate study at the University of Chicago and Toulouse, France. Borton served in the combat engineers in World War I. He spent some time in retail and wholesale grocery selling, and from 1923 to 1945 was Advertising and Sales Promotion director of La Salle Extension University, Chicago. He also edited a column on mail order advertising in *Advertising Age*.

Active in civic and advertising affairs for many years, Borton served as director of the Chicago Better Business Bureau during 1931-1945. He was a founder, and served as president of the Advertising Managers Club of Chicago, 1934-1935. During 1939-1940 he served as president of the Chicago Federated Advertising Club. He served as president of the Advertising Federation of America (1940-1941), and as board chairman (1941-1943). Borton was elected full-time president and general manager of the A.F.A. in July, 1945, and served in that capacity until 1957.

Borton has visited and addressed over 200 advertising and sales clubs, some of them from two to eight times, and has been said to know as many advertising people personally as any man in America. He has written much for advertising publications and books, and is in demand as a speaker for business and civic organizations and conventions. Borton is a member of the Advertising Advisory Committee of the U.S. Department of Commerce, and he has been vice president of the International Union of Advertising for six years. He is a director of the Advertising Club of New York and the Advertising Council. Borton is also treasurer of the North Carolina Society for Crippled Children and Adults, and is a professional member of the Ben Franklin Chapter of ADS.

Borton has also been awarded the Distinguished Service Key and the Golden Fifty Award by ADS, among various other awards by other organizations, states, firms, clubs, and cities.

1959—Neil H. Borden. Borden was born in Boulder, Colorado, in 1895. He received his bachelor's degree from the University of Colorado in 1919, and his master's degree from Harvard in 1922. Since that time he has served as assistant dean, assistant professor, associate professor, professor, and (currently) professor emeritus for the Harvard Graduate School of Business Administation.

Borden served in the Army during 1918. He has served in several high offices on planning boards, educational committees, etc., in Lexington and Winchester, Massachusetts. He served as vice president of the American Marketing Association in 1949, and as president during 1953-1954. Borden has served also as chairman of the Advertising Review Panel for the Brewing Industry from 1955 to the present. He has been a public trustee of the Marketing Science Institute since 1962. He has also been a consultant to the Indian Institute of Management at Ahmedabad, from 1963-1966. He is a member of the American Economic Association, Phi Betta Kappa, Alpha Tau Omega, and Acacia. Borden's writings are so significant that every student of advertising is undoubtedly familiar with them.

Numerous awards and honors have recognized the work of Neil H. Borden. He received Research Awards from the Kappa Tau Alpha Society and the American Marketing Association in 1945-1946. He was honored with the Distinguished Service Medal in Advertising from Syracuse University in 1949. He received the Paul D. Converse Award from the American Marketing Association in 1951, for advancing the science of marketing. He has been honored for his contributions to distribution and advertising education. In 1964 he received the Advertising Gold Medal Award of *Printer's Ink;* in 1965, the Victor Metaja Medal from the Austrian Society for the Scientific Study of Advertising.

The Borden's have four children. Neil Borden and his wife, Esther, now reside in Winchester, Massachusetts.

1961—Philip Ward Burton. Burton received his undergraduate degrees from Stanford University. He spent several of his early business years as a newspaper reporter and editor in San Jose, Palo Alto, and San Francisco.

Burton's other business experience has been diversified and extensive. He has served as creative director of the Bruce B. Brewer Advertising Agency, as account executive and copywriter of the Ruthrauff & Ryan Advertising Agency, as manager of medical promotion for Bell & Howell Company, and as copy editor of the advertising department of the Proctor & Gamble Company.

At one time, Burton served as a visiting professor at Florida State University. Other academic experience includes his chairmanship of the Advertising Department of the State University of Iowa. Currently, Burton serves as Chairman of the Advertising Department at Syracuse University.

Burton has published eight books and over 150 articles on advertising and public relations. Besides trade publications, his articles have appeared in the *Saturday Evening Post* and *This Week* magazine.

For four years Burton served as director of the Advertising Federation of America. He has also served two terms as national president of ADS. He has previously served on public relations committees for such trade associations as the American Association of Advertising Agencies and the Newspaper Advertising Executives Association. He has been consultant for many large firms, such as General Electric, National Cash Register, and Associated Business Publications. Burton has been listed in *Who's Who in America* for a number of years.

Burton is married and his family includes three children. He now resides in Skaneateles, New York.

1963—C. H. Sandage. Sandage was born in Hatfield, Missouri, in 1902. He was educated at the State University of Iowa, receiving his A.B. in 1926, his M.A. in 1927, and his PhD. in 1931. Sandage served as an assistant professor at Simpson College in 1927-1928 and at the University of Kansas in 1928-1929.

From 1929 to 1946, Sandage served as head of the Department of Marketing at Miami University (Ohio). He has also taught at the University of Cincinnati Evening College and at the University of California as a visiting professor. He served as a visiting professor of business research at the Harvard Graduate School of Business Administration in 1943-1944. Since 1946 Sandage, has served as professor and head of the Department of Advertising at the University of llinois.

Sandage served as chief of the Division of Transportation and Communications for the U.S. Department of Commerce (Bureau of the Census) during 1935-1937. He was vice president and director of research for the Institute of Transit Advertising during 1944-1946. He has been president of the Farm Research Institute since 1946, and has acted as consultant on advertising and marketing for the Federal Communications Commission from 1956 through 1958. He has done private consultation work for many various firms.

Sandage has written four major books (two with Vernon Fryburger) and has contributed to two others. He has contributed eight monographs and numerous magazine and journal articles. Sandage was director of the American Marketing Association from 1944-1947 and 1954-1955, and vice president in 1956-1957. He is a member of: American Economic Association, American Academy of Advertising, Association for Education in Journalism, American Association for Public Opinion Research, Alpha Delta Sigma, Delta Sigma Pi, Phi Betta Kappa, and Kappa Tau Alpha. He was the recipient of the *Printer's Ink* Gold Medal in 1964, and of a special award for contribution to advertising and advertising education by the American Association of Advertising Agencies in 1966.

1965—James Webb Young. Young was born in Covington, Kentucky, on January 20, 1886. With only sixth-grade schooling, Young went to work at the age of twelve. He later joined the J. Walter Thompson Company in 1912 as a copywriter in Cincinnati. Two years later he became manager of the Cincinnati office. In 1917, he moved to the company's New York office as vice president in charge of creative services; later that year, he became joint manager of the western operations with offices in Chicago.

In 1928, Young "retired," but continued on special assignments with the Thompson Company during the next fourteen years. He rejoined the company in 1941 as senior consultant and director, but he spent only six months at the New York headquarters while devoting the rest of his time to his ranch in Santa Fe, New Mexico.

During his so-called retirement, Young was even busier. During 1931-1938, he was professor of business history and advertising at the University of Chicago. With his son, Webb, he founded a business selling by mail the neckties "hand-woven by the mountain people of New Mexico." A study of advertising agency compensation he made in 1934 remains today the "bible on the subject."

From 1936 to 1941 he was also principal owner of *Sunset Magazine;* from 1939 to 1941 he served in Washington as director of the Bureau of Foreign and Domestic Commerce, and director of communications in the Office of Coordinator of Inter-American Affairs.

He is a founder, past chairman, and life director of the Advertising Council (formerly War Advertising Council). He is past president of the American Association of Advertising Agencies, and was named "Man of the Year" in 1945. He is the author of several books on advertising, the best known of which is *A Technique for Producing Ideas.* Young has three sons; he and his wife, Elizabeth, now live on their ranch in New Mexico.

1967—Charles W. "Chick" Collier. Collier attended the University of Missouri and St. Louis University where he studied journalism and advertising. Early in his career he served as advertising manager for a large retail store, a national advertiser, and a national trade magazine. He was field manager of Direct Mail Advertising Association for six years.

Before moving to the Pacific coast, Collier conducted the Chas. W. Collier & Associates firm in Detroit, which served the International Advertising Association, the Direct Mail Advertising Association, and the Detroit Board of Commerce.

In San Francisco, Collier served as advertising and sales manager of a large printing and publishing company. He also re-established his own public relations organization, and served the American Council on Public Relations in working with university programs. He was organizer and first Dean of the School of Advertising at Golden Gate College in San Francisco.

Mr. Collier was a member of the Joint Commission which recommended the merger of the Advertising Association of the West with the Advertising Federation of America. When the merger was approved, he was named Merger Administrator. When it was completed, he was elected first President of the new American Advertising Federation on February 6, 1967, and was re-elected in June, 1967.

Collier is a Director of The Advertising Council, Inc., and the Brand Names Foundation. He was a Forum Member of the U.S. Department of Commerce Committee on Advertising, which is not now operating.

Coinciding with one of his hobbies, Collier was founder of the Limited Editions Book Club of San Francisco. For three years, he served as director of the San Francisco Festival Association. He has served on boards of advertising clubs in St. Louis, Boston, Detroit and San Francisco. He was Western vice president of Alpha Delta Sigma for four years, and on ADS' 50th anniversary, he was selected as a member of the Golden Fifty.

APPENDIX G

Outstanding Chapter Awards
Donald W. Davis Award

Little is known about awards for outstanding chapters prior to 1940. Some chapters had been singled out during national conventions yet records for the early conventions were destroyed in most cases. Minutes from the 1928 national convention revealed that Outstanding Chapter Awards were presented to two schools for that year.

It was during the presidency of Ken R. Dyke in 1940 that a President's Cup Competition was discussed and established by the National Council. Due to World War II it was only given in 1941 before being withheld until after the war was over.

In 1948 the award was begun again and continued to be as a single award for the outstanding chapter until 1954. It was then that the National Council changed from one to two awards: Best Commercial Campaign and Best Public Service.

Again, in 1956, the titles were changed, this time for the Best Project Done in Cooperation with a Profesional Organization and for the Best Chapter Activities. The 1957 and 1958 awards went to best chapters in metropolitan and non-metropolitan areas.

The President's Cup Competition, as such, was ended in 1958 when New York University was given the cup permanently for having consistently had the best activities for the ten years from 1948-1958.

The 1959 chapter awards were entitled "Progress and Efficiency Award" and "Professional Competence Award." The Progress and Efficiency Award was renamed at the 1959 convention in Palo Alto as the Donald W. Davis Competition Award. Donald W. Davis had served as national president from 1947 to 1949. The Pennsylvania State University Chapter bears his name.

The Professional Competence Award was continued until 1962 at which time it was discontinued in favor of the one top chapter award, the Donald W. Davis Award. In addition to the one top chapter on the national basis each year, recognition certificates were given to the top chapter in each of the other four regions.

The top chapter awards presented to date include:

Date   Title of Award—Chapter (School)
1928   Outstanding Chapters — University of Missouri, University of Washington
1941   President's Cup Competition—New York University

1948 President's Cup Competition—Northwestern University
1949 President's Cup Competition—Emory University
1950 President's Cup Competition—New York University
1951 President's Cup Competition—University of Florida
1952 President's Cup Competition—Roosevelt University
1953 President's Cup Competition—University of Oklahoma
1954 President's Cup Competition (Public Service) — University of Iowa
President's Cup Competition (Commercial) — Roosevelt University
1955 President's Cup Competition (Public Service) — Pennsylvania State University
President's Cup Competition (Commercial) — New York University
1956 President's Cup Competition (Best Project) — University of Oregon
President's Cup Competition (Best Chapter) — University of Arizona
1957 President's Cup Competition (Metropolitan) — Babson Institute
President's Cup Competition (Non-Metropolitan) — Pennsylvania State University
1958 President's Cup Competition (Metropolitan) — Roosevelt University
President's Cup Competition (Non-Metropolitan) — Florida State University
1959 Progress and Efficiency Award — Florida State University
Professional Competence Award — Florida State University
1960 Donald W. Davis Award — Babson Institute
Professional Competence Award — City College New York
1961 Donald W. Davis Award — Franklin & Marshall College
Professional Competence Award — University of Arizona
1962 Donald W. Davis Award — University of Houston
Professional Competence Award — University of Arizona, Southern Illinois University
1963 *Donald W. Davis Award — University of Georgia;* Outstanding Midwest Chapter — University of Minnesota; Outstanding East Chapter — Franklin & Marshall College; Outstanding West Chapter — San Jose State College; Outstanding Southwest Chapter — University of Houston.
1964 *Donald W. Davis Award — Southern Illinois University;* Outstanding East Chapter — Franklin & Marshall College; Outstanding Southeast Chapter — University of Georgia; Outstanding Southwest Chapter — University of Houston; Outstanding West Chapter — San Jose State College
1965 *Donald W. Davis Award — Florida State University;* Outstanding Midwest Chapter — Southern Illinois University; Outstanding East Chapter — Babson Institute; Outstand-

ing West Chapter — San Jose State College; Outstanding
Southwest Chapter — Texas Christian University

1966   *Donald W. Davis Award — University of Georgia;* Out-
standing Southwest Chapter — Texas Technological Col-
lege; Outstanding Midwest Chapter — Southern Illinois
University; Outstanding East Chapter — University of
Rhode Island; Outstanding West Chapter — San Jose
State College

1967   *Donald W. Davis Award — Texas Technological College;*
Outstanding East Chapter — City College New York;
Outstanding Midwest Chapter — Southern Illinois Uni-
versity; Outstanding Southeast Chapter — University of
Georgia; Outstanding West Chapter — San Jose State
College

1968   *Donald W. Davis Award — Texas Technological College;*
Outstanding East Chapter — Fairleigh Dickinson Uni-
versity; Outstanding Midwest Chapter — Southern Illinois
University; Outstanding Southeast Chapter — University
of Georgia; Outstanding West Chapter — University of
Washington.

SECTION III
HISTORIES OF UNDERGRADUATE CHAPTERS
HISTORIES OF PROFESSIONAL CHAPTERS

Acknowledgment

Special acknowledgment should be given to the many persons who contributed to this section of this book. Many students and faculty advisors compiled and wrote the histories of the chapters.

It should also be noted that since the preparation of this book has been in progress for four years that many of the histories were written some time ago.

The editors are grateful to Gary L. Stevenson, a teaching assistant at Texas Tech in 1967-68, who organized most of the material in this section.

Raymond Rubicam Chapter
Arizona State University
Tempe, Arizona

Chapter History

The Raymond Rubicam Chapter of Alpha Delta Sigma was formally established at Arizona State University in 1953. Arizona State was then a state college, but in 1958, was recognized and renamed as a university. The chapter has several yearly activities. Each week a chapter member attends the Phoenix Advertising Club luncheons. The chapter works quite closely with this organization. Each year, during Campus Business Week, ADS sponsors various speakers, and during National Advertising Week, the chapter sponsors an advertising campaign on the campus. The annual sandwich board advertising campaign is the major project of the year. ADS at ASU tries to "bridge the gap" by having speakers at almost every meeting. The chapter has grown with Arizona State University and will continue to grow in Alpha Delta Sigma.

Several members of local agencies have spoken and given presentations at regular meetings. The formation of Ads Creative, a chapter-member agency, provides on-the-job experience for members. An end-of-the-year party closes out the year.

Biographical Sketch

Raymond Rubican is well-known to everyone familiar with advertising. He is co-founder and retired chairman and president of Young Rubicam, Inc., New York City. Mr. Rubicam has given advertising such famous phrases as: "the priceless ingredient" for Squibb; "the instrument of the immortals" for Steinway; and "no Rolls Royce has ever worn out."

Mr. Rubicam is a trustee of Colgate University, a member of the Committee for Economic Development, and a director of the American Institute of Foreign Trade. He has been a recipient of the Advertising and Selling Gold Medal Award for Distinguished Service to Advertising.

Elvin G. Wood Chapter
University of Arizona
Tucson, Arizona
John H. Wieland, Advisor

Chapter History

The Elwin G. Wood Chapter of ADS at the University of Arizona was installed on April 30. 1950, by Stanley Swanberg of San Francisco. The first major project was the sponsorship of the March of Dimes 1956 campaign in Tucson, for which the chapter won the President's Cup Award. From 1956 untl 1963, the chapter was among the top chapters in ADS, winning a first or second place award from the National Council every year except 1960.

The chapter has worked closely with the Tucson Advertising Club and has initiated a number of the Ad Club members as professional members of ADS. Chapter members always enter the Ayer's Three-Minute Speaking Contest sponsored by the Advertising Association of the West. On three occasions, members of the chapter have won district finals and advanced to the final contest during the A.A.W. conventions. In 1961 Joe De Nardo, the chapter president, won top honors at the A.A.W. Convention.

Other activities of the chapter have included: participation in the annual A.A.W. Advertising Week program; producing a radio program during Homecoming at the university; and annual publication of a desk blotter for fund-raising purposes.

Dr. Elwin G. Wood, advisor for the chapter, retired in 1963. Dr. John H. Wieland became the chapter advisor at that time.

Biographical Sketch

Dr. Elwin G. Wood received his bachelor's degree from Washington State College, where he also taught from 1920-1922. In 1924 he received his Ph.D. from the University of Wisconsin, earning his master's degree there sometime before. Wood is a native of Montana and a veteran of World War I. In 1920 he married Mabel Florence Clark, and they have two children.

Dr. Wood is a past district dean of the American Academy of Advertising. He is also a member of the American Marketing Association and the Advertising Association of the West. Dr. Wood was honored in 1963 with a Golden Anniversary Medal by ADS National Council for being "one of the outstanding contributors to advertising education during the first 50 years of ADS' history.

Since he became a faculty member of the University of Arizona in 1924, Dr. Wood has distinguished himself in the field of advertising education and in his work with youth groups. He helped organize the ADS chapter in 1950, the University of Arizona Junior Advertising Club of the Advertising Association of the West in 1950, and the Gamma Alpha Chi chapter in 1959. In 1965, the Tucson Advertising Club honored him by presenting him the club's first Silver Medal Award.

George W. Coleman Chapter
Babson Institute
Babson Park, Massachusetts
Edward J. McGee, Advisor

By Marvin Gould and John Stulbarg

Chapter History

On the evening of June 4, 1941, thirty-one men connected with Babson Institute were inducted as charter members into the George W. Coleman Chapter of Alpha Delta Sigma by members of the Bruce Barton Chapter at Boston University. Through the efforts of James E. Borendame Jr., '41, and Bertrand R. Canfield, Director of the Division of Distribution, ADS was founded at Babson. The chapter was named after the President Emeritus of the Institute, George W. Coleman. In May, 1943, the George W. Coleman Chapter was disbanded due to the fact that the student body diminished because of the American war effort. With the end of the war and the subsequent return of many former students, the George W. Coleman Chapter at the Institute was once again activated in October, 1945.

Since that time the fraternity has kept pace with the continuing expansion at Babson Institute. The George W. Coleman Chapter played an important role in the recent development of the new student union on campus. The members were successful in raising a considerable amount of money to contribute to the student fund. In return for their efforts, the George W. Coleman Chapter was given a room in the new student union. This recent development shows that the George W. Coleman Chapter continues to be as dynamic as the Institute itself.

Biographical Sketch

George W. Coleman led a very exciting life climaxed by his presidency of Babson Institute.

Dr. Coleman earned the name of one who cares for his fellow men. Admirers elected him president of the Associated Advertising Clubs of America, delegate-at-large to the Republican National Convention in 1911, and president of the Boston City Council in 1915.

Dr. Coleman was also founder of the Ford Hall Forum. Ford Hall held its first meeting on February 23, 1908.

In 1921, Dr. Coleman received his greatest honor. This was the presidency of Babson Institute. Under this man's wise guidance, the Institute advanced greatly. The administration building, Lyon Hall, the Richard Knight Auditorium, Bryant Hall, the Peavey Gymnasium, Park Manor South, the President's House (now the infirmary), Park Manor, and the Coleman Map Building, which appropriately bears his name were constructed while he was in office. He held the presidency until 1935.

Outstanding Members

GEORGE E. BEST, Class of 1941, Vice President and General Manager, Canada Sand Papers, Ltd.

LAWRENCE F. BRETTA, Class of 1953, Mayor of Somerville, Massachusetts.

DONALD F. DUNN, Class of 1949, Vice President of Control and Operations, Mass Brothers of Tampa, Florida.

ROGER A. GRAVER, Class of 1948, Division Manager, Encyclopedia Britannica.

CHARLES J. McCARTHY, Class of 1950, President, Standard Home Products, Holyoke, Massachusetts.

Bruce Barton Chapter
Boston University
Boston, Massachusetts

Chapter History

During the fall of 1924 a small group of advertising students in the College of Business Administration of Boston University met to formulate plans for the formation of an undergraduate ADS chapter on the campus. On March 18, 1925, the group was granted a charter by the National Council, making it the twelfth officially recognized local chapter of the fraterntiy.

By November, 1927, the membership had grown from eight undergraduates and one faculty member to a total of 40 undergraduate members. The chapter was also honored to receive permission from Bruce Barton to use his name to identify itself.

From its inception the Boston chapter has benefited from strong student leadership and devoted faculty guidance. Recently retired Professor Roger D. Washburn personifies the strong leaders the chapter has enjoyed. The chapter has won several *Linage* awards, and is credited with helping organize the Boston Alumni Association of ADS (the first of its kind) in 1939.

With a recent revision of the advertising program at Boston University, the future of the Bruce Barton Chapter seems bright indeed.

Biographical Sketch

Bruce Barton was born in Robins, Tennessee, on August 5, 1886. He received his A.B. from Amherst College in 1907, his

Litt.D. from Juanita College in 1925, and his L.L.D. from Amherst College in 1957. On October 2, 1913, he married Esther M. Randall. The Bartons had three children.

He began his career in 1907 as the managing editor of *Housekeeper* magazine. Afterwards, he became assistant sales manager for P. F. Collier and Son, and still later, the editor of *Every Week*.

From 1937-1939, Barton served in Congress as the Republican Representative from the 17th New York Congressional District. He was a member of Alpha Delta Phi and Phi Beta Kappa, serving as International President of Alpha Delta Phi from 1942-1947. Mr. Barton was chairman of the board of Batten, Barton, Dustine and Osborn, Inc., before his death in 1967. A noted author, some of his works were *Better Days* (1924), *The Man Nobody Knows* (1925), and *On the Up and Up* (1929).

Lowell Thomas Chapter
University of Colorado
Boulder, Colorado
Chris Burns, Advisor

Chapter History

The Lowell Thomas Chapter of Alpha Delta Sigma was begun at the University of Colorado on May 24, 1949. There were twelve original founders including the advisor, Bruce Smith, then instructor of advertising in the School of Journalism. Professor Chris Burns became advisor of the chapter in the Fall of 1950, and continues today. The chapter was named after the famed broadcaster, Lowell Thomas. A tape recording made by Thomas exorting new members is an important part of every initiation.

Each year the chapter initiates qualified undergraduates and local professional advertising men. The undergraduates serve as the nucleus of the collegiate chapter's activities. The professional members of ADS in Colorado meet with the students at rush parties and initiations and assist the chapter whenever possible.

During the school year the chapter meets socially on occasion. The main function of the group is to work on various advertising and marketing projects. The object of these projects is to acquaint the membership with some of the professional aspects of advertising in correlation with their classroom activities.

Biographical Sketch

Lowell Thomas was born in Woodington, Ohio, in 1892. He

received his B.A. and M.A. from Princeton University in 1916.

Thomas has been an outstanding figure in journalism for many years. He began his career as a reporter and editor of various newspapers in Cripple Creek, Colorado. He was a reporter for the *Chicago Journal* and an instructor in the English Department at Princeton University.

Lowell Thomas' ability to breathe life into the accounts of contemporary events led to his being appointed as chief of the civilian mission sent by President Woodrow Wilson to Europe to prepare a historical report of World War I.

Mr. Thomas first became famous as the discoverer and biographer of Count Felix von Luckner, the famed sea devil of World War I, and also wrote about Lawrence of Arabia, helping make Lawrence known on a worldwide basis.

He is the author of 46 biographical, travel and adventure books, among the latest being *The Seven Wonders of the World, History as You Heard It, and Sir Hubert Wilkins—His World of Adventure.*

Since the 1930's Thomas had become best known as a radio commentator. He was the producer-host of TV's "High Adventure's" series.

His interest in Alpha Delta Sigma inspired the founders of the University of Colorado Chapter to name their new organizatiaon in his honor.

Outstanding Members

E. LEE Fondren, 1965-1966 Chairman of the Board of A.F.A., and past President A.A.W. Mr. Fondren is Manager and Sales Director, KLZ Denver

CLAIR G. HENDERSON, past President of A.A.W. (1955), managing partner of Rippy, Henderson, Buckman & Co. The largest Denver-based AAAA agency.

JEAN K. TOOL, who as Colorado State Republican Chairman helped elect Colorado Governor John Love, and who also managed the campaign of gubernatorial candidate Winthrop Rockefeller (against Orval Faubus) in Arkansas. Mr. Tool is Vice President of Frye-Sills & Bridges, Denver agency.

Gardner Cowles Chapter
Drake University
Des Moines, Iowa

Chapter History

The Gardner Cowles Chapter at Drake University became the seventy-first chapter on May 8, 1964. Dr. Bill Mindak, University of Minnesota advisor and midwestern vice president of ADS, installed the chapter.

Dr. Roland Hicks was the chapter's first advisor, to be followed by Professor Edwin L. Sullivan in November, 1964. The first president of the chapter who reported to the national office was Thomas K. Lauterback.

The Gardner Cowles Chapter was founded by these 11 men; Bruce Brown, Denny Dunlap, Arthur Dwyer, Sanford Glickauf, James Goodwin, Peter Goodwill, Thomas Lauterback, Michael Podolsky, Dennis Waller, Richard Wernts, and Ted West.

Unfortunately, the chapter lost five of these brothers immediately after initiation because of graduation. This left five members with the job of getting the group established. Under the leadership of President Denny Waller, a few business meetings were held at the beginning until it was felt that the chapter was able to add new members. New initiates numbered five, including chapter advisor Neil Bernstein. During the remainder of the year, a luncheon and a dinner were held. The chapter handled the advertising for the campus variety show program, and the members served as tour guides for a Des Moines Ad Club tour of Meredith Hall, home of the Drake Journalism School.

During 1965 the chapter seemed to be on a much firmer footing. The members worked hard to make a name for themselves on campus and they are now trying to do the same with professionals through their "Roundtable" series.

Biographical Sketch

Gardner Cowles was born in Algona, Iowa, on January 31, 1903. He graduated from Phillips Exeter Academy in 1921 and received his A.B. from Harvard in 1925. Cowles received his LL.D. degree from Drake University in 1942. He has also received several other honorary degres.

Cowles became city editor of the *Des Moines Register* in 1925, and news editor in 1926. He was managing editor of the *Des Moines Register* and *Tribune* from 1927 through 1931. He became executive editor in 1931, and associate publisher in 1939; he has been president of the paper since 1943. He is president of Cowles Magazines & Broadcasting (publishers of *Look*), and director of General Development Corporation, R. H. Macy & Co., United Air Lines, Bankers Life Company; and was director of the Office of War Information during 1942-'43. He is a trustee of several major universities and other outstanding organizations. He also belongs to a number of social, trade, and professional Clubs.

Arthur A. Kron Chapter
Fairleigh Dickinson University
Teaneck, New Jersey

Daniel Pliskin, Advisor

Chapter History

On November 11, 1957, Professor Daniel Pliskin and a con- tingent of young ladies, students in advertising and marketing at Fairleigh Dickinson University, participated in the First Annual Career Conference conducted by the Advertising Women of New York at Fordham University. While there the idea of Alpha Delta Sigma was born for Fairleigh Dickinson University through the office of Professor Albert G. Romano of Fordham University. Professor Romano explained the significance of Alpha Delta Sigma and outlined the procedures to be followed. He pointed out that if a collegiate chapter was established at Fairleigh Dickinson University, it would be the first in the State of New Jersey. Furthermore, he indicated that the first step toward this goal would be the creation of an Advertising Club on the campus Following Professor Romano's *modus operandi*, an Advertising Club was established at Fairleigh Dickinson University shortly thereafter.

After a few years of successful operation, the former New Jersey Professional Chapter of Alpha Delta Sigma, upon hearing about the Fairlegh Dickinson University Advertising Club, in- vited the students to attend their meetings. After establishing pleasant rapport, the Professional Chapter indicated that they were eager to sponsor an undergraduate chapter at Fairleigh Dickinson University.

On February 26, 1960, Fairleigh Dickinson University made inquiries to the National Office concerning the formation of a chapter of Alpha Delta Sigma at Teaneck. Material was forwarded from Missouri, the National Office, and efforts were made to meet standing requirements. After considerable appraisal and corre- spondence, the bid for an Alpha Delta Sigma membership was rejected. This, of course, created a considerable amount of un- happiness on the campus.

The rejection, although disheartening, never really was a swan-song, since the Professional Chapter in New York and the students themselves continued to discuss the possibility of re- applying.

On April 16, 1963, Kurt Brown, corresponding secretary of the Advertising Club, requested information concerning the possibility of joining the national professional advertising fra- ternity. The National Offce forwarded the essential material and the first steps were made towards establishing the Arthur A. Kron Chapter of Fairleigh Dickinson University.

On December 16, 1963, Donald G. Hileman extended an offi- cial invitation to petition for a chapter. The formal petition was voted on and accepted in June, 1964. Since the semester was over, it was felt by the chartered members that the time to have the installation ceremonies would be the Fall of 1964.

Finally, all forces were gathered and the installation took place on Friday evening, November 20, 1964, during the Annual Founder's Day Dinner of the New York City Professional Chapter at the Advertising Club of New York.

Among those charter members who attended were: Arthur A. Kron, Professor Daniel Pliskin, faculty adviser, Jeffrey Alan Adler, George Biava, William Jon Blum, Ronald Henry Boyaiian, Kurt Brown, Charles O. Delisle, Peter R. Fisher, Steven Flehinger, Theodore Gibbons, Lawrence John Golczewski, Steven Klinkowize, Jr., and Donald Joseph Sullivan, Jr. Other charter members were David Laveton and Edward Robert Zarucha. The group was further honored by having Professor Albert G. Romano and a few Brothers from Fordham University participate in the ceremonies.

Dr. Noel P. Laird, National Treasurer, conducted the installation ceremony and attempted to initiate the group. However, as the ceremony was about to begin it was discovered that there were no ritual booklets. Consequently, the Chapter was installed, but not officially initiated until March 12, 1965, when Professor Romano and representatives from the Manhattan College Chapter performed the ritual ceremony at the Teaneck Campus of Fairleigh Dickinson University.

The first slate of officers for the Arthur A. Kron Chapter were: Steven Klinkowize, Jr., president; Lawrence J. Golczewski, vice president; Kurt Brown, professional vice president; Charles O. Delisle, social vice president; Peter R. Fisher, treasurer; Jeffrey A. Adler, recording secretary; William J. Blum, corresponding secretary; Donald J. Sullivan, Jr., sergeant-at-arms; Theodore Gibons, alumni secretary; George Biava, publicity director.

Biographical Sketch

The new Alpha Delta Sigma Chapter at Fairleigh Dickinson University became known as the Arthur A. Kron Chapter. Mr. Kron, a member of the Board of Trustees of Fairleigh Dickinson University, is chairman of the board and president, Gotham-Vladimir Advertising, Inc., New York. He is also president of the Board of Trustees of Englewood Hospital, Englewood, N.J., and honorary chairman, Northern Valley Chapter, American International Red Cross.

Active in a number of trade associations and past president of many of them, Mr. Kron was founder of the International Advertising Convention and was International Advertising "Man of the Year" in 1958. He is a resident of Teaneck, N.J.

**Leo Burnett Chapter
Ferris State College**

Big Rapids, Michigan
Roland Hicks, Robert A. Sprague, Advisors

By Duane G. Thon

Chapter History

The Leo Burnett Chapter of Alpha Delta Sigma was organized in 1963-64 as a result of a series of meetings held by Thomas Parker, Brian Klumpp, and Dr. Roland Hicks. The chapter was officially recognized on the campus òf Ferris State College February 28, 1964. Tom Parker was the primary force in getting the student chapter organized. He explained the functions of Alpha Delta Sigma to several marketing students and a chartered group was formed.

Through the efforts of Dr. Hicks the charter was brought before the National Council of Alpha Delta Sigma and was approved by them for installation May 31, 1964. Ten charter members were inducted on June 25 at an initiation presided over by Dr. Billy Ross, national president of Alpha Delta Sigma. The principal speaker at this induction ceremony was Professor John Crawford, Head of the Department of Advertising at Michigan State University.

The charter members include: Michael A. Barcy, Michael Davis Heideman, Gary F. Jenkins, Brian M. Klump, Thomas H. Lamoreaux, William R. Lepech, Scott A. McInnis, Thomas H. McSunas, Henry T. Parker, Thomas F. Parker, John J. Patterson, Ronald S. Sarkon, Graeme Stewart, Norman G. Striber, Robert F. Tarnopol, and Richard G. Webber.

Biographical Sketch

The Ferris State College of Alpha Delta Sigma is named after Leo Burnett, chairman of the board, Leo Burnett Company, Inc. His birthplace is St. Johns, Michigan, where he received his first exposure to advertising in his father's store.

The University of Michigan graduate's first agency experience was with the Homer McKee Company as a writer. He later joined the Erwin, Wassey and Company agency as vice President and creative head.

On August 5, 1935, with eight associates, he formed Leo Burnett Company, Inc. From three accounts in 1935, the company has grown to one of the largest in the country.

Mr. Burnett, married for forty-eight years, is the father of three children, and the grandfather of ten.

He has been a director of The Advertising Council since 1942 and is presently vice chairman of the board, director of the Chicago Better Business Bureau, and past director of the nonpartisan Register and Vote campaigns for The Advertising

Council in both 1952 and 1956.

In 1956, he was co-recipient of the *Printer's Ink* Gold Medal Award and in 1957 was named by Loyola University as one of Chicago's one hundred outstanding citizens.

Elon G. Borton Chapter
Florida State University
Tallahassee, Florida

Chapter History

The Elon G. Borton Chapter of Alpha Delta Sigma was formally installed on the Florida State University campus on June 1, 1953, becoming the 58th ADS chapter in the nation.

The chapter is named after one of America's outstanding leaders of advertising, Elon Borton. Former president of the Advertising Federation of America, Borton has been called "Mr. Advertising" by professional advertising men. Now retired, he lives in Chapel Hill, North Carolina.

The first faculty advisor was Dr. Royal H. Ray, Chairman of the Department of Advertising. The President during the first year was Louis Calderoni. Professor Richard Joel was advisor from 1955 to 1967.

Biographical Sketch

Elon G. Borton was born on a Michigan farm in 1889. He received his A.B. Degree from Greenville College in Illinois, studied law at the University of Chicago, and also studied at the University of Toulouse, France. He was a first sergeant in the combat engineers in World War I.

Mr. Borton was director of advertising and mail sales, LaSalle Extension University, Chicago, from 1923-1945; president of Chicago Federated Advertising Club from 1940-1941; president of the Advertising Managers' Club in Chicago from 1935-1936; president of A.F.A. from 1941-1942; chairman of A.F.A. from 1942-1943; and A.F.A. president and general manager from 1945-1957.

He is the author of "A.F.A. Statement of Principles" and "Questions and Answers About Advertising;" editor of "Directory of Advertising, Marketing, and Public Relations Education in the United States;" and columnist on direct mail for *Advertising Age* from 1943-1945 and 1957-1958.

Mr. Borton's A.D.S. honors are: professional member of the Ben Franklin Chapter at Penn State University; Honorary Member of the Paul Thompson Chapter at the University of Texas; Distinguished Service Key; Golden Fifty Award; and Charles R. Nichols Cup for The Greatest Contribution to Advertising Education since 1955.

H. W. Prentis, Jr., Chapter
Franklin and Marshall College
Lancaster, Pennsylvania

Chapter History

The H. W. Prentis, Jr., Chapter was installed on the Franklin and Marshall College campus 27 years ago on May 29, 1937. Arthur Hallen, national secretary-treasurer, initiated and installed 28 students with Dr. Noel P. Laird, professor of Economics and Business Administration, as chapter advisor. Also initiated were former college president, Dr. John A. Shaeffer, and former dean, Richard W. Bomberger. The chapter developed from the Distribution Society which had functioned for several years. One of the charter members, Hiram P. Ball, Pittsburgh industrialist, is now a member of the college Board of Trustees.

Today the chapter is unique in that it is a small, slective, closely knit and exceptionally active organization for its size, not withstanding the fact that an advertising major is no longer offered in this liberal arts institution. The 13th oldest collegiate institution in the U.S., Franklin and Marshall College was originally chartered in 1787.

Recently the chapter placed first in the Donald W. Davis activities award competition. In recent times it was third, fourth, or fifth in the annual national competition.

Biographical Sketch

Henning W. Prentis, Jr., for whom the Franklin and Marshall College chapter was named, was born in St. Louis, Missouri, July 11, 1884, and died in Lancaster, Pa., October 29, 1959. He received his BA from the University of Missouri in 1903 and his M.A. from the University of Cincinnati in 1907. He was one of America's most distinguished citizens. During his life, twelve institutions awarded him honorary doctoral degrees.

Before joining the Armstrong Cork Company in 1907 he had served as secretary to the president of the University of Missouri and as secretary of the University of Cincinnati. He was manager of Armstrong's first advertising department from 1911 to 1920 and became general sales manager in 1920. He was elected a member of the Board of Directors and one of its vice presidents in 1926, and was promoted to first vice president in 1929. Prentis was elected president of the Armstrong Cork Company in 1934 and elected Chairman of the Board in 1950, an office he continued to hold until his death.

He was a director of many organizations, a well known speaker and writer, trustee of six educational institutions (including F. & M. College), and a good friend of Alpha Delta Sigma.

He was a member of the Franklin and Marshall College chapter, which is honored to bear his name.

Outstanding Members

ROBERT A. McLAUGHLIN, Vice President, Fiber Glass Division of Pittsburgh Plate Glass Co.

JAMES KILPATRICK, Vice President, First National Bank, Newark, New Jersey.

WILLIAM L. RUTH, President and Treasurer, William G. Leininger Co., and President Treasurer of the Wilton Hosiery Co., both of Mohnton, Pa.

MAJOR JAMES G. Henderson, Director of the Salvation Army Social Welfare Services, Greater New York Metropolitan area

HIRAM P. BALL, President, Ball Chemical Co., Glenshaw, Pa.

THEODORE A. DISTLER, (LL.D., 1957 from F. & M.) F. & M. College President Emeritus, Lancaster, Pa.

Samuel C. Dobbs Chapter
University of Georgia
Athens, Georgia
Alen Fletcher, Advisor

By Carlos L. Zellner

Chapter History

Chartered on April 30, 1954, the University of Georgia chapter became the sixtieth chapter of ADS formed in the United States. It was named for Samuel C. Dobbs, former advertising manager and later President of the world-famous Coca-Cola Company.

Professor Leonard J. Hippchen, an ADS member at the University of Texas, was the first chapter advisor. Professor Hamilton Frazier Moore followed Mr. Hippchen as faculty advisor upon the former's invitation to become a professional member on November 17, 1955.

The University of Georgia chapter won honorable mention in the chapter activities division in 1956 and honorable mention in the non-metropolitan division of the President's Award competition in 1958. During the 1962-63 school year, the Dobbs Chapter took three giant steps forward and captured the Donald W. Davis Award for the most outstanding chapter in the nation and has remained in the top ten ranking since that time.

In 1955 the Georgia chapter organized a student advertising agency, which has subsequently become a major professional activity of the school. Journalism production credit is given to students for participation in its projects. Ad Lab, as it was named, is directed by a member of ADS and is under the supervision of the head of the advertising-public relations sequence of study. Most of the projects are handled as a public service for the School and University, community organizations, and charitable causes. However, Ad Lab successfully handled several small advertising accounts for local business firms. A pioneer development in the teaching of advertising, Ad Lab has proven a tremendous success.

Biographical Sketch

A poor farm boy and a multi-millionaire—two personalities, yet one and the same—marked the outerlimits of the career of Samuel Candler Dobbs.

An illiterate farm boy who rose to become one of the great and dynamic forces in the advertising profession and president of the Coca-Cola Company, Dobbs was one of the fathers of modern advertising. At the age of forty-one, having already established a distinguished reputation for himself in advertising and sales for Coca-Cola, he was, in 1909, named President of the Associated Advertising Clubs of America (later the Advertising Federation of America). He served two terms—two years that saw great changes take place in the policies and organization of advertising in the United States.

Mr. Dobbs believed advertising is valuable only if true. It was in his acceptance speech as president of the national group of advertising clubs in Louisville, Kentucky, that Mr. Dobbs inaugurated a campaign for truth in advertising. From then on, he and the Association waged an unrelenting war against wildcat advertising schemes and crooked promoters. He and his organization drew up rules of ethics, barred misleading ads, and generally raised the tone of advertising to the position of honesty and good taste that it enjoys today. His work won for him the title of "founding father of organized advertising in America."

During his presidency, he traveled 45,000 miles at his own expense and spread the doctrine of "Truth in Advertising" far and wide. The crusade he launched seemed at first almost a lone and personal battle, but the torch he carried spread into flame from one end of the country to another. He retired from office recognized as an internationally known figure in the advertising world.

—Presented at Chicago Convention of Advertising Federation of America, June 16, 1953.

A. B. Penny Chapter
University of Houston

Chapter History

From the matrix of metropolis Houston, steeped in oil, industry and space, the University of Houston has emerged as one of America's fastest growing universities. A unique Communication Arts Department within the College of Letters and Sciences and a fine curriculum in the College of Business Administration offer students interesting avenues to the study of advertising.

Student interest crystalized in 1948 with the founding of the University of Houston Advertising Club. The club applied to Alpha Delta Sigma in 1950, and was inaugurated as the A .B. Penny Chapter the following year. Among the 26 charter members was Jack Valenti, formally a Presidential Advisor and now President of Motion Picture Association.

The chapter won the Donald W. Davis Award for 1961-62, was honored by the installation of former Chapter President Tim Alban as National Student Vice President in 1962, and received Junior Membership in the Houston Advertising Club in 1963. Former Chapter President John Daigle served as Student Regional Vice President.

Biographical Sketch

Professional discipline, honesty, engaging personality, and an interest in young people are the extraordinary qualities of Alvis Burnett (Abe) Penney. He retired in 1962 as Public Relations Advisor for the Humble Oil and Refining Company. During his colorful career Abe was legend for his patriotic, civic, and professional activities. He served as President of the Houston Advertising Club, Governor of Advertising Federation of America, President of Industrial Advertising Association of Houston, National Vice President of AFA, and was commissioned an "Arkansas Traveler." Abe now enjoys exercising his talent for writing. He has completed one novel, *Three Cheers from River Bend*, and is hard at work on another.

Virgil D. Reed Chapter
Indiana University
Bloomington, Indiana
Jean Halterman, Advisor

Chapter History

The Virgil Reed chapter of Alpha Delta Sigma was founded

in 1932. Since its inception at Indiana University, ADS suffered a period of growing pains and struggled for recognition from the faculty and students.

The initial membership centered mainly around business students interested in marketing, with the chapter becoming a subsidiary of the Marketing Club. With the advent of broader concepts, the Virgil Reed chapter has grown into one of the largest membership of the sixty-one chapters in the United States.

Under the expert tutelage of Professor Jean Halterman, Dwight Riter, and Edward Van Riper, the chapter began an energetic rush program designed to attract the man whose future was in the advertising field. On December 5, 1963, 41 new initiates joined ADS in the realization that better learning and knowledge in the complex and growing field of advertising was now reality.

Not satisfied with merely being the largest chapter of ADS in the United States, the Virgil Reed chapter of Indiana University is determined to achieve greater recognition in professional and social activities.

The chapter sponsors the "coffee hour" at the Indiana University Marketing Seminar that has top executives in the fields of marketing and advertising presenting the growing scope of the fields today.

Charles H. Dennis Chapter
University of Illinois
Urbana, Illinois

Chapter History

The Charles H. Dennis Chapter of Alpha Delta Sigma was actually installed twice at the University of Illinois; the first chapter was installed in 1914 and became inactive in 1932. Eleven years later, March 27, 1943, the present chapter was installed by a team from the University of Missouri.

This second chapter was the successor to Gamma Theta Phi, founded in 1931. This vigorous local organization dedicated itself, according to its constitution, to "Truth, Acuracy, Impartiality, Sincerity, and Courage in Journalism."

World War II, of course, was hard on the fraternity; and finally when the lone draft-exempt member was graduated, its activities were suspended. The chapter was re-activated April 5, 1946, and has continued on an active basis throughout the past eighteen years.

The original chapter on the campus chose to honor one of their illustrious alumni, Charles H. Dennis, by taking his name for the chapter.

Biographical Sketch

Charles H. Dennis was a famous editor. He was associated with the *Chicago Daily News* for 50 years, at one time or another holding almost every editorial position—including that of Editor-in-Chief. He was Editor Emeritus of the *Daily News* when he died on February 8, 1943, at the age of 83.

At the University of Illinios, Mr. Dennis was editor-in-chief of the *Daily Illini*, the campus newspaper, in his senior year. He was instrumental in helping change that publication (then called the *Illini*) from a monthly to a semi-monthly. He was elected to Phi Beta Kappa and was president of his class in his junior year. He graduated in 1881, was given an honorary Master of Arts degree by the University in 1905, and was at one time president of the University's Alumni Association.

L. N. Flint Chapter
Kansas University
Lawrence, Kansas
Mel Adams, Advisor

By Dave Anderson

Chapter History

The earliest advertising organization on the campus of the University of Kansas was the Advertising Club. Records indicate that this organziation was formed in either 1919 or 1920. This organization, on February 25, 1925, became the Lou Holland Chapter of Alpha Delta Sigma.

In 1925 the Kansas chapter had only seven members. The president was Andrew Wise and the secretary was Carl Coffelt. The other five members were Ellis Van Camp, Clark Rose, Myron Taggert, Elliott McKean, and Othel Sherwood.

At the first formal meeting of the Kansas chapter of Alpha Delta Sigma, L. N. Flint and W. A. Dill, both instructors in journalism, were made honorary members.

Kansas was then the 13th chapter in the nation. Kansas and Missouri had the only chapters of Alpha Delta Sigma in the entire Missouri Valley.

In the first year, Wise represented Kansas at the Associated Advertising Clubs of the World in Houston, Texas. At that meeting were more than 5,000 delegates, representing 26 countries.

Then the Depression struck and men's minds were filled with the problems of day-to-day living. In 1929 the chapter had no members, and in 1930 the charter was lost.

But Alpha Delta Sigma was not lost to the University of Kansas. Professors of journalism and former members kept alive the ideals of Alpha Delta Sigma. Finally, on May 9, 1942, the L. N. Flint chapter of Alpha Delta Sigma was granted a new charter.

Initiation of the eight new members was conducted by members of the Missouri chapter. The eight members were Mel Adams, Charlie Carr, Art Cook, Cliff Crain, LeMozne Frederick, Wally Kunkel, Wilbur McCool, and John Pope.

Then the war years stripped the universities across the country of their men. During the war years, only two men were enrolled in the School of Journalism at Kansas University.

Finally, on May 22, 1947, the first post-war meeting of Alpha Delta Sigma was held. At this meeting 13 pledges were initiated by 4 former Kansas charter members.

During the last few years the Kansas chapter of Alpha Delta Sigma has attended meetings at the Ad Clubs in Kansas City and Topeka. It has sponsored speakers from across the nation in the field of advertising, and has invited both students and professional people to hear these speakers. One day each school year is set aside as "Advertising Day on Campus" and speakers are invited to speak before interested students. This has been so successful that the School of Journalism dismisses classes on the day these speakers are to appear.

Biographical Sketch

L. N. Flint was one of the most beloved men in the newspaper business. He was a commanding force for good in Kansas journalism for more than 40 years. He believed that a newspaper should have a conscience.

L. N. Flint was born in Thayer on October 8, 1875. He attended Lawrence High School and went on to graduate from Kansas University with a degree in philosophy in 1897. After being principal of Olathe High School, he became a teacher at Lawrence High. From 1901-1905, he became editor of the *Manhattan Nationalist*.

In 1905 L. N. Fint became the first general secretary of the Kansas University Alumni Association. He became the editor of the graduate magazine in 1916. He was the author of three texts.

He organized the annual conferences of high school editors and annual meetings of Kansas editors in 1920. In 1931 he organized the Kansas Editors' Hall of Fame.

A member of the Kansas Editorial Association and Phi Beta Kappa, L. N. Flint was past President of the American Association of Schools and Departments of Journalism and past President of the K. U. Alumni Association. He organized the K. U. Press Club and the Kansas Council of Teachers of Journalism.

The Journalism Building at Kansas University was named in his honor. The Kansas chapter of Alpha Delta Sigma was named in his honor in 1941.

L. N. Flint was a pioneer teacher and administrator who fought to establish journalism as a respected major curriculum in universities and to win the cooperation of editors and publishers. He took an active interest in everyone around him and was always ready with sympathy and advice.

As a teacher he inspired the best work his students could do. Called "Daddy" Flint by students and colleagues, he trained students whose names are by-words in American journalism.

Professor Flint began teaching as an instructor in journalism in 1906 and became chairman of the newly created Department of Journalism.

L. N. "Daddy' Flint, Chairman of the Department of Journalism from 1916 to 1941, died at the age of 79 from a hip fracture after suffering a fall. He died Friday, September 30, at the University of Kansas Medical Center.

The Kansas Council of Teachers created the L. N. Flint Loan, a scholarship in his honor.

L. N. Flint, the teacher, the journalist, the gentleman, is gone ... but he will never be forgotten while his name and deeds remain engraved in the hearts of all whom he helped and encouraged.

Outstanding Members

MAC F. CAHAL, Publisher, *General Practice Magazine* in Kansas City, Missouri.

DALE O'BRIEN, President, Mayer and O'Brien Public Relations in Chicago, New York, and Holywood.

MILTON L. PEEK, Ad Manager, *Ladies Home Journal.*

LESTER SUHLER, Vice President, *Look Magazine.*

ROBERT M. TRUMP, Vice President and Account Executive, Foote, Cone, Belding Inc., Chicago.

BURT COCHRAN, Pacific Coast Manager, McCann-Erickson Agency, Los Angeles.

JOHN HARVEY, Account Executive, Leo Burnett Inc., Chicago.

LEO FLANAGAN, owner of public relations firm in Chicago.

HARRY TURNER, JR., President of the National Association of Ad Distributors.

E. Julian Herndon Chapter
Little Rock University
Little Rock, Arkansas
Gene G. McCoy, Advisor

By Donald W. Keene

Chapter History

The Little Rock University chapter of ADS was founded during the fall of 1966, largely through the efforts of the Little Rock Advertising Club and Mr. Gene G. McCoy.

Advertising was first offered during the 1966-'67 school year, and the first degree with the major was offered in 1968.

ADS at Little Rock University had nine charter members. Today that number has climbed to 25 members—all with a major or minor in advertising.

L.R.U. sent five delegates and an advisor to the national convention in Houston during their first official semester as an active chapter of Alpha Delta Sigma.

The members of ADS at Little Rock attend all of the meetings of the Little Rock Advertising Club. In this way they take an active step in bridging the gap between the classroom and the professional world.

The members of ADS make up the advertising staff of the school paper, *Forum*, and the school annual, *Trojan*.

The Little Rock chapter meets twice a month to cover all school and social business, and twice a month with the Little Rock Ad Club to hear professional speakers and converse with the members.

Biographical Sketch

The Little Rock chapter honors E. Julian Herndon, who, for nearly forty years, served the *Arkansas Democrat* as vice president and advertising director. Julian Herndon got his start in newspaper advertising in his home town of Richmond, Virginia, by working in the advertising departments of both Richmond newspapers. Then he moved to Raleigh, North Carolina, to assume the job of advertising manager of the *News and Osverver*. In 1920 he went to Fort Worth, Texas, joining the *Record* (later merged with Hearst's *Star-Telegram*) as national advertising manager. He moved to the *Arkansas Democrat* in 1925 where he remained until his death in 1965.

In addition to his professional experience, Mr. Herndon gave much time to development of the programs of the Ad Clubs, the Advertising Federation of America, and the newspaper advertising organizations. He received the AFA-AAW-*Printer's Ink* "Silver Medal" award; he was Governor of the Tenth District of the AFA; he served both the Fort Worth and Little Rock Ad Clubs as president; and he was a charter member of the Midwest Newspapers Executives Association, an organization he served as president in 1934. As Gene McCoy says, "He was one of the finest gentlemen I've ever known!"

William Bernbach Chapter
Long Island University
Brooklyn, New York
August St. John, Advisor

By John T. Petersen

Chapter History

The William Bernbach Chapter of Alpha Delta Sigma is located at Long Island University. It was founded in 1956 by Professor Carl Rosner. Mitchel Sherman, account executive at Cunningham and Walsh, was the first president. The chapter is young, yet at last report it was the second largest in the country.

In the past the chapter has tried to bring its members into close contact with leaders in the advertising field. To accomplish this, seminars have been staged, and speakers have been invited by the chapter to speak to the students of marketing as well as members of the chapter. Tours of some of the top advertising agencies in New York City have been arranged both as an introduction to leaders in the field and as a method of supplying first hand knowledge of the advertising field.

The chapter is a member of the Metropolitan Collegiate Marketing Council and takes an active part in the activities of the council. One of the programs is the "Intro" program. This program is designed to provide students with the opportunity to obtain interviews for job positions after graduation. Another program is that of securing part time on-the-job training for students through the offices of the American Marketing Association.

Biographical Sketch

William Bernbach was born in New York City in 1911 and attended public schools in the city. He received a Bachelor of Arts degree from New York University in 1932 where he majored in English and also studied music.

His first job during the depression years was as an office boy in New York with Schenley Distillers. While working in the mailroom, he wrote an ad for a Schenley whiskey that was printed word-for-word and got him a job in the company's advertising department. Later he worked as a ghost writer at the New York World's Fair and as a copywriter for the William Weintraub Agency.

Following a stint in the United States Army and a job in post-war planning with Coty Inc., Bernbach joined Grey Advertising as a copywriter and soon became Grey's vice president in charge of copy and art. On June 1, 1949, Bernbach and

Ned Doyle, who was also with Grey, joined with Maxwell Dane who had been running a small advertising agency of his own, to form Doyle, Dane, Bernbach.

The agency started with the Ohrbach's account and a philosophy of low pressure, uncluttered advertising built on honest, striking ideas, but no gimmicks—in short, as Bernbach has described it, "advertising that is provocative but with a purpose." Within a decade the agency's billings had soared to more than 40 million dollars, and today DDB is billing about 230 million dollars. Bernbach is a director of the American Association of Advertising Agencies and has been chairman of its Committee on Improving Artistic Content.

Outstanding Members

MITCHELL SHERMAN, Class of 1956, VP-Account Supervisor, Cunningham and Walch.

HORACE MALFA, Class of 1956, VP-Account Supervisor, Cunningham and Walsh.

PAUL ZUCKERMAN, Class of 1956, Assistant Media Director, Ogilvy, Benson and Mather.

LEROY BENJAMIN, Class of 1958, VP, Audits and Survey Inc,, a research firm.

LEONARD GALPA, Creative Director, Sudler and Hennessey.

Eldridge Peterson Chapter
Manhattan College
Riverdale, New York
Alfred Manduley, Advisor

By Ronald F. Vazzano

Chapter History

On May 21, 1957 the following telegram arrived at Manhattan College:

"To Prof. John Enders
Manhattan College, Riverdale
CONGRATULATIONS ENTHUSIASTIC MAJORITY OF CHAPTERS VOTES APPROVAL YOUR PETITION. PLEASE PROCEED WITH INSTALLATION PLANS. LETTER FOLLOWS.

MILTON GROSS"

This was it. Manhattan College had been admitted into the ranks of Alpha Delta Sigma.

In the many busy months preceeding, this had been the sole goal of the founding fathers. This was the something that Manhattan had needed, a professional fraternity that would help its marketing majors make the long step from academic knowledge to practical application in the business world.

The notion of consolidating the students of Marketing into a chapter of ADS had originated in the spring of 1956. The Marketing Club had just finished attending the Marketing Conference, and Professor John Enders, an ADS member from his years at N.Y.U., mentioned the Fraternity and its aims to Alfred Manduley, then a marketing junior. This was all that Mr. Manduley needed. He immediately started to sound out and recruit interested marketing majors. A petitioning organization was set up in the Club's first fall meetings, where it received an enthusiastic approval.

To produce financial proof of their sincerity the members conducted a raffle. And, in May of 1957, the infant chapter was accepted by the National Headquarters of ADS.

Finally, on the evening of June 13 at the New York Advertising Club, the Eldridge Petersen Chapter of Alpha Delta Sigma was born. Six distinguished professional members and twenty-nine undergraduates went through the initiation and induction ceremonies.

Biographical Sketch

Eldridge Peterson, for whom the Manhattan College Chapter of Alpha Delta Sigma has been named, is a man well known throughout the City of New York. In fact, because of his prominence as a publisher, he is familiar to the entire country.

Born March 1, 1905, Mr. Peterson showed great scholastic promise as a young lad. When the time came for him to go to college, he chose New York University as the place to further his education. Upon graduation in 1926, he joined the ranks of *Printer's Ink Magazine,* as a reporter. He held this position until 1938 when he was promoted to News Editor. Futher promotions soon followed: Associate Editor, Executive Editor, and Editor in 1946. In 1956, he assumed the position of Publisher of the magazine.

Through the years Mr. Peterson has indulged in numerous outside activities. He was the editor of the National Conference of Business Papers, and director of the Advertising Club of New York. Among other fraternal organizations he is a brother in both Delta Sigma Pi, a business fraternity, and Sigma Delta Chi, the journalism fraternity.

Currently, Mr. Peterson edits the fund-raising publications at Pace College in New York City.

Chapter History

The C. Brooks Smeeten Chapter of ADS at Marquette was founded on April 12, 1954, under co-sponsors C. Brooks Smeeten of Business Administration and Clifford L. Helbert of Journalism.

Two major traditions of the chapter are the annual advertising tour to Chicago (held over the semester break), and the annual Sweetheart Contest (held in November).

The professional activities of ADS at Marquette include tours of firms involved in advertising, and the appearance of professional speakers. Each of these activities takes place once a month. During the annual tour to Chicago such firms as J.Walter Thompson and Foote, Cone & Belding are visited. An advertising symposium is also held annually, and the most recent version had the theme of ''The Ethical Responsibility of the Advertiser.'' Pledging occurs twice a year for the chapter.

The main social activity is the sweetheart selection, and the sweetheart acts as fraternity hostess at all university functions. Other social activities are occasional parties and an annual dinner dance held at the end of each year.

In January, 1958, the Lucus-McDonnell Pledge Award was established. The award takes the form of a trophy, and is presented to a pledge based on his attitude, performance, and service to the fraternity.

For a number of years, the fraternity had conducted a Career Day for young people interested in advertising. More recently, the fraternity has been sponsoring the annual symposium. This activity helps stimulate a great deal of enthusiasm among the brothers and other interested individuals as well. The history of ADS at Marquette has been marked by continued progress in ''bridging the gap between advertising theory and experience'' for its brothers.

Biographical Sketch

Professor C. Brooks Smeeten has been at Marquette since September 1, 1950. Professor Smeeten had formerly taught at Notre Dame during 1940-1946. He holds the Bachelor of Science and Master of Business Administration degrees from Northwestern University.

Professor Smeeten has not only been outstanding in his academic career, but he is also highly acknowledged in the advertising world for his continued contributions to the profession. In his eleven years as sponsor of ADS at Marquette, he has devoted much time and energy to the attainment of fraternity goals.

Charles G. Mortimer Chapter
University of Maryland
College Park, Maryland
Dr. Roy Ashmen, Advisor

By Dr. Roy Ashmen

Chapter History

The Charles G. Mortimer Chapter of Alpha Delta Sigma at the University of Maryland was installed on May 13, 1960.

A letter in April, 1959, from Dr. Roy Ashmen, University of Maryland, to Milton Gross, National Secretary, requesting information on the procedure for establishing a chapter, heralded the chapter's gestation period, so to speak. To meet the paper work requirements, obtain official approvals, and secure the minimum ten initial pledges appeared on the surface to constitute a simple task. This conception was erroneous.

In early 1960, the chances for the chapter seeing the light of day appeared rather dim indeed. The fact is that some of the most energetic pledges had already graduated and moved away. An emergency approach was needed. The handful of pledges remaining were persuaded to sit down at a war advertising council in April and plan recruiting strategy. After much discussion, an organized and systematic plan of attack evolved which was vigorously implemented , and resulted in the birth of the chapter. Twenty men were initiated. Since this was accomplished in the latter part of the spring semester, the success of the effort was considered no less than phenomenal.

The first ten charter members of the chapter were Dr. Roy Ashmen (advisor), Calvin Longacre, Bradley W. Becker, William Cook, Ralph L. Vitale, Joel K. Rubenstein, Harold Gershowitz, Wayne H. Bethards, Kenneth S. Fedder, and Ernest Freda. The long wait for membership would appear to entitle several of these men to be here listed at least for their faith and financial fortitude. Calvin Longacre should be singled out, however, for spearheading the initial campaign in the spring and fall of 1959.

The following are the past presidents of the chapter: Calvin Longacre (pro tem), William Cook, Robert E. Geiger, Donald Box, Phillip V. Johnson, Richard J. Rose, Larry A. Pearson, Charles C. Hinkel, and William P. Thomas, Jr. The newly elected president is Harold Hoffman.

Space does not permit eulogizing all of those who have helped to "bridge the gap" in the nation's capital. Kudos to them and to the student officers and members who have given unstintingly of their time and energy, and whose loyal support has given continued impetus to the chapter's growth. Many have earned accolades.

Biographical Sketch

The Alpha Delta Sigma Chapter at the University of Maryland bears the name of Charles G. Mortimer.

In his 1959 report to stockholders, Charles G. Mortimer, President of the General Foods Corporation, offered an explanation of the "Why" of his company's advertising expenditures that has become a classic. "Advertising, he said, "develops such a large and dependable volume of sales that the company can keep its plants running at high efficiency, can utilize its personnel to full advantage, can turn its inventories and materials rapidly, and can protect the future value of its stock by maintaining a sound rate of company growth."

Viewing advertising from the corporate apex, and with a distinguished career in advertising and marketing behind him, Mr. Mortimer was able to subordinate the usual departmental explanation of advertising's worth and relate advertising explicitly to total corporate objectives. As so conceived, advertising thus becomes a significant instrument of general management, a dynamic determinant of growth, a potent propellant of business and economic progress. In our society, as corporations go, so goes the economy.

Joining General Foods in 1928, after several years experience as an advertising agency account executive and also as a director of sales, Mr. Mortimer was named Vice President in charge of Advertising in 1943. In 1947 he was made responsible for the complete marketing function, becoming Executive Vice President in 1952, President in 1954, and Chairman of the Corporation in 1959.

Mr. Mortimer is former chairman of the Association of National Advertisers and of the Advertising Council and has served on the Business Advisory Council of the U. S. Department of Commerce. He attended Stevens Institute of Technology and holds honorary degrees from several institutions of higher education. He has been honored elsewhere on numerous occasions.

Ward Archer Chapter
Memphis State University
Memphis, Tennessee

Chapter History

The Ward Archer Chapter at Memphis State University was officially installed on May 19, 1967. Dr. Donald G. Hileman, national executive secretary, was the installing officer.

The chapter's first advisor was Professor Al Westland, and the first president was Dick Cooper.

Don Francisco Chapter
Michigan State University
East Lansing, Michigan
Gary Bradbury, Advisor

By *Richard J. Preiss*

Chapter History

The Alpha Delta Sigma chapter at Michigan State University was established in 1949. Its founders and first advisors were Joseph A. Del Porto and Alan Scott.

In 1955 Frank B. Senger came to Michigan State from the University of Illinois. Senger was advisor to the Illinois Alpha Delta Sigma chapter from 1948 to 1954. During this time he was also the Midwest Vice President of Alpha Delta Sigma. Seeing the plight at Michigan State, Senger reorganized the chapter in 1956 and again became Midwest Vice President (1956-57). In reorganizing Alpha Delta Sigma, Senger realized that there was a need for including women advertising students in the organiza- tion. This need was provided for by creating a woman auxillary. The members of the auxillary have no real membership in Alpha Delta Sigma nor any voting power, but they do take part in the many activities the chapter sponsors.

In 1953 Senger resigned as advisor and Louis Wolter became the new advisor.

Biographical Sketch

The Michigan State University chapter of Alpha Delta Sigma is named in honor of Don Francisco, a graduate of the class of 1914. Although Francisco graduated with a degree in botany he was the first graduate to enter the advertising feld.

He went to the West Coast after leaving Michigan State College to work for the California Orange Growers. While in California he realized that oranges were not nationally accepted. The problem, as Francisco saw it, was both the promotion of oranges and the need of refrigerated transportation of the fruits. Under his influence Union Pacific built some of the first re- frigerated cars in America. This made it possible to have fresh, ripe oranges anywhere in the U.S.

The next step Francisco undertook was the promotion of oranges. At that time, drinking orange juice or eating oranges was done only during holidays. Francisco did all the promotion, including copy and layout, research, and media selection.. The orange market grew unbelievably fast, and other orange growers of California were getting into the field. Francisco realized the California Orange Growers needed an "image" to distinguish their oranges from others. It was to be an image of "quality." The Sunkist Orange was born. Francisco was responsible for the name, for the method of picking and stamping the oranges with Sunkist trademark, and for the capture of a major part of the orange market in the U.S.

Samuel C. Gale Chapter
University of Minnesota
Minneapolis, Minnesota

Chapter History

The Minnesota Chapter of Alpha Delta Sigma was started in 1925, but unfortunately was inactive for many years. It was reactivated in 1959 as the Samuel C. Gale Chapter. In April of 1961, the chapter hosted the ADS National Convention. Speakers and guests at the convention included such prominent people as Jack Baxter of Creative House, P. C. Peterson, executive vice president of Bell & Howell, James Fish of General Mill, and Peter Schruth of the *Saturday Evening Post*.

In 1962-63 the Minnesota chapter was awarded the Outstanding Regional Chapter Award by ADS. In the same year, the chapter was the runner-up for the Donald W. Davis Award, which is given annually to the fraternity's best chapter. In 1963-64, the chapter president served as mid-west Regional Vice President.

The years 1964-65 found ADS becoming very active in the School of Journalism at Minnesota. All the advertising students on the Journalism School Liaison Committee were active ADS members.

The Samuel C. Gale Chapter has close affiliations with the other advertising clubs in the Twin Cities area. As a member of this chapter, one automatically becomes a member of the Minneapolis Junior Advertising Club. The Junior Ad Club membership opens the door to many talks by prominent professionals from every phase of advertising. The chapter also enjoys close contact with the Minneapolis Advertising Club.

Biographical Sketch

The University of Minnesota Chapter of Alpha Delta Sigma is extremely proud and fortunate to be named for one of America's top five advertising figures, Samuel C. Gale.

Mr. Gale was associated with General Mills Inc. and its predecessor company, Washburn Crosby Co., from 1921 until his retirement in 1955. He held the jobs of advertising manager (1921-26), vice president in charge of advertising, home services, public service and market analysis (1943-55), and he was a consultant in marketing, advertising, and public relations until his death in early 1961.

While he was with General Mills, Mr. Gale created the famous "Betty Crocker" personality.

Mr. Gale was chairman of the board of the National Advertising Council (1950-51). He was prominent in civic and community service projects as well as advertising. He was vice chairman of the Citizen's National Commission for Public Schools (1953-56), chairman of the Minnesota Governor's Commission on Higher Education, and a member of the Minneapolis Commission on Public Education, the Foreign Policy Association and the American Association of the United Nations Groups.

Mr. Gale was co-author of a book entitled *Minnesota's Stake in the Future of Higher Education*, 1956-70.

Outstanding Members

RAY MITHUN—Chairman of the Board, Campbell-Mithun.
JOYCE SWANN—Publisher, *Minneapolis Star and Tribune.*
R. W. STAFFORD—Executive Vice President, Knox-Reeves Advertising.
JAMES FISH—Vice President in charge of Advertising, General Mills.
THOMAS KILBRIDE—President, Minneapolis Advertising Club.
DAVID COWELL—The Cowell Press.
FRANK MILLER—Vice President, Knox-Reeves Advertising.

George McLean Chapter
University of Mississippi
Jackson, Mississippi
S. Gale Denley, Advisor

By Joseph L. White

Chapter History

The George McLean Chapter of Alpha Delta Sigma was chartered May 23, 1952, at the University of Mississippi. Installation was performed by the Memphis professional chapter. Milton Gross, national secretary, was guest of honor at a luncheon following the installation. Seven undergraduates and four professional members became charter initiates.

The University of Mississippi undergraduate chapter was the culmination of the work of the Ole Miss Advertising Club which was organized in 1948. The advertising club actively participated in sponsoring lectures, advertising projects and institutes on the campus. Close liaison was maintained with the Memphis professional chapter which ultimately sponsored the installation of ADS at the University.

From 1952 to 1960 the Mississippi chapter has initiated an average of ten undergraduuates annually. Activities were stepped up and it is a healthy organization both financially and as a service organization.

The chapter has sponsored some ten professional lectures annually; it is co-sponsor of the Mississippi High School Press Institute and a workshop on advertising for retailers. Members of the fraternity meet with the Memphis professional chapter twice annually—in social and business meetings. Alumni of the chapter have attained successful careers in advertising, and very few have turned to other fields of work.

In 1960, because of several factors—including a drop in advertising enrollment—the chapter was deactivated. However, activities of the remnant club continued on approximately the same level as when the unit had national affiliation.

The chapter was reactivated in 1964 under the leadership of Prof. Walter Hurt.

Biographical Sketch

As publisher of the *Tupelo Daily Journal*, George McLean has been a leader in promoting his area of Mississippi from a poverty stricken farming economy to one of the most prosperous industrial-agricultural regions of the South. The community development program which he fostered through his newspaper has long drawn international attention. It has been widely copied throughout the nation. It has been the frequent subject of study by visiting committees from under-developed nations of the world.

During the past quarter-century Mr. McLean built a struggling weekly newspaper into a model small daily which, in advertising and circulation, is the strongest in the United States in proportion to trade area population. The advertising promotion method of his newspaper has been a major stimulus to the prosperity of Northeast Mississippi.

Mr. McLean, 65, is still an active and effective leader. He attended the University of Mississippi and Southwestern University, where he earned M.A. and B.A. degrees. He served as a faculty member at Southwestern prior to the purchase of the Tupelo newspaper. He served as a Naval Officer during World War II. He is the holder of numerous awards and honors for his work in dealership, publishing, and writing.

John B. Powell Chapter
University of Missouri
Columbia, Missouri

Chapter History

The history of the John B. Powell Chapter, the fraternity's first chapter, will be found in Chapter 2, of the book entitled "The First Chapter."

Biographical information about John B. Powell, the founder of Alpha Delta Sigma, will also be found in that chapter.

Claude M. Bolser Chapter
City College of New York
New York, New York
David Hymes, Advisor

By Barry Finkenberg

Chapter History

Alpha Delta Sigma had its birth at City College of New York in 1937. Through the dedicated work of ten individuals, a milestone was reached in the field of advertising. William H. Johns, former President and Chairman of the Board of Batten, Barton, Durstine & Osborne, was the first of the illustrious men from the business community to become a part of the chapter. In 1937 the founding brothers of the CCNY chapter decided to name the chapter after William H. Johns.

In 1961 the chapter unanimously decided to rename itself the Claude M. Bolser Chapter. The chapter is quite pleased that two of the founding brothers of The William H. Johns Chapter, Alfred Miller and Harry Greisman, are still active members in the chapter.

During its 30 years of existence in CCNY, ADS has won both fame and recognition. A project which the chapter entered in the Babson University contest received a 1st place trophy. In 1955 the publication, *The Bridge*, received the Kleppner-Linage Award for that year. In 1960 the CCNY chapter won the Professional Competence Award for the creation of the best and most successful advertising project of the year. The Eldridge Peterson Award for the most active chapter in the New York metropolitan area was won by the chapter many times.

For 30 years the CCNY chapter of Alpha Delta Sigma has been a fruitful and active organization.

Biographical Sketch

In 1961 the CCNY chapter of Alpha Delta Sigma decided to rename itself the Claude M. Bolser Chapter. There could not have been a better choice for a new name. Claude M. Bolser pumped energy, enthusiasm and training into City College undergraduates for fourteen years.

Claude M. Bolser was the youngest 75-year-old person one could meet. He was still active in 1967 as the Executive Secretary of the League of Advertising Agencies. He was a bundle of energy that didn't want to stop. This was evident at the chapter dinners where the person who got around the most and made the most interesting speeches—Claude M. Bolser.

Mr. Bolser helped build respect for the CCNY advertising man in general, and the ADS man in particular, by inaugurating the Advertising Work-In-Training Program in 1947, and by leading the way in reorganizing and developing new and more intensive advertising courses at City College.

Claude Bolser taught and lectured at Indiana University (his alma mater), Columbia University, and Rutgers University, besides CCNY. He also created marketing and merchandising concepts for many top companies. Among these companies are the Florida Citrus Commission and the Mutual Life Insurance Company of New York.

Outstanding Members

DR. WALTER A. GAW, 1st recipient of the Alfred Erickson Award for Advertising Education, 1964. Author: *Advertising: Methods and Media*.

DAVID HYMES, Author: *Advertising Production and the Graphic Arts*.

MAURY LERMAN, Creative Director, Ted Bates and Company.

ALLAN SACKS, Account Executive, Young and Rubicam.

MURRY GROSS, Vice President of the Television Bureau of Advertising.

JACK CASPER, Vice President, Alden Advertising Agency.

George Burton Hotchkiss Chapter
New York University
New York, New York

Chapter History

The George Burton Hotchkiss Chapter at New York University was charted in 1933 as an honorary organization for marketing and advertising students. Since then other chapters have been founded.

Each year members organize and execute projects which give them experience in handling various aspects of practical marketing assignments. By winning first place three times in the annual inter-chapter competition, the George Burton Hotchkiss Chapter has won permanent possession of the Alpha Delta Sigma cup.

In addition to undergraduate members, graduate members and evening students, this chapter honors outstanding practitioners by electing some of them to professional membership. The roster of the George Burton Hotchkiss Chapter professional members reads like a "Who's Who in Advertising."

Membership to undergraduate ranks is by election. Only students in good standing who have attained an average of "B" or better in 12 points of advanced marketing courses may be considered. Successful candidates are formally initiated at the annual Marketing Banquet.

Among the various activities the chapter participates in are, a research project designed to determine the buying habits of the students at New York University, the setting up of a school advertising agency, and a stimulating series of lectures in the field of advertising and marketing.

In 1966 the chapter was proud to elect Mr. Norman Strouse to professional membership. He will be formally initiated in June at the Annual Marketing Banquet. Mr. Strouse is the President and Chief Executive Officer of the J. Walter Thompson Co.

Biographical Sketch

Professor George Burton Hotchkiss, for whom the chapter was named, was one of the pioneers in marketing instruction. During his years of teaching, he is said to have influenced many of the top copy men in the advertising business.

Mr. Hotchkiss was a reporter on the *New York Evening Sun*, marketing consultant for the James F. Newcomb & Co. agency, and a copy writer for the George Batten Co. agency, while serving as a professor at New York University.

As senior faculty member at NYU (45 years), he was for many years head of the marketing department. He was professor of marketing from 1927 until his retirement in June, 1950, when he received the honorary degree of Doctor of Letters.

He was one of the organizers of the National Association of Teachers in Marketing and Advertising and was among the early proponents for merging it with the present American Marketing Association.

Winner of a poetry prize while at Yale, he continued his interest in English composition and wrote three textbooks in Business English. He wrote many advertising books, some of which were adopted as texts in various advertising courses.

Ralph Starr Butler, retired vice president of General Foods had this comment about Professor Hotchkiss. "In the transition of advertising from its small beginning to a major tool of business,

George Burton Hotchkiss was one of the group of men who gave to the developing vocation the needed qualities of dignity, integrity, and stature. His character, scholarship and devotion to the highest ideals are a legacy for which the advertising world will long be indebted."

Alpha Delta Sigma at N.Y.U. is very proud to bear the name of such a great man.

Outstanding Members

Professor William J. McKeon is not only a teacher at N.Y.U., but he is also one of its distinguished graduates. He graduated from the School of Commerce, Accounts and Finance in 1931 and he graduated from the Graduate School of Business Administration in 1934. From 1947-50 he was an Assistant Professor of Marketing and is presently an Associate Professor of Marketing.

Prof. McKeon has a fine business record. From 1934-41 he worked for Johns-Manville in the field of Sales Promotion and Research. He was also the editor of *Power Specialist*. From 1943-47, Prof. McKeon was the Promotion Mgr. for *Family Circle* magazine.

As a writer, he has also proven himself. He is the author and editor of several books and articles in the field of sales psychology and copy testing.

Presently Prof McKeon is a consultant to business in the field of market planning and promotion.

Among his other accomplishments, Prof. McKeon is a member of Alpha Delta Sigma, Delta Mu Delta, the American Marketing Association and Theta Chi.

The brotherhood of the George Burton Hotchkiss Chapter of Alpha Delta Sigma is extremely grateful that Prof. McKeon has taken such a keen interest in our chapter, and that he has given of himself willingly whenever we have needed his assistance.

William Wrigley, Jr. Chapter
University of Oklahoma
Norman, Oklahoma
Robert L. Bryson, Jr., Advisor

By Robert L. Bryson, Jr.

Chapter History

In the spring of 1924, two students and a faculty member from the University of Oklahoma School of Journalism visited the University of Missouri to lay ground work for establishing an O. U. chapter of Alpha Delta Sigma.

With encouragement and support from the John B. Powell chapter at Missouri, the Sooner Advertising Club at O. U. was installed as the 11th chapter of ADS in April, 1924. Charter members included seven students and the advisor, Arthur Hallam, who later became national secretary of ADS.

The newly organzied O. U. chapter, named in honor of William Wrigley, Jr., was one of five chapters represented at the first national convention in Columbia, Mo., in 1924.

Although the O. U. chapter became inactive in 1931, it was reactivated in the fall of 1946 with Leslie H. Rice as advisor. In the late 1940's the chapter sponsored "Huckster's Hop" and "Rothschild's Day," two annual activities that attracted campus-wide participation. The chapter's "Get Out the Vote" campaign in 1952 won first award in the president's cup project.

With the exception of two years while he was on leave of absence, Professor Rice served as advisor until 1959. During his tenure, he was elected regional vice president for two terms.

J. M. Poyner, Jr. served as advisor from 1950 to 1964 and was followed by Robert L. Bryson, Jr., current chapter advisor.

Biographical Sketch

The career of William Wrigley, Jr. is probably one of the most fascinating and romantic to be found in the annals of American salesmanship.

He was born in 1861 in Philadelphia. With $32 capital he went to Chicago in 1891, where, after gaining experience selling soap and baking powder, he started the chewing gum business which was destined to become the greatest enterprise of its kind in the world.

In a 1947 letter to the ADS chapter at O. U., his son, Phillip K. Wrigley, wrote, "My father was probably one of the greatest believers in advertising that ever lived, and during the early days of the Wm. Wrigley Jr. Company he personally wrote practically all of the advertising. He always regarded advertising as one of the most important parts of the company's business, if not the most important; and in later years he continued to directly supervise the advertising at all times."

One who consistently applied the power of advertising to his business, Wrigley once said, "Advertising is pretty much like running a furnace. You've got to keep on shoveling coal. Once you stop stoking, the fire goes out. It's strange that some people's imagination can't compass this fact."

Outstanding Members

HUGH C. GILLICK—Advertising Manager, Sunray-DX Oil Company.

FRANK EUGENE HEASTON—Vice President, Director of
Marketing and Member of the Board of Directors, Gardner
Advertising Co.
MORGAN V. HUNTER—Associate Advertising Manager, Procter
& Gamble.
DR. JOHN E. MERTES—Past National Dean, American Aca-
demy of Advertising.
ORB C. REEDER—Production Manager, Wall Street Journal.
LOWE RUNKLE—President, Lowe Runkle Co.

H. T. Vance Chapter
Orgeon State University
Corvallis, Oregon
Irwin C. Harris, Advisor

By Irwin C. Harris

Chapter History

Oregon State University is unique among schools with Alpha
Delta Sigma chapters throughout the country. Oregon State does
not have a department of advertising and offers only three courses
in the field through the School of Business and Technology—
yet Alpha Delta Sigma has flourished at OSU since its founding
back in 1926.

It has been possible to maintain a high level of operation
because of continued faculty support, a well organized business
staff of the student daily newspaper, professional help from the
Department of Journalism and the downtown *Corvallis Gazette-
Times,* and cooperation from the Oregon Advertising Club.

In fact, one of the reasons for establishing an ADS chapter
at Oregon State was to help fill the void resulting from the
absence of an advertising curriculum. Since the chapter was
founded, it has been a regular policy to bring professional advertising people to the campus from Portland to talk to the ADS
members on the various phases and philosophies of advertising.
These talks have been supplemented by field trips to the Portland
agencies and newspapers, and short workshops.

Biographical Sketch

H. T. Vance, for whom the Oregon State Chapter of Alpha
Delta Sigma was named, not only developed the first course in
advertising to be offered at OSU but also organized the Department of Secretarial Science in the School of Business and Technology.

Born in Westchester, Pa., on January 8, 1876, and a 1901 graduate of Drexel Institute of Philadelphia, Professor Vance came west and served as a department head at Oregon State from 1920 until his death in a car accident in 1942. Professor Vance was one of the principal founders in the establishment of an ADS chapter at OSU in 1926. He maintained an active interest in the fraternity throughout the remainder of his life.

W. F. G. Thacher Chapter
University of Oregon
Eugene, Oregon

Chapter History

The W. F. G. Thacher Chapter of ADS was founded at the University of Oregon in 1921.

Chapter activities include a variety of functions. The ADS chapter handles the entire promotion for ''Mothers' Weekend'' on the campus. Besides providing valuable experience for new and old members, this activity serves as a source of funds for the chapter.

Each spring the W. F. G. Thacher Chapter elects an ADS Campus Queen, who reigns over various activities. The chapter's most festive activity is their annual beer and steak feed. On the academic side, the chapter awards a $100 Senior Scholarship every year.

Biographical Sketch

The ADS chapter at the University of Oregon was named after W. F. Goodwin Thacher—a professor of English. Those students who chose his name must have had a great deal of foresight, for Professor Thacher has represented the spirit of our fraternity, through his many years of dedication to the advertising profession.

Professor Thacher helped establish the Advertising Department at the University of Oregon, and he also helped develop it into a full curriculum of study. Within a few short years of the school's existence, he organized and maintained a ''summer scholarship'' placement program for students. In 1942, he was called upon to preside over the national fraternity, and he guided it during the difficult years of World War II.

Since then the Oregon chapter has tried to follow his example. The chapter believes fervently in a strong academic background in advertising . . . one which Professor Thacher made possible for its members

Donald W. Davis Chapter
Pennsylvania State University
University Park, Pennsylvania
Kim B. Rotzoll, Advisor

By Kim B. Rotzoll

Chapter History

The Benjamin Franklin Chapter of ADS was founded in 1933 when only three advertising courses were offered by the School of Journalism. The Penn State chapter sought from the outset to "bridge the gap" between campus and business by offering the membership the opportunity to meet and exchange views with respected members of the advertising business.

ADS at Penn State celebrated its 25th anniversary in 1958 with C. James Proud, president of the Advertising Federation of America, as featured speaker. It had been a productive 25 years.

Organizations bear the imprint of people. Donald W. Davis was the guiding force of the Benjamin Franklin chapter until his death in 1959. The chapter now proudly bears his name. Roland Hicks became Eastern Region Vice President in 1961 and the chapter hosted the Eastern Region Convention in 1962.

Through the years the chapter has been a four-time winner of national inter-chapter awards.

Biographical Sketch

Donald W. Davis was born on July 11, 1896, and died June 29, 1959.

He was elected to the Advertising Hall of Fame (1962) in recognition of a lifetime effort dedicated to advertising. Recognizing its importance as a social and economic force, he upheld the highest ideals as a working advertising man, as a leader in professional organizations, as a writer and speaker on advertising, and as an inspired teacher of thousands of students. He has often been called the "Mr. Chips" of advertising.

He began his career on the Springfield, Massachusetts *Republican* and *Daily News* in 1919 and became the Advertising Director in 1929.

In advertising organization work, he was a leader in improving advertising and explaining its role in society through professional associations. He served as president of the Springfield Advertising Club in 1930-31, vice president of the Advertising Federation of America in the 1920's, governor of the First District of AFA from 1932 to 1934, and national president of ADS in 1947-49. He edited the exhaustive "AFA Directory of Advertising, Public Relations and Marketing Education" in the United States in 1951.

His most enduring monument, of course, was his work for Alpha Delta Sigma, for he is credited with revitalizing the professional advertising fraternity and expanding its scope while serving as its president for two years.

As a writer and speaker, he ably presented his philosophy on advertising to tens of thousands of professionals and non-professionals. His most enduring contribution as a writer is his widely used textbook, *Basic Text in Advertising.*

As an educator, he taught university courses in advertising for 37 years out of the 40 years he was engaged in advertising. In 1922 he began teaching at the Springfield Division of Northwestern University. In 1922 he also accepted an invitation to establish a curriculum in advertising at Pennsylvania State University. Under his leadership, the University's enrollment in advertising grew to be the largest in the country. The many thousands of students across the land who testify to his instruction and inspiration are his greatest memorial.

It is significant that the following appeared in the School of Journalism's statement nominating him for membership in the Advertising Hall of Fame.

"His influence will be longest felt and his contributions longest noted in his work for Alpha Delta Sigma. He is credited with revitalizing the fraternity and extending its scope while national president. On a leave of absence as professor of advertising . . . he visited every active chapter. During his presidency the number of chapters rose from twenty-five to thirty-four. As one of Davis' associates has said: 'It was he who put into words the basic function of Alpha Delta Sigma: Bridging the Gap Between Advertising Theory and Experience.' "

Herbert Hall Palmer Chapter
University of Rhode Island
Kingston, Rhode Island

Chapter History

On Monday afternoon, May 23, 1949, the Herbert Hall Palmer Chapter of Alpha Delta Sigma at the University of Rhode Island was installed. Twenty-four students and one faculty member were initiated by members of the George W. Coleman Chapter of Babson Institute. Among those present were National President Donald W. Davis and Professor Herbert H. Palmer, for whom the chapter was named.

Professor Palmer, the new chapter's advisor, is a former National President of Alpha Delta Sigma.

That evening at a banquet attended by the installing officers, the new members and guests received a greeting from the school's president, Carl R. Woodward. Other speakers included Professor Bertrand R. Canfield, then national treasurer of ADS. Professor Herber H. Palmer, Dean John F. Quinn, and Mrs. Louis C. FitzGerald of FitzGerald, Inc., Providence. Mr. FitzGerald spoke on the possibilities of advertising in television.

The toastmaster was Professor Herbert M. Hofford, a charter member of the Penn State chapter and at that time director of public relations for the school.

The chapter's first officers were: George A. Gilbert, president; Bruce G. Zimmerman, vice president; Edwin B. Lowe, treasurer; Theodore L. Zitserman, secretary; and William A Avison, corresponding secretary.

Biographical Sketch

Herbert Hall Palmer joined the Rhode Island State College faculty as an assistant professor in the fall of 1942. Previously he had served on the faculty of Syracuse University and had held high school teaching jobs in Louisville, Kentucky; Cambridge, Mass.; and Boston, Mass.

Profesor Palmer received a Bachelor of Art degree from Amherst College with the class of 1907. His academic honors include membership to Phi Beta Kappa and Phi Kappa Phi.

In 1947 he was promoted to professor and head of the Department of Marketing and Advertising at the University of Rhode Island. During his early years at Rhode Island the name of the school had been changed to the University of Rhode Island. He retired from the school in 1953.

Professor Palmer served as national president of ADS from 1931 to 1933. He was advisor of the ADS chapter at the University of Rhode Island from the founding in 1949 until 1953 when Dr. Larry Bresch replaced him.

During his teaching career he authored two books, both published by McGraw-Hill Book Company.

George D. Gaw Chapter
Roosevelt University
Chicago, Illinois
Robert E. J. Snyder, Advisor

Chapter History

In 1947, the George D. Gaw Chapter of Alpha Delta Sigma, at Roosevelt University in Chicago, was formed in cooperation with Charles Wolfe, head of the Advertising Department, and the Roosevelt Alumni.

In 1948, Professor Brandel Works became advisor. During his term of supervision, the chapter received these awards: Chapter Achievement Award for Commercial Campaign, 1954; President's Competition—First Place, 1958; and Benjamin Franklin Award—Curtis Publishing Company.

In 1952, from the ranks of the chapter, the A.D.S. Advertising Agency was formed. The agency is still in operation today and is under the supervision of the current advisor, Dr. Robert E. J. Snyder, who succeeded Professor Works in 1965. As a student-operated advertising agency, it provides a rare opportunity for students to gain actual advertising agency experience, thus consistent with Alpha Delta Sigma's objective of "bridging the gap." Students who participate solicit and service small business accounts in the Chicago area. This helps them gain first-hand experience of the problems and procedures discussed in the classroom, while also earning some money. In the March 31, 1952, issue of *Advertising Age*," the agency was noted as billing better than $500 a month.

In 1954, the George D. Gaw Chapter, in cooperation with other university chapters in the Chicago area, sponsored the National Alpha Delta Sigma Convention.

One of the most outstanding recent activities of the Gaw Chapter is the raising of funds for the restoration of the world-famous Auditorium Theater. The famous landmark, which belongs to Roosevelt University, is the world's most acoustically perfect theater.

Another chapter activity is a monthly "Creative Workshop" created and instructed by prominent ADS Alumnus, Jack Baxter. Baxter was "Copywriter of the Year" in 1960-1961, creative director of Leo Burnett Company, president of Creative House, and currently president of Advertising Talent Center in Chicago. Mr. Baxter conducts this workshop exclusively for the Gaw Chapter.

Biographical Sketch

The Roosevelt University Chapter of A.D.S. has long been proud to bear the name of George D. Gaw. Although Gaw was never a member of ADS, he always showed a keen interest in it and recognized the necessity and importance of the student chapters.

During his career, Gaw founded the O'Hara Envelope Company. One of his greatest innovations and contributions was the window envelope.

In 1933, the World's Fair was in Chicago. Thousands of visitors and dignitaries from across the country and around the world flocked to the "Windy City." With a friendly handshake and warm smile, the Fair's Official Greeter, George D. Gaw, welcomed them and made them feel at home.

In 1945, Gaw and Louis Cheskin founded the Color Research Institute, an organization which conducted market research in the fields of packaging and advertising.

Gaw retired from the Color Research Institute in 1950 and became a consultant for the Envelope Manufacturer's Association. He remained in this position until his death in 1966.

The Roosevelt University Chapter of Alpha Delta Sigma has realized a great deal of pride and a truly distinct challenge in living up to the name of George D. Gaw.

Hugh Thomas Chapter
San Francisco State College
San Francisco, California

Chapter History

The Hugh Thomas Chapter at San Francisco State College became the seventy-sixth chartered chapter on November 17, 1966. Representing the National Council for the installation was Randy Smith.

Initially the chapter had co-advisors, Dr. Jack Tenge and Dr. Stan Johnson. Dr. Tenge is professor of marketing and Dr. Johnson is chairman of the department of marketing at the college.

The first officers for the chapter included Bill Dowler, president; Charles Betz, vice president; Jon T. Weatherwax, treasurer; and Steve Courtney, secretary.

Alan Cundall, creative director of Honig, Cooper and Harrigton, was the speaker at the initiation dinner.

Alvin Long Chapter
San Jose State College
San Jose, California
Jerry Lynn, Advisor

Chapter History

"A professional fraternity means even more after you are out of school." This statement was made by Mr. Carl R. Hoffmann.

Mr. Hoffman, who has been a veteran in the advertising industry for more than thirty years and a teacher of advertising at San Jose State College for an additional fourteen years, meant that a professional fraternity such as Alpha Delta Sigma can offer a student more rewards that extend even beyond his graduation.

Mr. Hoffman and a handful of dedicated men made this ideal their blueprint in establishing an ADS chapter. They wanted an ADS chapter that would offer more than social rewards. So, they, as did the original founders of ADS at the University of Missouri, felt that the all-important ingredient of professionalism was necessary to learn from important leaders in the profession, and to learn from their example and experience.

In the spirng of 1947, a chapter of Alpha Delta Sigma was founded on the campus of San Jose State College. Its original membership was only twelve. The chapter was given the name of Alvin Long who was the owner of San Jose's largest advertising agency.

Members of the Alvin Long Chapter at San Jose State College attend a luncheon once a month with the professional chapter in San Francisco. Members feel they are very lucky to have such a strong alumni chapter in the region. The alumni help them to plan field trips to agencies as well as other companies related to advertising.

Since its original and meager beginning ADS at San Jose State has grown into a leading chapter. It is a unique chapter in that for seventeen years it has been dedicated to helping the student make the transition from campus to career.

Biographical Sketch

Mr. Alvin Long graduated from Stockton High School in Stockton, California, shortly after the turn of the century. He started his career with a local newspaper, but later moved to San Jose and opened his own one-man advertising agency. At first, Long Advertising, Inc. did only retail ads (Mr. Long getting accounts, working up ads, buying time and space and billing all himself). After more than fifty years of business, Long Advertising, Inc. has many national and international accounts.

Carolina Chapter
University of South Carolina
Columbia, South Carolina
Perry J. Ashley, Advisor

Chapter History

The Carolina Chapter at the University of South Carolina became the eightieth chapter to be installed by the national organization on October 4, 1968.

Dr. Frazier Moore, head of the advertising program at the University of Georgia and Professors George Abney and Lou Wolters of the same faculty participated in the installation and initiation. Ober Tyus, a graduate student at the University of Georgia and a former regional student vice president of ADS also participated.

The new chapter did not take the name of an outstanding person in advertising at the time of installation but plans to in the future. To find such a person a search is being made for an outstanding advertising practitioner who is an alumni of the University of South Carolina.

Dr. Donald G. Hileman, executive director of Alpha Delta Sigma, installed the new chapter and initiated the eighteen charter members. Among the new initiates were Dr. Albert T. Scroggins, Dean of the School of Journalism, and Dr. Perry J. Ashley, assistant professor and chapter advisor. The first chapter president was Jerry Jay Bender.

Other charter members include: Charles Warner Alexander, Donald F. Barton, Rudy Coward, F. Coates Crewe, Leonard Carter Crewe III, Timothy Stephen Crowley, Sr., William Holt Duncan, Thomas John Greene, Jack H. Hicks, Jr., Robert Isbell Ward Huddleston Lang, Van T. Newman, Edwin Ernest Riley, Jr. Robert Everett Skenes, and James F. Wenthe.

Barton, Duncan, Isbell, Coward, and Newman were initiated as professional members.

Charles H. Sandage Chapter
Southern Illinois University
Carbondale, Illinois
Donald G. Hileman, Advisor

By Donald G. Hileman

Chapter History

Since its inception the Charles H. Sandage chapter at Southern Illinois University has been one of the fraternity's finest. Just two months after the chapter was started (June 1, 1959) its advisor, president and vice president participated in the national convention held at Stanford University in August. The chapter has been represented by its advisor, president and at least a minimum of three other student members at every national and regional meeting of the fraternity since that date. In many years the unofficial delegates from S.I.U. numbered ten or more.

In its second year, 1960-61, the chapter placed among the top five chapters in the country and has remained among this elite group in all but one of the eight succeeding years. In that year the chapter placed 10th. In 1963-'64 the chapter received the Donald W. Davis award as ADS' top chapter, and it has received the award for the top chapter in the Midwest since the inception of the award.

The chapter is consistently one of the first to meet all its financial and other committments to the national chapter, and has always been eager to provide leadership when needed. For example, it has established the only professional chapter directly associated with a university, in an attempt to establish a formal structure for maintaining communication and contact with its alumni. Through this chapter S.I.U. alumni and professionals contribute time, talent and money to the S.I.U. ADS undergraduate chapter and the professional advertising program in the Department of Journalism.

Two of the chapter's advisors have served in the two top national positions of the fraternity. In 1961, Dr. Donald G. Hileman was appointed National Executive Secretary, a position he still holds. The National Headquarters of the fraternity have been located on the S.I.U. campus for the past seven years.

In 1963 co-advisor Billy I. Ross was elected to the National Presidency and served in this capacity for four years. He has since joined the faculty of Texas Technological College. In the fall of 1963, Dr. Hileman became editor of *Linage*. Co-advisor C. Dennis Schick served as Associate Editor of the publication.

Other recognition received by the chapter and its members include: In 1959-'60, Jerry Lynn (2nd place in the Cigar Institute promotion); in 1961-'62, the Professional Competence Award; Bob Wylie, elected Midwest Student Vice President in 1961-'62; Ron Geskey and Walt Waschick, individual awards in the Florida State Creative Sweepstakes in 1964-'65 and 1965-'66; the chapter award in 1964-'65 for the most entries in the Creative Sweepstakes competition; and Steve Templeton, the Sprite competition in 1966-'67. Members have received many awards, scholarships, etc., other than those specifically associated with ADS.

The presidents for the chapter have been: 1959-'61, John Finch; 1960-'61, Mike Nixon; 1961-'62, Bob Wylie; 1962-'63, Larry McCoy; 1963-'64, Don Burnett; 1964-'65, Stan Nicpon; 1965-'66, Larry Mann; 1st half 1966-'67, Bob Quaglia; 2nd half 1966-'67, Bob Taylor; and 1967-'68, Steve Templeton.

Biographical Sketch

For more than a score of years the name of Dr. Charles Harold Sandage and advertising education have been synonomous. The men of Alpha Delta Sigma at Southern Illinois University were honored that Dr. Sandage would allow their chapter to bear his name.

Much could be said about Dr. Sandage's work prior to going to the University of Illinois shortly after World War II but it has been in the past twenty years that his greatest influence on advertising education has taken place. He was author of a text for the basic advertising course; the text—now in its seventh edition—remains one of the most widely used for the course. He has written other books and articles since.

His greatest sphere of influence, however, comes through the doctoral program at the University of Illinois. This program has produced more than fifty teachers of advertising for our nation's colleges and universities. His establishment of the James Webb Young Fund at the University of Illinois has served to help future teachers of advertising to study at that university, and has set the pattern for the establishment of such funds elsewhere.

Early in his tenure at Illinois, he and Earle Ludgin pioneered a cooperative venture bringing representatives of the American Association of Advertising Agencies and advertising educators closer together. This program of the Central Region of the A.A.A.A. is today one of the finest practitioner-educator cooperative programs in existence.

He has been a leader in the Division of Advertising of the Association of Education for Journalism. In the American Academy of Advertising he has spearheaded the development of a new academic journal for advertising.

In 1963 Alpha Delta Sigma awarded the Nichols Cup to Dr. Sandage for his outstanding contribution to advertising education; in 1965 he became the first educator to be awarded the AFA-*Printer's Ink* Gold Medal Award for outstanding service to advertising.

Outstanding Members

Advertising education at Southern Illinois University, although among the 26 accredited programs by the American Council for Education in Journalism, is relatively young in a historical sense. It was in 1957 that the first advertising majors received their degrees. Thus, while most of its graduates, few of whom are above 30, have already distinguished themselves by becoming valuable employees for their organizations, none have achieved national acclaim. Among the chapter's professional members, Mark Cooper is a past President and General Manager of the Advertising Federation of America.

Will C. Grant Chapter
Southern Methodist University

By Dr. Jerry E. Drake

Chapter History

During the 1949-50 academic year the officers of the Southern Methodist University Students Ad League made application for membership in Alpha Delta Sigma.

The Students Ad League had been operating effectively for several years, and had a membership of 45, including student as well as professional members. The entire group of 45 became charter members of the S.M.U. chapter when it was installed on May 8, 1950 by Professor Ernest Sharpe, who was Southwestern Vice President of Alpha Delta Sigma at that time.

Our charter members decided to name the S.M.U. chapter for Will C. Grant, who is an ex-student of S.M.U., and was the founder of Grant Advertsing, Inc.

Since the Will C. Grant Chapter was installed, we have never failed to send a delegate to the national convention. Seven years after the formation of our chapter, the national convention was held in Dallas, with S.M.U. being the host chapter. That convention year (1957) was the first time that the National Convention was held in the Southwest, and at that time the S.M.U. faculty sponsor was elected Southwestern Vice President of Alpha Delta Sigma. During his administration, new chapters were installed by him at Texas Tech, Texas Christian University, and at Texas A.&M. University.

The Will C. Grant chapter of Alpha Delta Sigma enjoys a close working relationship with the Dallas Ad League, the Dallas Sales and Marketing Executives Club, and the North Texas Chapter of the American Marketing Association. Our chapter also has close working relationships with other student organizations on the S.M.U. campus, and is helpful in providing publicity and promotion for many school-wide events.

Biographical Sketch

The Southern Methodist University chapter of Alpha Delta Sigma is named for Will C. Grant, founder and currently chairman of the board and chief executive officer of Grant Advertising, Incorporated.

Mr Grant is a native Dallasite, and an alumnus of Southern Methodist University. While in college he was a member of Phi Delta Theta fraternity, and was very active in campus extracurricular activities. Among other things, he served as head cheerleader, and was the recipient of the R. E. L. Saner Oratorical Award. In June, 1955, his alma mater conferred the L.L.D.

degree upon him.

Grant Advertising, Inc. was established in Dallas in 1934 The Chicago office was opened in 1935. The agency, in the meantime, has spread to international proportions and is one of the largest advertising agencies in the country. Mr. Grant, as well as his agency, has done a great deal to encourage and improve advertising education. In recognition of his contributions to advertising, the National Council of Alpha Delta Sigma, at its 1961 national convention in Minneapolis, conferred upon Mr. Grant the Sixth Degree Key, which is the highest award conferred by Alpha Delta Sigma.

Howard Willoughby Chapter
Stanford University
Palo Alto, California

Chapter History

In February, 1939, nine Stanford students petitioned the national offices of Alpha Delta Sigma for the establishment of a local chapter of the fraternity at Leland Stanford, Jr., University. These students formed a cross-section of the top men on the business staffs of all the student publications. Cifford F. Weigle, an assistant professor, was the faculty advisor for the group. Now he is the Executive Head of the Department of Communications at Stanford. Howard Willoughby, then of Foster & Kleiser in San Francisco, was professional advisor and an invaluable aid in organizing the chapter, which was eventually named after him. The charter was officially granted on March 5, 1939, at a meeting in San Francisco.

Biographical Sketch

A native of Wisconsin, Howard Willoughby spent his early years in Santa Barbara, California. He graduated from the University of California at Berkeley, and now lives in Piedmont.

He retired as Executive Vice President and Director of the Lane Magazine Company (publishers of *Sunset Magazine*) and Manager of the company's San Francisco office. Previous to joining Lane Co. in 1944, Mr. Willoughby served as Director and Vice President in charge of sales with Foster & Kleiser Company. In 1939 he helped organize the Stanford University Chapter of Alpha Delta Sigma, which was eventually named after him. Widely known in western advertising and business circles, Mr. Willoughby has served twice as senior vice president of the Advertising Assoication of the West, has been President of the San Francisco Advertising Club, and has been Natonal President of Alpha Delta Sigma.

Chapter History

The Arthur J. Brewster Chapter of Alpha Delta Sigma received its charter on May 5, 1925. Formal installation ceremonies, also held at that time, officially made it a part of the organization.

The charter members were: A. J. Brewster, H. H. Palmer, Alonzo Palmer, W. A. Bruce, Walter Thompson, George Ryan, Paul Carpenter, Harold Cree, W. Stanley Reese, Jr., Irving Potter, Irving C. Harney, Howard M. Barker, Richard Wilbur, Truman O. Young, Donald T. Pomroy, and Robert Fellows.

But before ADS, came the Advertising and Selling Club and Sigma Mu Beta, local advertising fraternity.

At the first regular meeting of the Advertising and Selling Club, December 6, 1920, Mr. Drayer outlined the purpose behind the starting of the Syracue University Advertising and Selling Club. The constitution and by-laws were formally submitted and approved, followed by the election and installation of officers.

The first mention of Sigma Mu Beta occurred at the March 15, 1921, meeting when it was suggested that the Advertising and Selling Club be formed into a fraternity. Accordingly, a committee was appointed to draw up an appropriate constitution and submit a name for such a fraternity. On April 4 a constitution and the name Sigma Mu Beta were presented and approved by the members. A little later Sigma Mu Beta accepted its first honorary members. Among those elected at a May 2 meeting was Professor A. J. Brewster, who has come to mean so much to the Syracuse Chapter of Alpha Delta, which today bears his name.

The following year Professor Palmer was also elected to honorary membership in Sigma Mu Beta. A charter member of the Brewster Chapter of Alpha Delta Sigma and a Past President of the national fraternity, Professor Palmer, along with Professor Brewster, has worked tirelessly through the years to make the Syracuse chapter of ADS what it is today.

Then on May 14, 1922, Brother P. Taylor discussed the possibilities and benefits that would be gained by Sigma Mu Beta going national. This is where Alpha Delta Sigma came into the picture. After talking over the merits of the University of Missouri's chapter of Alpha Delta Sigma, national advertising fraternity, a committee was appointed to correspond with that national organization and report its findings.

On October 23, 1924, the members of Sigma Mu Beta voted to petition Alpha Delta Sigma for national affiliation.

In the following Spring, a charter was granted, and the University chapter, named the Brewster Chapter, started on its successful career.

The first year of Alpha Delta Sigma at Syracuse was guided by Mr. Don Pomeroy as President, and Mr. Irving Harney as Vice President.

Dennis M. McGill Chapter
Texas A&M University
College Station, Texas

Chapter History

The A&M Advertising Club was organized in 1956, composed of students from the Department of Journalism. The club's objectives were to help its members meet advertising professionals, attend Texas advertising meetings, and develop a professional attitude.

In 1958, the A&M Ad Club set as its main goal the establishment of an Alpha Delta Sigma chapter on the A&M campus.

In February, 1961, after receiving permission from college officials, the A&M Ad Club submitted an elaborate 64--page petition to Alpha Delta Sigma for membership. The petition was a detailed presentation of the club's organization, history, and activities. Their petition was accepted. On March 25, 1961, the club was installed into ADS at the University of Houston. The chapter was named for its initial sponsor, Wesley D. Calvert. The membership numbered 21.

Every year, four or five students are selected to attend the Dallas Ad League Tour which lasts for two days. Tours are taken of advertising agencies and radio and television facilities in the Dallas area. One student and a sponsor attend the National Convention. On years in which the National Convention is not held, members attend an Ad Forum sponsored by the Houston Ad Club. Here, top people in advertising from across the country speak to professionals and students alike. The regional convention is usually held in conjunction with this.

After the ADS chapter was started, members began to graduate and activity dwindled. However, in the fall of 1965, the club began to gain strength again. In the spring of 1966, five members were initiated, bringing total membership to nine.

In 1967 the chapter was renamed the Dennis M. McGill Chapter. Before his death in 1967 Mr. McGill had been a Dallas advertising executive.

Biographical Sketch

Dennis M. McGill worked for Guiberson Corporation, Dallas, for 23 years before his death in 1967. He started in accounting and then served 22 years as head of advertising.

Mr. McGill was born in Dallas, attended Southern Methodist University and then received his degree from the University of Texas. He and his wife, Dorys, had one son, Dennis, and one daughter, Denna.

He was active in the American Industrial Advertising Association, serving in many of the national offices.

The Dallas Chapter of the AIAA gave to the A&M Chapter a stereo phonograph for the advertising laboratory in Mr. McGill's honor. The chapter also gave a ten-year plaque on which the name of the outstanding member of the A&M Chapter will be placed each year.

Outstanding Members

A great number of the graduates in advertising of the Department of Journalism at Texas A&M University cannot be linked to the Alpha Deta Sigma chapter, since it received its charter in 1961 and these men were earlier graduates.

Since the military program at A&M claims most male graduates for two, three, or four years of service immediately after their graduation, those who have gone out since the chapter was formed are just entering their professional careers. The Texas A&M Chapter has many chapter graduates who need only time to place them in the ranks of "outstanding graduates serving in the advertising profession."

Thomas L. Yates Chapter
Texas Christian University
Fort Worth, Texas

Chapter History

The Thomas L. Yates chapter of Alpha Delta Sigma at Texas Christian University was installed in the spring of 1959. Fifteen undergraduate and five professional members were initiated into the chapter in a ceremony that was held in the TCU student center.

The chapter was named after Thomas L. Yates, president of an advertising agency bearing his name, and then a member of the ADS Professional Advisory Board.

Installation of the chapter was handled by Southwestern Vice President Jerry Drake, Southern Methodist University.

Professional members initiated at the time of the chapter installation included Dr. Max R. Haddick, journalism department chairman; Dr. Sam Leifeste, marketing department chairman; Amon G. Carter, Jr.; Mickey Schmid, North Texas Advertising Co.; and Roy Bacus, WBAP, Fort Worth.

J. Culver Hill Chapter
Texas Technological College
Lubbock, Texas
Billy I. Ross, Advisor

By Freddie Koenig, Jr.

Chapter History

The Alpha Delta Sigma Chapter at Texas Technological College began as the Tech Ad Club. Jim Watts, president; and Phil Orman, vice president; were determined to become affiliated with ADS nationally. On their fourth application, with the help of faculty member Bill Whitted, their application was sent to New York City and accepted. They were told the main reason for their previous rejections was the structure of the Tech advertising program.

The University of Houston and the University of Texas ADS chapters came to Lubbock to install the new chapter in 1958. At the installation dinner in the Palm Room, Phil Orman was installed as the first president and Travis Cupp was elected first vice president. The chapter was named after J. Culver Hill, advertising and promotion director of Hemphill Wells Co., because of his outstanding leadership in advertising, both on the Tech campus and as a practitioner in Lubbock.

In 1958 there were 23 members, and the first pledge project was started. In 1959, the officers of the chapter formed the "Advertising Association," an advertising agency with offices above Brown's Varsity Shop. They handled about 15 accounts, with the largest being High Plains Water Conservation District. The agency was so successful that each officer was offered a job with one of the companies.

Members of the Association were: Bill Whitted, Jim Watts, Jerry Morton, Phil Orman, Travis Cupp, and Ray Lemons.

The Alpha Delta Sigma Chapter on the Tech campus has grown from a small struggling club in 1958 to the number one chapter in the nation in 1966-67. In 1966-67 Texas Tech received the Donald W. Davis award as the best chapter of Alpha Delta Sigma in the nation. An important part of the reason that it received this honor was the co-sponsorship of the best Advertising Recognition Week Program in the nation in 1966-67.

This was quite a successful climb for a chapter that had struggled so hard for initial recognition.

Biographical Sketch

J. Culvert Hill was born March 14, 1910, in Nocono, Texas, but has lived in Lubbock so long that he calls it his "home."

He graduated from Texas Technological College in 1932 with a degree in economics, even though he had taken every related advertising course that Tech offered. He studied basic commercial art, yet no degree was offered at that time.

Today, his two biggest interests are advertising and Texas Tech. Mr. Hill has a long history connected with Tech, going back to the day Tech was founded. As the cornerstone was layed that big day in Tech's history, J. Culver Hill was the boy who helped raise the United States and Texas flags; that night at the banquet he checked in Governor Pat Neff's hat. Talking to him about that night brings a smile, because he was playing with and wearing the Governor's hat when Governor Neff came to the checkout to leave.

All of the Hill family are interested in art. His wife paints china and his son, Rodney C. Hill, is employed by Kennith L. Bentzen, an architect of Houston, Texas.

Hemphill Wells Company has been his only employer since high school. Hill started as a delivery boy on a bicycle, then moved to display advertising, and after college was placed in charge of the advertising department.

In 1944, Hill joined the Navy. He served as a communication officer and attained the rank of full Lieutenant.

Hill returned to Hemphill Wells and found that the store had grown so large that the advertising and display departments were divided. The company offered him his pick, and he took the advertising department. For the last 15 years Hill has been a director of the firm and vice president in charge of advertising and promotion.

In 1958, Phil Orman and Jim Watts, both Tech students, visited Hill and told him of their plans to petition ADS for a charter. They asked Hill for his permission to name the new chapter after him. Hill consented and the new Alpha Delta Sigma Chapter on the Tech campus was named in his honor.

The awards Mr. Hill has received are more than this page allows. Some of the many related to the field of advertising include:

President of Retail Merchants Association, 1966
First President of Lubbock Ad Club
On the Retail Advisory Board, *Department Store Journal*
First to get the Lubbock Silver Medal Award, presented by *Printer's Ink*
President of The Ex-Student's Association, 1956
On the Board of Directors of Texas Tech
Awards for work in Chamber of Commerce
Chairman of Salvation Army Advisory Committee
Lubbock Beautification Committee Chairman
Community Chest Award for Excellence for heading up Advertising Committee
Listed in Who's Who in Advertising.

Paul J. Thompson Chapter
University of Texas
Austin, Texas
Ernest A. Sharpe, Advisor

By E. Sharpe

Chapter History

Professor Paul J. Thompson, for whom the Texas chapter is named and its first faculty advisor, on many occasions credited Robert M. Gray, a student at The University of Texas in 1928, as the person most responsible for organizing and founding the ADS chapter at Texas. Mr Gray went on to achieve national fame in advertising, presently being national advertising and sales promotion manager of Humble Oil Company. About the beginnings of the UT chapter, Mr. Gray has written: "Originally the chapter was called the Frank Holland Chapter and it was later renamed for Professor Paul J. Thompson.... Other persons who were in the original chapter were Judd Miller, now Collector of Internal Revenue, Austin, Texas, and Dale Miller, well known in Washington, D.C." Frank Holland was the founder of *Holland's Magazine*, a popular regional magazine in the South for several decades. Paul J. Thompson taught journalism and advertising at Texas from 1919 to 1963, and headed the Journalism School from 1927 to 1958.

During the Depression years of the early 1930's, the Texas chapter became inactive. It was revived in 1947 with twenty-five members and Ernest A. Sharpe, instructor in advertising at that time, became faculty advisor. During the peak of the post-World War II veteran enrollment at Texas, the chapter membership reached an all-time high of eighty active members. Since the reactivation in 1947, several hundred members have been initiated into the chapter. From its professional members and alumni have come one national president and several regional vice presidents—Ernest A. Sharpe, John E. McGary, Robert Van Voorhis, and Charles H. Lewis.

Biographical Sketch

A native of Kahoka, Missouri, and a journalism graduate from the University of Missouri in 1914, Paul J. Thompson worked in the field of weekly newspapers prior to joining the faculty of the School of Journalism at The University of Texas in 1919 to teach advertising and journalism. With a student, Robert M. Gray, he founded the chapter of ADS at Texas, first named for Frank Holland, prominent publisher of a regional magazine. In the

1930's the Texas chapter was renamed for Professor Thompson.

He headed the School of Journalism at Texas from 1927 to 1958, and continued to teach until his retirement in 1963. He was one of the pioneers of both journalism and advertising education in the United States and a national leader in these fields. Among his prominent honors and offices, he was the first Missouri graduate to be given the famed Missouri "Distinguished Service in Journalism Award;" he was president of the American Association of Schools and Departments of Journalism in the late 1940's; he was one of the leaders who established the accreditation system for journalism education in the United States.

Outstanding Members

ROBERT M. GRAY, National Advertising and Sales Promotion Manager, Humble Oil Company, Houston; Past Chairman, Advertising Federation of America.

RAY W. BONTA, former National Advertising Manager, presently Manager, Audio-Visual Communication, The General Electric Company, Schenectady, N.Y. (Bonta is a professional member of the Texas chapter.)

Robert W. Jones Chapter
University of Washington
Seattle, Washington
Arnold Gooder, Advisor

By Robert E. Wintersteen

Chapter History

The Robert W. Jones Chapter of Alpha Delta Sigma was the fourth chapter to be installed into the new advertising fraternity in 1923.

The chapter's advisor and pioneer advertising educator, Robert W. Jones, was honored when the chapter members voted to name the chapter after him. In 1929, Professor Jones became national president of the fraternity.

One of the highlights in the early history of the organization was in 1931 when the chapter was host to the national convention. The convention was attended by delegates from 16 other chapters throughout the United States. Gleen Goodard and Dick Williams were co-chairmen for the program.

In the more recent years the Robert W. Jones Chapter has continued to be one of the most active chapters of Alpha Delta Sigma.

Biographical Sketch

The late Professor Robert W. Jones, whose name the University of Washington Chapter of Alpha Delta Sigma bears, served as National President of ADS from 1929-31. He was the first member to receive the Sixth Degree Key, the highest honor our fraternity can bestow.

Professor Jones was a graduate of the University of Missouri, where he received both his Bachelor of Arts and Bachelor of Law degrees. While serving as the head of the University of South Dakota School of Journalism, he received his master's degree in economics.

The genial professor of journalism and advertising is well-remembered at the University of Washington where he taught for 30 years, from 1920-50. Jones utilized his law background in evolving two of his justly famous courses: Law of the Press and the Legal Restrictions of Advertising. The latter, the first of its kind, has become a model for similar courses throughout the country.

His practical approach to journalism and advertising was strongly reflected in his teaching. While intrigued by "cute" ads as attention-getters, he constantly emphasized that attention was only a first step; the product had to be sold. Every advertising class he conducted was admonished: "Hats don't sell hams—hams sell hams. *Always* put a ham in a ham ad."

Professor Emeritus Robert W. Jones died October 1, 1951, following many years service to Alpha Delta Sigma and to the profession of advertising.

P. I. Reed Chapter
West Virginia University
Morgantown, West Virginia
W. R. Summers Jr., Advisor

Chapter History

The P. I. Reed Chapter of Alpha Delta Sigma is one of the youngest chapters. The chapter was installed on December 12, 1964, with 29 charter members of which 16 were professional members. The initiation rolls show a total of 60 student and professional members since the chapter's installation. Through the guidance of Professor William R. Summers, Jr., of the West Virginia University School of Journalism, requirements for the charter to Alpha Delta Sigma were fulfilled and plans for the first initiation of the national profesional advertising fraternity for men on the West Virginia University campus were started.

On the morning of December 12, 1964, Professor Summers

saw his long dream of an ADS chapter on the WVU campus become a reality as he and Dr. Noel P. Laird, national treasurer for ADS, initiated tweve undergraduate and seventeen pro fessional members into the P. I. Reed Chapter of Alpha Delta Sigma.

The P. I. Reed Chapter was named after Dr. P. I. Reed, founder and director emeritus of the WVU School of Journalism. Dr. Reed was also initiated as one of seventeen charter professional members.

Over one year before plans for the first initiation were finalized the first future undergraduate members were in the middle of their pledge project of distributing both shave lotion and cigars to other university students. Finally all the hurdles of forming the fraternity on the WVU were cleared and the first members were initiated.

The ceremonies of that first initiation were held in classroom of Martin Hall on the WVU campus. They were followed by a banquet at the University Montainlair and a get-together reception at Professor Summers' home.

The chapter annually selects "West Virginia's Advertising Man of the Year," which is announced at the School of Journalism's annual alumni banquet in May of each year. The chapter meets monthly to hear an address and meet a professional man in advertising.

The first officers of the P. I. Reed chapter were Brian R Smith, president; Peter A. Pignetti, vice president; and Michael E. McCormick, secretary-treasurer.

Biographical Sketch

The chapter is named after Dr. P. I. Reed, founder and director emeritus of the School of Journalism. Dr. Reed joined the WVU staff as an English teacher in 1920. In 1922 he offered the first course in journalism; and later became the first teacher of advertising in the state. From that beginning of a single course, he guided and directed the development of journalism and advertising education to a departmental status, with the department finally growing to a separate school. He retired in 1958 and is still living in Morgantown.

Dr. Reed is a charter professional member of the ADS chapter bearing his name. He is the author of many books, former president of Kappa Tau Alpha, and president or high ranking officer in many national journalism organizations.

Western Michigan University Chapter
Western Michigan University
Kalamazoo, Michigan
Zane Cannon and William Japinga, Advisors

By Zane Cannon

Chapter History

The Western Michigan University Chapter of Alpha Delta Sigma was installed on December 10, 1967. Mr. Kent Westrate, national professional vice president, presided. Immediately following the ADS ritual, Mr. Westrate initiated—on behalf of GAX National Council—six Western Michigan University coeds as members-at-large of Gamma Alpha Chi. This new colony of GAX will actively participate in activities of the university's ADS chapter.

Guest speakers at the installation and ensuing banquet were Dr. James Miller, President of Western Michigan University, and Dr. Arnold E. Schneider, Dean of the School of Business. Professors Zane Cannon and Wiliam Japinga, co-sponsors, introduced new Alpha Delta Sigma officers: Chester Trybus, president; John Rudberg, vice president; James Donoghue, treasurer; and Bruce Remington, secretary.

Western Michigan University Chapter of ADS is the largest undergraduate chapter ever granted a charter—having 82 charter members. Perhaps this is indicative of the continued interest and growth of "professionalization of advertising through education." All 82 members are more interested in quality than quantity. They're a new chapter, their history is yet to be made. All the new members feel they can be counted on to contribute.

The first official business meeting was held in January, 1968. Their first professional guest was Lee Fondren, national president of ADS.

Biographical Sketch

The National Council approved the formal petition request that this new undergraduate chapter be installed as the Western Michigan University Chapter of ADS. Whenever a meaningful selection can be made, the chapter will change its name to honor an outstanding advertising man who has helped the chapter.

The David Ogilvy Chapter
Youngstown University
Youngstown, Ohio
William Flad, Advisor

By William S. Flad

Chapter History

During the 1964 "Inside Advertising Week" Convention a

professor from a Midwestern university was told about the advertising program at Youngstown University and he suggested that the school would be good "material" for a new chapter of Alpha Delta Sigma. He said that he would get in touch with Dr. Donald Hileman, National Secretary, about this.

A few weeks later a letter from Dr. Hileman was received inviting Youngstown University to submit an application to charter a new chapter of ADS. The Dean of the School of Business Administration thought this was an excellent idea, and the advertising students were most enthusiastic. The necessary forms were filled in and mailed to Dr. Hileman, along with a Youngstown University catalog. Copies of the curriculum sheets for majors in advertising and for majors in commercial art were also sent.

All of this material was reviewed by the ADS National Council. Later, a letter was received stating that Youngstown University had been accepted as a new chapter of the fraternity.

On May 22, 1965, 71 students and the chapter advisor were installed as charter members of the David Ogilvy chapter of ADS at a banquet at the Voyager Motor Inn in Youngstown. Dr. Noel Laird, National Treasurer, came from Franklin and Marshall College to install the chapter and he was assisted by Richard Barrett, a local ADS alumnus who had graduated from Franklin and Marshall. The charter membership at Youngstown was the largest group ever installed by Alpha Delta Sigma at that time.

Biographical Sketch

David Ogilvy was born in 1911 in West Horsley, England. Educated at Fettes, in Edinburgh, and Christ Church, Oxford, he started his career as a chef in the kitchens of the Hotel Majestic in Paris. He went on from Paris to sell cooking stoves in Scotland, and later emigrated to America to become associate director of Dr. George Gallup's Audience Research Institute at Princeton.

During World War II, Mr. Ogilvy was on Sir William Stephenson's staff in British Security Co-ordination, and served as Second Secretary at the British Embassy in Washington. After the war, he founded the advertising agency known today as Ogilvy, Benson and Mather. Mr. Ogilvy, his wife and son, live in New York City, and also have a farm in Lancaster County, Pennsylvania.

Atlanta Professional Chapter
Atlanta, Georgia

Chapter History

The May, 1953, issue of *Linage* carried the story about Atlanta Alpha Delta Sigma alumni banding together to form Alumni chapter number fourteen. Thirteen members signed the petition for the chapter that was granted on March 19, 1953. Charles W. Reep was appointed as temporay chairman at the first meeting.

In the application for a chapter, the alumni said, "As you may already know, the Division of Journalism at Emory University is to be disbanded in the near future, and with this move our ties to Alpha Delta Sigma will be removed. As we desire to remain in contact with each other, it is our wish to establish an alumni group whereby we can meet periodically to re-kindle the spirit of Benjamin Franklin."

The School of Journalism at Emory University was disbanded, but the professional chapter of Atlanta still is very active.

The charter members of the chapter included: I. B. Williams, Jr., John Peacock, Roy C. Owen, Jr., George P. Crumby, Jr., Hugh G. Cates, Ralph E. Russell, James A. Young, Edward R. Wright, Jr., Fred T. Hogue, Jr., Charles W. Reep, Richard Joel, Donald H. Waddington, Jr., and William B. Gray.

Chicago Professional Chapter
509 S. Wabash, Chicago, Illinois

By Jim Kobs

Chapter History

In January, 1933, Mr. Joe Probst (ADS, University of Wisconsin) wrote to Mr. Arthur Hallam, National Grand Secretary of Alpha Delta Sigma, for a list of alumni living in the Chicago area. A list of 53 ADS graduates was mailed to Mr. Probst, and he sent out a notice announcing the organization of the *first* Alumni Chapter of the fraternity.

The intitial meeting was held November 7, 1933. Many of the alumni notified were in attendance, along with Mr. Hallam . . . who came down from the University of Wisconsin for the meeting.

During the following years, the Chicago Alumni Chapter was used by National as a model for other alumni groups in Boston, Los Angeles, and San Francisco. As World War II neared, the chapter became inactive during the late 1930's.

In 1948, the Chicago chapter was completely reorganized, and received its official charter. It has been meeting monthly ever since, and has built up an enviable record among the fraternity's alumni groups.

Now known as the Chicago Professional Chapter of ADS, it hosted the National Convention in 1955, and again a few years later. In 1964, it was chosen to host the 50th Anniversary observance of the fraternity's founding. And it was at this meeting that President Bill Ross announced the National Round-Up Program.

Also in 1964, the chapter offered a five-week seminar entitled "Advertising 1964," which was conducted at Roosevelt University by professional admen.

Current chapter activities include monthly dinner meetings with guest speakers . . . annual Founders' Day meetings . . . an employment service for members and local undergraduates . . . and a scholarship program for advertising students in the Chicago area.

Outstanding Members

A few of the chapter's prominent current members include:

FAIRFAX M. CONE—Chairman Executive Committee, Foote, Cone & Belding.

IRVING D. AUSPITZ—Senior Vice President, Arthur Meyerhoff Associates.

GEORGE LAZARUS—Advertising Columnist, Chicago Daily News.

KENT WESTRATE—Account Supervisor, Lilienfield & Company, and National Professional Vice President of ADS.

KEN EDWARDS—Advertising Manager, Culligan, Inc., and Sales Promotion Executive of the Year, 1964.

Dallas Professional Chapter
Dallas, Texas

Although still carried as an active chapter, little has been heard from the Dallas Professional Chapter. The last president reported by the chapter was James W. Kumpf.

An attempt was being made in 1968 by A. E. "Ziggy" Nicholson, former Texas Tech undergraduate president, to reform the group.

Houston Professional Chapter
Houston, Texas

Chapter History

The Houston Professional Chapter of Alpha Delta Sigma was started in the latter part of the 1940's by a group of University of Texas graudates working in the area. The early meetings served as social gatherings more than business meetings.

Some of the members instrumental in getting the chapter started inculded: Bill Browder, Foote, Cone, & Belding, Houston; Dick Mims, head of Ace Rican Health Studios; Jean Brown, president of Rives, Dyke Co., Houston; Ken Rice, semi-retired, Dallas; Ralph Davis, McCann-Erickson; and John McGary, partner in a Houston agency until his death in 1962.

In the mid-1950's the organization became a little more formal under the presidency of Harry Dollahite, and later Robert Van Voorhis. It was during this period that the chapter served the true function of "bridging the gap" from the undergraduate chapters to the professional field of advertising. John McGary and Charles Lewis also served terms as president during the 1950's.

While serving as Southwestern Vice President in the early 1960's, Charles Lewis worked with the members in trying a new direction for professional chapters. The idea was to have members who had just graduated from collegiate chapters to serve as officers. This would allow those members who just arrived in Houston to work with an active advertising organization. It also freed the older members to move on into the membership of the Houston Advertising Club, which works very closely with the professional chapters of ADS and Gamma Alpha Chi.

The 1968 president of the chapter is Richard Albitz, KPRC Radio-TV.

Memphis Professional Chapter
Memphis, Tennessee

By Dallas Nelson

Chapter History

Alpha Delta Sigma was a post World War II offspring of the mother chapter at the University of Missouri. Four of the seven charter members were Missouri graduates, Frank Berfield, Harry Dollahite, Charles Montgomery and Dallas Nelson. The other three were Bailey Campbell, Milton Fortas and Ralph Moriarty.

Frank Berfield (Missouri '48) was the first president, and held the meetings in his apartment which he shared with Dallas Nelson. These early-day meetings were like a floating crap game, moving every month to a different house. Parties were held on the same basis.

The programs consisted mostly of choosing a topic and wringing it out in a bull session. Occasionally the members would hold an on-site meeting at a place of business. Nearly every printer, engraver, photographer, TV station, radio station, newspaper, or whatever, has hosted ADS at one time or another.

By the mid-fifties, as the group grew to 20-25 members, the programs became slightly more formalized. Speakers were invited and the monthly meetings were moved to the University Club.

The easy-going, good-natured conviviality of the early days has prevailed to date. ADS Memphis has made no attempt to compete with the Advertising Club of Memphis. Membership has remained select. It's a fun group. No projects. The last one suggested was proposed over ten years ago. Harry Dollahite, then a salesman for Memphis Publishing Co., suggested that the chapter prepare a direct mail campaign to encourage Main Street merchants to put street numbers on their doors. The caustic comments melded to sound like the bullhorn on a Mississippi river barge—"B-o-o-o-o-o!"

Today ADS Memphis has 36 members and convenes regularly every third Thursday at the Tennessee Club.

Greater Miami Professional Chapter
Miami, Florida

Chapter History

During the Spring months of 1955 about 25 members of Alpha Delta Sigma got together and decided to meet regularly to cement friendships and to work together in assisting the George E. Merrick Chapter at the University of Miami. Approximately 50 percent of the original members of this chapter had been initiated as Professionals, some at the George E. Merrick Chapter and others at various chapters throughout the country. Some had been a part of previous attempts to start such an alumni and professional chapter in Miami, but had seen it fail to operate on a continuing basis.

One of the things that put this chapter on a sound, permanent basis was the establishment of a Constitution and By-Laws with the following purpose stated at the beginning:

> To provide Alumni and Professional members of Alpha Delta Sigma, working and residing in Southeastern Florida, with frequent meetings covering advertising, selling and marketing subjects; to provide for social activities; to exchange information: and to help Alpha Delta Sigma undergraduates "Bridge the Gap."

At the time this chapter was founded and for several years afterwards, the George E. Merrick Chapter at the University had a good sponsor and ran along smoothly, requiring little assistance from this chapter. Nevertheless, it assisted them in their forums, tours and initiations. As a result they initiated very few Professionals and, because most of the members came from other parts of the country, they returned there after graduation. The professional chapter was not able to gain much in membership from them and the chapter could not grow and progress as desired. So, with permission of National ADS Headquarters, the professional chapter started initiating a limited number (maximum of 8 per year) of Professionals each year. These Professionals, along with new Alumni members moving into the area, have increased membership to 65 for the 1965-66 fiscal year.

Meetings have been held almost monthly and attendance averages around 35. (In July and December ADS Professionals join in the Advertising Club Social Functions—A Splash Party and a Christmas Party). Many of the meetings are held at plants and firms operating in some phase of advertising. Undergraduate members of the George E. Merrick Chapter are always invited to these meetings.

The Professionals initiated in November, 1962, were given the responsibility of putting on a meeting in early 1963, and thus began an annual event which has grown to sizeable proportions. They staged pantomine type spoofs of some advertising and called it "Fibs and Boast." A larger version was staged at the Annual Installation Dinner in June that year and it has been an annual event since then. The name was changed in 1965 to "Waysgoose" because Sigma Delta Chi, who had been staging an annual "Ribs and Boasts" in which they rib politicians, claimed infringement. During the last two years the event has been open to the public and well atended.

In 1965 this chapter handled the arrangements for what has been called the finest and most successful National Convention cf ADS. This convention was held at the Carillon Hotel on Miami Beach and attracted over 100 delegates from chapters all over the U. S.

Outstanding Members

PAUL R. GREENWAY—Governor, Fourth District Advertising Federation of America; Vice President of Advertising Federation of America; recipient of AFA-Printer's Ink Silver Medal Award.

HORACE W. SCOTT (deceased)—Governor, Fourth District Advertising Federation of America; recipient of Alpha Delta Sigma Golden Fifty Award.

CHARLES H. WHITEBROOK—Governor, Fourth District Advertising Federation of America, Vice President of Advertising Federation of America; recipient of AFA-Printer's Ink Medal Award.

L. L. "DUKE" ZIMMERMAN—Governor, Fourth District Advertising Federation of America; recipient of Alpha Delta Sigma Golden Fifty Award and AFA-Printer's Ink Silver Medal Award.

Milwaukee Professional Chapter
Milwaukee, Wisconsin

The Milwaukee Professional Chapter was founded in the mid-1950's. The founder and first president for the group was Howard Shaw, who later was president of the Chicago Professional Chapter.

The last reported president for the chapter was Bruce Robertson.

Minneapolis Professional Chapter
Minneapolis, Minnesota

Conrad Razidlo was listed as president of the Minneapolis Professional Chapter as the history went to press. The Minneapolis chapter did not submit a chapter history.

New Jersey Professional Chapter

Chapter History

The New Jersey Professional chapter of Alpha Delta Sigma was formed on Tuesday, January 29, 1952. For the first meeting the chapter attempted to gather together all professional advertising and sales personnel residing in New Jersey, who were members of Alpha Delta Sigma chapters in their undergraduate days.

The members elected at the first meeting included: Fred M. Hurwitt, Bloomfield, N.J., president; Nicholas W. Walton, Montclair, N.J., vice president; and Wister D. Shreve, Arlington, N.J., secretary-treasurer.

One of the main objects of the new chapter was to assist and give free advertising, marketing, and sales promotion aid to worthwhile New Jersey charitable and civic organizations who need profesional help.

New York Professional Chapter
New York, N.Y.

Chapter History

The glimmer that became the New York Alumni Chapter of Alpha Delta Sigma started in 1947 when eight NYU graduates—all ADS—thought they should get together periodically to continue the relationships they established while attending the School of Commerce. They planned to meet about once a month in various restaurants around New York. Attendance usually ran about 50 percent for a total of four members.

Approximately two years elapsed in this embryonic stage. In late 1949, with the help of the National Secretary, the New York Alumni Chapter was launched. A membership drive soon raised the total from eight to sixty, and included Alumni from undergraduate chapters all over the country.

Today, the roster lists approximately 300 names, some active, others dormant. Many inactive members, however, have done their share to contribute to the growth of the organization and deservingly now relax while the younger men carry on.

Current activities of the New York Chapter consist of monthly meetings with a guest speaker. Such meetings are held in various locations around the city and are alternating lunch and dinner sessions.

Highlight of the year's activities is usually a banquet, which includes an impressive array of industry leaders on the dais, as well as on the speaker's platform.

In addition, the Chapter's Newsletter serves as an aid to members for job relocation, and for other such assistance.

Northern California Professional Chapter
San Francisco, California

By William F. Fielder

Chapter History

In the Spring of 1937, twenty-four years after the ADS Fraternity was founded, the first alumni chapter was organized in San Francisco by a few University of California alumni, with the urging of Professor Charles Raymond and the active support of Charles W. Collier, who had been made a professional member in 1934 by the Charles Raymond Chapter (established in 1927).

Another professional member, Don E. Gilman from the University of Oregon (W.F.G. Thacher Chapter—established in 1924), who was National President during 1937-38, encouraged the founding of the San Francisco Alumni Chapter (name changed in 1951 to Northern California Alumni Chapter), prior to the Silver Jubilee Convention in Los Angeles in the Spring of 1938.

The moving spirit among the young advertising men was John W. Eggers, a Phi Beta Kappa and Alpha Delta Sigma member, who had graduated from California in 1934 and became the first president of the San Francisco Alumni Chapter.

The United States then was beginning to recover from the Depression. The Alumni Chapter's job of bridging the gap between theory and practice was begun by the young alumni men obtaining the cooperation of outstanding advertising men in managerial positions and initiating them as professional members (then called Honorary).

Among the professional members initiated in 1937 was Wilmot P. Rogers, Director of Advertising and Promotion of California Packing Corporation. He was chapter president, following Eggers, during the remainder of 1937-38. Another professional member, Hugh W. Thomas, beloved by all, was president during 1938-39. It was during this period that an undergraduate chapter was established at Stanford University in 1939, followed by one at San Jose State College in 1940. The fourth Bay Area undergraduate chapter, at San Francisco State College and named in honor of the late Hugh W. Thomas, was founded in 1965.

The Stanford expansion was sparked by professional member Howard Willoughby, who had been elected National President for 1938-39 at the Silver Jubilee Convention, and for whom the Stanford Chapter was named.

Other professional members of the San Francisco Alumni Chapter included Alvin Long, for whom the San Jose State Chapter was named, and Lou E. Townsend, who became National President in 1941-42 and led all ADS Chapters in the United States in promoting the sale of War Bonds.

For the 1939-40 year the alumni elected a president who had been president of the Charles Raymond Chapter in the Class of 1931, Ernest A. Mennell. The 1940-41 president was Mc-Cullough Campbell who had studied under Professor Raymond in the class of 1926. He became a professional member in 1937.

Then came the war and the years immediately following during which Stanley Heyman and Ben D. Nixon, both professional members, served as Chapter presidents. Chapter members under their guidance helped in defense work, war manpower, recruitment, and helped ADS members returning to advertising from military service.

The post-war years were difficult for the three undergraduate chapters. One of the most diligent alumni chapter workers in strengthening these chapters was Charles W. Collier, who was president during the 1948-49 term. The following year another professional member, Charles W. Reed, while president, introduced the advertising orientation program with the Department of Journalism at San Jose State College.

"Outstanding among the various ADS projects whose purpose is to 'bridge the gap' is the apprentice program which the San Francisco Alumni Chapter put into operation for the benefit of three Bay Area Chapters in 1950."

This recognition by the National Fraternity was published following the 1950-51 term of Stuart O. Harding. Harding had been an undergraduate member of the Charles Raymond Chapter,

Class of 1936. He became active in the Alumni Chapter early in the war. In addition to his apprentice program, he was particularly helpful to ADS members in securing employment in advertising. For many years following World War II, Stu Harding was Job Placement Chairman of the Northern California Alumni Chapter of ADS.

Another member of the Northern California Chapter who served with distinction was Walter Guild, National President in 1960-61. Mr. Guild, along with Bill Dumont, Chick Collier and Howard Willoughby, has been honored as a recipient of the Ben Franklin Award.

Presidents of the Northern California Alumni Chapter since 1950, in order, were: Stanley Colberson, Peter Schulz, Richard Newell, William Anderson, William Ayres, Duncan Scott, Morton McDonald, George Briggs, Floyd Pickett, William Dumont, Jack Wallace, Bern Bernardini, Jack Wildman, Martel Scroggin, Jerry Gibbons, Randy Smith, and Victor Bacigalupi.

Puget Sound Professional Chapter
Seattle, Washington

Chapter History

More than 40 members and guests attended the first meeting of the Pudget Sound Profesional Chapter of Alpha Delta Sigma on January 27, 1967, at the Benjamin Franklin Hotel in Seattle. It was a joint meeting with the undergraduate chapter from the University of Washington.

Monte Solkover, Seattle Advertising Agency, president of the professional chapter, and Dave Smith, undergraduate president, presided. Guests included Professors Daniel S. Warner, Willis Winter and Arnold Gooder from the University of Washington School of Communications.

The program for the first meeting was the 1967 version of "The Wonderful World of Advertising," a film, slide and tape presentation produced by the Seattle Advertising Club.

One of the first projects assumed by the professional chapter was the responsibility for the summer internship program for advertising students from the University of Washington and Seattle University. Chapter chairmen are Carl Bengtson, *North Central Outlook*, vice president for undergraduate relations, and Frank Welch, Frederick E. Baker Advertising, vice president for professional relations.

The charter members of the chapter included: Bruce Baker, Carl Bengtson, Robert Davidge, Jack Wallace, Peter Hemp, Folke Olsen, Will Pascoe, Harry Pearson, Monte Solkover, Jack Wallace, and Frank Welch.

Other elected officers were: Hemp, secretary; and Olsen, treasurer.

Southern California Professional Chapter
Los Angeles, California

Chapter History

Although a complete history of the Southern California Professional chapter could not be obtained, the March 1956 issue of *Linage* carried a story about the former presidents of the chapter. The chapter, one of the first alumni chapters, was founded in 1937. It was one of the most active chapters until recent years. The names of its former presidents reads like a Who's Who in Advertising: Eric Smith, 1938; Milton V. Carlson, 1939; Edward Keeler, 1942-46; Carl Johnson, 1947; Martin R. Klitten, 1948; Howard McKay, 1949; Russell Z. Eller, 1950; Gene Duckwall, 1951; Harry Witt, 1952; Ted Stromberger, 1953; and Roi Rider, 1954.

At the meeting in 1956, Executive Service Awards were presented to each of the past presidents, their names inscribed on a handsome plaque which was hung in the Statler Hotel, quarters of the Los Angeles Advertising Club.

Known presidents since that meeting include: Phil Dexheimer, 1955; Norman B. Moeler, 1956; Joseph G. Mohl, 1957; Maurie Webster, 1958; Rol Rider, 1959; Jack Laffin, 1960; Pete Schulz, 1961; and the last president of record was Kendall J. Mau.

Southern Illinois University Professional Chapter
Carbondale, Illinois

Chapter History

The S.I.U. Professional Chapter was formed April 27, 1963 on an experimental basis in an attempt to establish a formal organization and procedure for the university chapters to maintain communication and contact with its anumni.

The S.I.U. Professional Chapter meets only two times a year, at Homecoming in the Fall and in the Spring during Journalism Week. Members are charged $5 annual dues, $2 of which goes to National Headquarters to pay their national dues and $3 is placed in an ADS Loan Fund, available to ADS members currently in school and on the campus.

Jack Brundage of the Advertising Department of the *Southern Illinoisan*, an area newspaper with headquarters in Carbondale, has served as president of the group since its inception.

In addition to returning to campus for the fall and spring meetings, members are readily available to assist the S.I.U. undergraduate chapter in whatever ways needed.

Washington Professional Chapter
Washington, D.C.

By C. E. Anderson, Jr.

Chapter History

In June. 1962, Lieutenant W. D. Collins, USN, made the first serious inquiry about putting together an ADS professional chapter in the nation's capitol. What would have apparently succeeded did not. Lieutenant Collins was transferred to a new assignment with the Atlantic Fleet at Norfolk, Virginia.

In November, 1964, Charles Anderson, an advertising copywriter and just out of the University of Maryland's ADS Chapter, started organizing where Lt. Collins left off. ADS alumni in the metropoitan Washington area were located and invited to become the nucleus of a Washington Professional Chapter of the fraternity. Most of the alumni were enthusiastic about the idea and quickly consented to help charter the Chapter.

Three months later (February 2, 1965), the Washington Professional Chapter produced a charter group consisting of 17 newly initiated professionals and 24 alumni . . . 41 in all—the largest installation in the history of the Fraternity. Ceremonies were held at the Statler-Hilton Hotel in Washington under the sponorship of the Advertising Federation of America.

The highly professional membership included many of Washington's advertising greats: President of the Advertising Club, heads of the two largest advertising agencies, President of the Advertising Council. Former Editor and Publisher of *Printer's Ink*. ad managers from a score of firms. ad agency people, public relations people and professors of advertising from several local universities.

Founder Anderson was elected as the Chapter's first president during installation ceremonies. Other officers included first vice president, Len Oxenberg; second vice president, L. Q. Bradley; secretary. Charles Hinkel; and treasurer, J. A. Brownridge. A five-man Advisory Comittee was appointed by the president and chaired by Don Wilkins.

For their organizational efforts in helping to make the Washington Chapter a reality, Anderson awarded Messrs. Wilkins, Ashmen and Hinkel the chapter's highest award, the Outstanding Service Key. Awards were preceded by a "welcome" from the ADS National Professional Vice President who flew in from Chicago for the Installation. Kent Westrate did a truly fine job of coordinating organizational efforts between the National Council and the Washington Chapter.

Late in March, 1965, the Chapter held a Spring Banquet at the National Press Club featuring guest speaker Lee Fondren— an ADS alumnus, ADS national officer and Chairman of the

Advertising Federation of America. Mr. Fondren delivered his famous "Advertising 1980" . . . an Orson Wellian preview of advertising's bleak future at the hands of government over-control and regulation.

At the national convention held in April, 1965, the Chapter President and Second Vice President were given a first-hand look at the entire Fraternity assembled together. Both returned with a much broader knowledge of how and why the National Advertising Fraternity functions, together with a few ideas on possible new sources of income. Thus was born the ADS Merchandise Program which to date has produced an official decal and a promise of more items to come. All profit from the sale of merchandise to individuals and chapters will go toward the strengthening of the National treasury. The Washington Chapter provided and will continue to provide organizational direction and creative service to make this Merchandise Program a financial cornerstone of the Fraternity.

In September, 1965, general elections were held, although somewhat early, to assure continuity with National's fiscal year beginning October 1st. Len Oxenberg, first vice president of the Chapter, was unanimously elected to the presidency along with his vigorous platform of new activities to boost interest both in and outside the Chapter, and to strike an even closer rapport with the nearby undergraduate chapter of ADS at the University of Maryland. Past President Anderson moved to chairman of the five-man Advisory Committee. Ceremonies marking the occasion were held at the National Wildlife Federation.

What began in 1964 as a dozen or so has mushroomed into the largest and most active chapter in the Fraternity. ADS is at last a reality in the nation's capitol.